GOLDY

The Life and Times of Oliver Goldsmith

"Where shall I meet a soul of such purity as
that which resides in thy breast! Sure thou
hast been nurtured by the bill of the Shin
Shin, or sucked the breasts of the provident
Gin Hiung. The melody of thy voice could
rob the Chong Fou of her whelps, or inveigle
the Boh that lives in the midst of the waters"

GOLDSMITH, *The Citizen of the World*

GOLDY

The Life and Times of
OLIVER GOLDSMITH

~~~~~~

"Kindness and gentleness are never out of fashion; it is these in Goldsmith which make him our contemporary"—!

W. D. HOWELLS, *My Literary Passions*

~~~~~~

by

OSCAR SHERWIN

TWAYNE PUBLISHERS, INC. • NEW YORK

To
TREV
AND
HIS PETS

FOREWORD

(A VERSION based on fact—the fact of reality—by research—and the fact of artistic imagination—from the core of Goldsmith's writing.)

CONTENTS

CONTENTS

GOLDY
The Life and Times of Oliver Goldsmith

~~~~~~~~~~~~~~~~~~~~~~~~~~~~~~~~~~~~~

CHAPTER 1

PROLOGUE:
A CITIZEN OF THE WORLD

"You men of Europe," says our Chinese philosopher, Lien Chi Altangi, as he brushes a grain of snuff from his sky blue coat, "think nothing of a voyage by sea. With us of China a man who has been from sight of land is regarded upon his return with admiration. I have known some provinces where there is not even a name for the ocean. What a strange people, therefore, am I got amongst, who have founded an empire on this unstable element, who build cities upon billows that rise higher than the mountains of Tipartala, and make the deep more formidable than the wildest tempest!" . . . A thick clumsy mass of bloom-colored waistcoat and breeches stirs in the next seat. Pale round face, pitted with smallpox, protruding upper lip and two great wrinkles between the eyebrows.

Lien goes on. "The English seem as silent as the Japanese, yet vainer than the inhabitants of Siam. Upon my arrival I attributed that reserve to modesty, which, I now find, has its origin in pride.

"A few days ago, passing by one of their prisons, I could not avoid stopping, in order to listen to a dialogue which I thought might afford me some entertainment. The con-

versation was carried on between a debtor through the grate
of his prison, a porter, who had stopped to rest his burden,
and a soldier at the window. The subject was upon a
threatened invasion from France, and each seemed extremely anxious to rescue his country from the impending
danger.

" 'For my part,' cries the prisoner, 'the greatest of my
apprehensions is for our freedom. If the French should conquer, what would become of English liberty? My dear
friends, liberty is the Englishman's prerogative; we must
preserve that at the expense of our lives; of that the French
shall never deprive us. It is not to be expected that men
who are slaves themselves would preserve our freedom
should they happen to conquer.'

" 'Ay, slaves,' cries the porter, 'they are all slaves, fit
only to carry burdens, every one of them. Before I could
stoop to slavery may this be my poison! (and he holds the
goblet in his hand), may this be my poison!—but I would
sooner list for a soldier.'

"The soldier, taking the goblet from his friend with much
awe, fervently cries out, 'It is not so much our liberties, as
our religion that would suffer by such a change; ay, our
religion, my lads. May the devil sink me into flames (such
was the solemnity of his adjuration), if the French should
come over, but our religion would be utterly undone!'—So
saying, instead of a libation, he applies the goblet to his
lips and confirms his sentiments with a ceremony of the
most persevering devotion.

"In short, every man here pretends to be a politician;
even the fair sex are sometimes found to mix the severity
of national altercation with the blandishments of love, and
often become conquerors by more weapons of destruction
than their eyes. . . ."

Patrons are laying their pennies at the bar, which make
them free of the rooms, and then calling for what they
desire—coffee steaming hot, or punch, or plain brandy, or
maybe a pipe of tobacco. The barmaid, a fine lady who

stands pulling a rope and screaming like a peacock against rainy weather, is pinned up by herself in a little pew, and all people bow to her as they pass by. She is armed with those principal badges of her honorable station in life—the chalk and sponge. Waiters are learning the tavern trip by running up the balcony and down again.

The company is mixed. Young noblemen in figured silks and laces are rubbing shoulders unawares with well-dressed highwaymen or expert thieves from Whitefriar's.

Aimwell—"Pray, sir, han't I seen your face at Will's Coffee House?"

Gibbet—"Yes, sir, and at White's, too."

The outward room is in a buzz of politics, but the knot of theorists sits in the inner room. The whole Spanish monarchy is disposed of and all the line of Bourbons provided for in less than a quarter of an hour. Then on to Pitt and Fox and whether taxation is tyranny or not. . . . While the coffee boys are crying, "Fresh coffee, fresh coffee, gentlemen! Bohea tea, will ye ha' fresh coffee, gentlemen?"

Lien Chi Altangi rises to make his apologies. He is very sorry; he cannot await Alderman Trump; he cannot accompany his friend and Mr. Trump to the Devil Tavern. In short, he is to wait upon my Lord at the Star and Garter. My Lord, equally distinguished for rank, politeness, taste, and understanding, has got some pretty things from China— miniature temples, sprawling dragons, squatting pagods, and clumsy mandarins—and he most passionately desires the pleasure of his acquaintance. But is it possible . . . ?

It is not possible. The round bellied alderman who breathes the foggy air of the city requires more solid diet than the light kickshaws of our meager persons of quality. My lord, or Sir John, after having whiled away an hour or two at the parliament house, drives to the Star and Garter to regale on macaroni or piddle with an Ortolan; while the merchant who has plodded all the morning in the Alley sits down to a turtle feast at the Crown or the Kings' Arms and crams himself with Calipash and Calipee.

GOLDY

Lien Chi Altangi says adieu, makes an impassive, jerky bow as he passes the barmaid, and glides swiftly out of the house. His friend now calls for quill, ink, and paper, and drawing himself near the table, writes:

"To Mr.——, Merchant in London.

"The schoolmen had formerly a very exact way of computing the abilities of their saints or authors. Escobar, for instance, was said to have learning as five, genius as four, and gravity as seven. Caramuel was greater than he. His learning was as eight, his genius as six, and his gravity as thirteen. Were I to estimate the merits of our Chinese Philosopher by the same scale, I would not hesitate to state his genius still higher; but as to his learning and gravity, these, I think, might safely be marked as nine hundred and ninety-nine, within one degree of absolute frigidity. . . ."

A hearty slap on the back, and a "Good day to you, Goldy," is rapped out in loud tones. Our friend looks up quickly and frowns. It is honest Tom Davies, publisher, bookseller, and critic of Russell Street, Covent Garden, who waves his hand and strolls away. And Oliver Goldsmith mutters as he turns to his blotted page—"Now to be clapped on the back by Tom Davies is humiliating enough. But I wish he wouldn't call me Goldy whatever Dr. Johnson does."

CHAPTER 2

THE MISTAKES OF A NIGHT

IN THE YEAR 1718 Charles Goldsmith, a young Irish Protestant clergyman, descended of a clerical family, marries Ann Jones. Though his father has some property, he is a younger son. His wife, whose father is the Reverend Oliver Jones, master of the diocesan school at Elphin, brings a very small dowry. He himself has not been able to earn a living. In a word, while his heart is great, his prudence is not.

For twelve years after his marriage, his means of support are both very narrow and very precarious. He farms a little land, officiates occasionally in the parish of Kilkenny West, in the county of Westmeath, the rector of which is his wife's uncle, and is regularly curate in charge of Pallas in the parish of Forgney. Pallas is a wretched hamlet far from any highroad on a dreary plain which in wet weather is often a lake.

By 1730 four children are born. On an uncertain stipend, which averages forty pounds a year, another birth is a new burden. But on the tenth of November, a fifth child, Oliver, makes his appearance.

As Charles Goldsmith's fortune is but small, he lives up to the very limit of it. He has no intentions of leaving his children money, for that is dross. He is resolved they shall

[17]

have learning, for learning, he observes, is better than silver or gold. For this purpose, he undertakes to instruct them himself and takes as much pains to form their morals as to improve their understanding. They are told that universal benevolence is what first cemented society; they are taught to consider all the wants of mankind as their own, to regard the human face with affection and esteem. He winds them up to be mere machines of pity and renders them incapable of withstanding the slightest impulse made either by real or fictitious distress. In a word, they are perfectly instructed in the art of giving away thousands before they are taught the more necessary qualifications of earning a farthing.

Thus refined out of all their suspicion by his lessons and divested of even the little cunning which nature has given them, they resemble, upon their first entrance into the busy and insidious world, those gladiators who were exposed without armor in the amphitheaters of Rome. . . .

Charles Goldsmith's chief task is to endeavor to inculcate virtue. He thus sets a resolution to become acquainted with every man in the parish, exhorting the married men to temperance and the bachelors to matrimony, so that in a few years it is a common saying that there are three strange wants at Pallas—a parson wanting pride, young men wanting wives, and alehouses wanting customers.

Matrimony is always one of his favorite topics, and he writes several sermons to prove its happiness. But there is a peculiar tenet which he makes a point of supporting—for he maintains with Whiston that it is unlawful for a priest of the Church of England, after the death of his first wife, to take a second; or to express it in a word, he values himself upon being a strict monogamist.

The death of the rector of Kilkenny West improves his fortune, for in 1730 he succeeds to this living of his wife's uncle. His income is raised nearly to two hundred pounds a year, and so the family moves from Pallas to a respectable house and farm on the verge of the pretty little village of Lissoy.

[18]

The first born Margaret dies in childhood, and the family, at this time consisting of Catherine, Henry, Jane, and Oliver, born in Pallas, or Elphin (where the widow of the Reverend Oliver Jones still lives) is in the next ten years increased by Maurice, Charles, and John, born at Lissoy.

The youngest, as the eldest, dies in youth. Charles in 1769 departs for Jamaica to seek his fortune and after a long self exile dies in a poor lodging in Somers' town; Maurice is put to the trade of a cabinet maker, keeps a meager shop in Charlestown in the county of Roscommon and departs from a miserable life in 1792; Henry follows his father's calling and dies as he has lived, a humble village preacher and schoolmaster; Catherine marries a wealthy husband, Mr. Hodson; Jane, a poor one, Mr. Johnstone, and both die in Athlone.

"The Goldsmiths are a strange family," confess three different branches of them in as many different quarters of Ireland. "They rarely act like other people. Their hearts are always in the right place, but their heads seem to be doing anything but what they ought."

Oliver's education begins when he is three years old. That is, he is gathered under the wings of one of those good old motherly dames found in every village, who cluck together the whole callow brood of the neighborhood to teach them letters and keep them out of harm's way. In Lissoy, Mistress Elizabeth Delap, for that is her name, has flourished in this capacity for fifty years. But Oliver is hopelessly dull and stupid. At the age of six he is handed over to the village school, kept by Mr. Thomas Byrne, retired quartermaster of an Irish regiment that has served in Marlborough's Spanish Wars. Paddy Byrne, as he is familiarly called, is more given to shoulder a crutch and show how the fields were won than to inculcate what is called the Humanities; and his knowledge of the wild legends of the Irish hovel is at once deeper and more sympathetic than that of Agamemnon and Achilles, Ulysses and Aeneas. On windy days when the smoke swirls about the room as if it has quarrelled with the chimney flue, the little boys in their long frieze coats listen enchanted to the schoolmaster's wonderful tales about ghosts, banshees, and fairies, about the great rapparee chiefs Baldearg O'Donnell and Galloping Hogan, and about the exploits of Peterborough and Stanhope, the surprise of Monjuich, and the glorious disaster of Brihuega.

Oliver comes away from Paddy Byrne much as he went, in point of learning. But certain wandering, unsettled tastes have been implanted in him.

Yet to give Paddy Byrne his due, the Master delights in translating Virgil's *Eclogues* into Irish verse *ex tempore,* and young Oliver responds by trying his own hand at writing verse. His father and mother are overjoyed at this display of genius, but Oliver, dissatisfied with his poems, burns them as soon as he has written them. Except one, which remains and gains him a paternal reward of gingerbread.

There is company at tea, and Oliver is asked to hand the kettle, but the handle being too hot, he takes up the front skirt of his coat to put between him and it. Unfortunately the ladies perceive something which makes them laugh immoderately, and Oliver, immediately noticing the cause of their laughter, promises his father to write some verses on it. I insert them here:

> Theseus did see as Poets say
> Dark Hell and its abysses,
> But had not half so Sharp an Eye
> As our young Charming Misses.
>
> For they could through boys breeches peep
> And view whate'er he had there;
> It seemed to Blush and they all Laughed
> Because the face was all Bare.
>
> They laughed at that
> Which sometimes Else
> Might give them greatest pleasure.

How quickly they could see the thing
Which was their darling treasure.

(It may be noted that the household at Lissoy is anything
but squeamish.)

An attack of confluent smallpox halts Oliver's attendance
at the Lissoy school, and when he recovers, it is with his
naturally plain face disfigured into such grotesque ugliness
that it is difficult to look at him without laughing.

"Why Noll!" exclaims a visitor, "you are become a fright!
When do you mean to get handsome again?"

Oliver moves in silence to the window. The speaker, a
reckless and notorious scapegrace of the Goldsmith family,
repeats the question with a worse sneer, and the boy retorts,
"I mean to get better, sir, when you do."

There is company one day at a small dance given by his
uncle. During a pause between two country dances, the
party is greatly surprised by little Noll quickly jumping up
and dancing impromptu *à pas seul* about the room. His droll
face and clumsy figure amuse the fiddler so much that he
bursts out laughing, and pointing to the dancer, exclaims,
"Aesop!" Aesop stops, looks round at the player, and without hesitation calls out,

"Our herald hath proclaimed this saying:
See Aesop dancing, and his monkey playing."

To get him out of sight for a time, Oliver is now tossed
about from school to school in his native part of Ireland—
first at Elphin, which has formerly been taught by his grand-
father, the Reverend Oliver Jones, then at Athlone, nearer
home, and finally at Edgeworthstown. He gradually gets on
in Latin and prepares for the University. He is fond of Ovid
and Horace, likes Tacitus after a while, but hates Cicero,
and delights in Livy. At every school we hear of him as a
shy, thick, awkward boy, the constant butt of his companions
and thought by most of them as little better than a fool.
He is quick to take offence, though feverishly ready to for-

give, and it is impossible for him to harbor resentment. To his masters, he is one of the most generous, good for nothing, amiable little creatures that have ever conjugated the verb *"tupto,"* I beat, *"tuptomai,"* I am whipped.

As Cornelius Kelly, the wag of Ardagh, is walking down the road smoking his pipe, there comes along a young bantam cock of a fellow, who pulls up his horse and says to him, as patronizing as if he were King George himself, "Can you tell me, my man, if there's any place hereabouts where a gentleman can lie for the night? None of your cabins," he adds, flourishing his whip, "but a place where a gentleman that can pay for real comfort will be at home. The best house in the district is what I'm looking for, my good fellow," he says again.

"Is it the very best house hereabouts, you're looking for?" Kelly asks.

"And what else would a gentleman like me be wanting?"

"Well, then," says Kelly, "you see that house half a mile down the road," pointing to the home of the great Squire Featherston. "That's the best in Ardagh."

"There's good quarters there?"

"As good as any in all Ireland," the wag replies, taking the pipe out of his mouth and smiling.

"Well, then, good night to you, my man," and he rides off.

It is the close of Oliver Goldsmith's last holidays, and he is on his way to Edgeworthstown, a Rosinante beneath him, a guinea in his pocket, and a light heart in his breast. A delicious taste of independence has beguiled him to a loitering, lingering, pleasant enjoyment of the journey, and now at nightfall, instead of finding himself under Schoolmaster Hughes's roof, he is in Ardagh, a few miles out of the way.

But following Cornelius Kelly's directions, he arrives at Squire Featherston's. With an authoritative air, he orders the servant to take his bare-boned racer to the stables, knocks at the door, and demands a night's lodging and a dinner. Everything bespeaks a hospitable country inn. There is the goodly display of cold meats, game, pies, cheese, and pastries on view in the glazed cupboard in the hall. There is the floor formed of large tiles scrubbed clean and sanded. The chairs are of spindled Windsor type with Hogarth backs. There is a panelled settle, some oaken stools, and a "cricket" table. And at the back of the fireplace, on an iron crane, is a cauldron of stew.

Mr. Featherston sees the young man's mistake and humors it. He is content to play Boniface for a while instead of the Squire, to be bullied a trifle, instead of being made obeisance to. He stands and waits for his guest.

"We have in the larder, I believe, a joint of cold beef, a leg of cold veal, a ham, and a pigeon's pie, from which we should be honored to have you select your meal. I can especially vouch for the merits of the pie."

"None of your cold victuals for me."

Mr. Featherston is taken aback—expresses his regrets and hastens to confer with the hostess. In a short time a goodly feast is spread. There is an immense joint of roast beef at the head of the table and a leg of mutton of equal bulk at the bottom, together with two large dishes of potatoes and French beans. With the potatoes there is butter sauce and in glass jars some pickled onions, which give a particular relish to the beef. Then for dessert there are grapes, walnuts, apples, crackers, and two sorts of pie. . . .

The supper gives Oliver so much satisfaction that he orders a bottle of wine. And the attentive landlord is not only forced to drink with him, but with like familiar condescension the wife and pretty daughter are invited to the supper room. There he sits in the best armchair, with the squire and mistress both standing up, and his legs crossed before him as comfortable as a lord. While he sings the ballad tune:

GOLDY

In Scarlet Town, where I was born
There was a fair maid dwellin'
Who made the youths sigh *Well-a-day!*
Her name was Barbara Allen. . . .

Before going to bed, he proceeds to give special instructions for a hot cake to breakfast, and it is not till he has dispatched this latter meal and is regarding his guinea with a pathetic look that the truth is told him by the good natured squire. Then the short, thick, ungainly young fellow in riding boots with a cockade in his hat blurts out his apologies and flees in confusion.

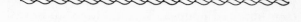

CHAPTER 3

BURGERSDICIUS AND
SMIGLECIUS

HENRY HAS DISTINGUISHED HIMSELF at the University and obtained a scholarship. His father now trusts that he will push forward for that comfortable provision, a fellowship, and then to higher dignities and emoluments. Henry, however, has the unworldliness of his race. Returning to the country during the succeeding vacation, he marries for love, of course relinquishes all his collegiate prospects and advantages, sets up a school in his father's neighborhood, and buries his talents and requirements for the remainder of his life in a curacy providing forty pounds a year.

Another matrimonial event occurs not long afterwards in the Goldsmith family to disturb the equanimity of its worthy head. This is the clandestine marriage of his daughter Catherine to a Mr. Daniel Hodson, a gentleman of property, who at the time is availing himself of Henry Goldsmith's services as a private tutor. As the youth is of wealthy parentage, it is thought a lucky match for the Goldsmith family, but tidings of the event sting the bride's father to the soul. Proud of his integrity and jealous of that good name which is his chief possession, he sees himself and his family subjected to the degrading suspicion of promoting a mercenary match. To ward off the imputation, and to show Mrs. Hodson that his daughter is no "penniless lass" with only "a lang pedigree" to her name, he furnishes as a marriage portion, four hundred pounds. To raise the sum in cash is impossible. But he assigns to Mr. Hodson his little farm and the income of his tithes until the money shall be raised.

By this arrangement all the rest of the family is pinched at the time and some of them permanently. If Oliver is to go to the University now, it must not be as a "pensioner," as brother Henry has gone, but in the lower grade of a "sizar."

There are five classes of students in Trinity College— noblemen, noblemen's sons, fellow-commoners, pensioners, and sizars, or poor scholars. The sizar has his commons and tuition free and pays a nominal sum for his chambers. To obtain these advantages he is expected to come more advanced in classical learning, to show himself a good scholar, and being clad in a coarse black gown and a red cap, to perform the duties of a housemaid upstairs and those of a scullion in the fellows' hall. In the morning he sweeps the court and scrubs the floor; in the afternoon he carries up dishes from the kitchen to the fellows' dining table; and in the evening he waits till the fellows have dined.

At this prospect Oliver recoils. He would rather, he declares, be bound to some trade. But Uncle Contarine, that is, the Reverend Thomas Contarine, clergyman of Oran, near Roscommon, intercedes and persuades him to yield. This worthy man, who has been the college companion of Bishop Berkeley and is possessed of some means, has married the sister of Goldsmith's father, but is now a widower with an only child Jane. No one has liked the boy better all along than Uncle Contarine. Already he has helped to maintain him at school, and during the holidays opened his house to him. Whatever affection would have gone to a son of his own, is transferred to his nephew Oliver. He insists that Oliver must go to college. What matters being a sizar? He was a sizar himself, and has he fared the worse for it?

The youth goes to Dublin, shows by passing the necessary examination that the time at school has not altogether been thrown away, and on the eleventh of June, 1745, is admitted at Trinity College, the last in a list of eight sizars who so present themselves.

The gaiety of a brawl with pistol shots and flashes of steel is indulged in every night in every grade of society in Dublin. This is called fun. In Ireland it is generally understood that no such good feeling exists as that which has been cemented by bloodshed.

Irish youth are high spirited and disdain any work not considered "fit for a gentleman." The professions are sneered at. An attorney-at-law is looked down upon as a slave in the southern colonies of America; a physician is on a social level with a horse dealer; and any man connected with commerce must never presume to sit down in the same room as a "gentleman." There are "a gentleman," "a real gentleman," "a gentleman to the backbone," and two or three other varieties.

Manners are barbarous. In the volume on etiquette entitled *Hints to Introduce Decorum at City Feasts and Sundry Ordinaries in Dublin,* the guest is cautioned not to be eager for the first cut from any joint at a banquet and not to have his plate heaped with meat and vegetables. Two pounds weight, roughly speaking, is suggested as reasonable to start with. It is inadvisable for the guest to drag the leg of a fowl through his teeth in order to secure his property in it and then to lay it by to pick at his leisure. And the author discountenances throwing rejected scraps of meat off one's plate into the dish. . . . Tables groan with abundance, but there is neither order nor good taste in the establishments. Burgundy is usually drunk during the dinner, which begins as early as two o'clock, and then whisky punch is freely indulged in until long past midnight.

The pleasure loving people have their courts, their assemblies, their routs, and their drawing rooms. They have a pretty fair conceit of themselves as patrons of the drama and carry their zeal for its welfare to such a length that every theater manager is bankrupt. For a full century the English stage gets its greatest ornaments from Dublin, and Dublin people discuss the theater, fête artists of the theater, and in fact do everything for the theater short of going to the theater. . . .

Trinity College is *Imperium in Imperio*—an aggregate of exclusiveness in comparison with which White's is a common tap room and Almack's a beer shop in the Borough. The college, though situated in the very center of Dublin, is a separate and distinct corporation in itself. It has its own laws and its own rules, and only upon some notable occasion, such as the celebration of the Battle of the Boyne, does it join hands with the city. Then it sends representatives to the procession that marches round the statue of William III and salutes the leaden figure of the great Prince of Orange.

The academic dress is pretty enough. It consists of a square cap resembling what you may see painted over grocer shops on the head of the Chinese Emperor, long black gowns differing according to the rank or standing of the wearer, some as full tassels as a livery servant's and some as plain as a parish sexton's. Add to these a small ornament projecting out from under the chin like gills, and called a band, and I believe you know the whole.

In Dublin College the Muses blush to be seen, and the only Graces that appear are Silence, Stupidity, and Sorrow. The fellows provide a wisdom that none can use. Barbara Celarent has both more music and more meaning than the hymns of Callimachus or the luminous and instructive pages of Thucydides. They sup on syllogisms, are enamored of their cobwebs, and bigoted in their by-laws. The whole library of a college youth consists of a Locke and a Murray with an Elrington's Euclid thumbed into importance.

First the student steers his course through the crabbed rules of logic, nicely showing how syllogistically well-formed arguments may strike opposition dumb. Then he roams through the pleasing scene of physics, explores the wondrous laws of motion and the nature of the liquid world. This done, he proceeds to where the aspiring mind views all the motions of the heavenly orbs and discerns the eclipse's course. Again he wanders through the moral world and now turns his eyes to the elegance of Greece and Rome— and when all is over, he hastens to the refuge of foaming bowls of punch.

In the evening the gilded youth sallies forth through the college gates to the diversions of the city. He is a prim young fellow with a cue or Adonis, plastered rather than powdered and appearing like the twigs of a gooseberry bush in a deep snow. He wears a pleated shirt ruffled at the hands and bosom, coat with a cape reaching like an old wife's tippet halfway down his back, shoulders crusted or iced over with a white as thick as a twelfth cake, milk white stockings, velvet breeches with silver buckles at the knees, tassels hanging halfway down his legs, Spanish leather pumps without heels and peaked toes seeming to stare the wearer in the face, fine buckles near as big as a coachhorse covering his instep and half his foot, and on his head a diminutive hat hardly bigger than a square inch of gingerbread at a country fair, gallantly cocked and adorned with a silver button and loop. In this manner with white gloves upon his hands, if he has no rings, and a white staff as tall as himself, he goes forth to delve in the mysteries of Bacchus and Venus. . . Towards midnight the fellows plunge through the streets to rake the body of sanctified youths into the college, some out of the watch house and some out of the kennel. . . .

Lord Chesterfield declares in 1731 that the education offered at Trinity is "indisputably better" than that at the English universities—but he does not mention the standards of taste prevailing there. Undoubtedly the College is improving. There is a fine library building, a new dining room (poorly constructed), and a handsome three hundred foot façade. But as there are many empty shelves in the most superb library and few modern publications, there is some ground for the severity of the following little epigram:

GOLDY

"Our Alma Mater like a whore,
Worn out with age and sin,
Paints and adorns herself the more,
The more she rots within."

Yet the Provost, Dr. Richard Baldwin, insists that the faculty perform the duties assigned to them—a startling innovation.

The gilded coach of the Lord Lieutenant with its six horses and outriders in gorgeous liveries, with its cavalry escort in all the bravery of helmet and saber, is driving down the broad college green straight for the college gates. Behind are noble chariots painted in all colors, with panels carved and gilded in many devices, every vehicle with four horses and postillions and half a dozen silken lackeys clinging in a double row on the footboard behind. . . . While lounging at the gate a small, thickset, plainfaced sizar in dingy garments gazes on the flowing stream, vivid and full of color, which rolls by him. . . .

Little goes well with poor Goldy in his student course. He has a menial position, a learned brute for his tutor, and few inclinations to the study exacted. But he is not without his consolations—he can sing a song well and at a new insult or outrage can blow off excitement through his flute with a kind of "mechanical vehemence." At the worst he has a knack at hoping.

His Edgeworthstown schoolfellow, John Beatty, a sizar too, shares his rooms which adjoin the library of a building numbered thirty-five.

A Trinity wag (John Winstanley) describes the typical dormitory room:

Imprimis, there's a *Table* blotted;
A tatter'd *Hanging* all besnotted;
A *Bed* of Flocks, as one may rank it,
Reduc'd to Rug, and half a Blanket. . . .
A *Penny-pot* and *Bason*, this
Design'd for *Water*, that for *Piss*. . . .

A rusty *Fork*, a blunted *Whittle*,
To cut his *Table* and his *Vittle*.
Item, if I am not mistaken,
A *Mouse-trap*, with a bit of *Bacon*. . . .
And *Chairs* a couple (I forget 'em)
But each of them without a Bottom.

In his spare time, after playing his flute and singing his Irish songs, Goldsmith amuses himself by scratching his name on the window pane.

He has his chums—Edward Mills, his relative, Robert Bryanton, also his relative, of whom he is fond, Lauchlan Macleane, and some others. Flood and Edmund Burke, both then in the college, barely notice him.

Theaker Wilder, Goldsmith's tutor, is a strong-bodied savage. Once upon receiving an accidental flick from a coachman's whip, he springs from the pavement to the box of the moving coach, and fells the driver to the ground. On another occasion, when he encounters a group of students dousing a troublesome bailiff under the College Pump, pretending to intervene for the man, he calls out, "Gentlemen, gentlemen, for the love of God, don't be so cruel as to nail his ears to the pump"—whereupon the students immediately act on the hint. The man is nailed up by one ear and left by his tormentors bleeding and shouting. Years later Goldsmith often declares that his tutor is "the most depraved profligate and licentious being in human shape." Yet Theaker Wilder is (at times) reportedly human. Meeting a young lady at a crossing where she cannot pass him without walking in the mud, he stops opposite her, and gazing for a moment on her face, lays his hands on each side and kisses her. He then nods familiarly at the astonished girl, and saying, "Take that, Miss, for being so handsome," steps out of the way, and lets her pass.

Mr. Wilder is devoted to logic and the exact sciences. Goldsmith is fond of the classics. The cold logic of Burgersdicius and the dreary subtleties of Smiglecius equally repel him. "Hideous Burgersdicius," Burke calls him, and dubs his famous logic "blackguard stuff, a hoard of exploded nonsense, the scum of pedantry and the refuse of the bog-house school of philosophy." Goldsmith thus expresses his opinion of Smiglecius:

"Wise Aristotle and Smiglecius
    By rationations specious
Have strove to prove with great precision,
    With definition and division,
Homo est ratione preditum,
    But for my soul I cannot credit 'em."

But mathematics is Mr. Wilder's intellectual passion and the same strength, agility, and ferocity which drive him into brawls with hackney coachmen, he carries to the demonstrations of Euclid.

Thomas Gray to his friend West—"It is very possible that two and two make four, but I would not give four farthings to demonstrate this ever so dearly; and if these be the profits of life, give me the amusements of it. The people I behold all around me, it seems, know all this and more, and yet I do not know one of them who inspires me with any ambition of being like him."

Wilder endeavors to force his favorite studies upon his student, insults him when he stands up in class, ridicules him as awkward and ugly, and at times indulges in personal violence. The pupil's shame and resentment harden into reckless idleness, and the college career of Oliver Goldsmith is proclaimed a wretched failure.

At the commencement of 1747, a year and a half after he has entered college, Goldsmith's father dies. The scanty sums required for his support are stopped altogether. His poverty is now relieved by occasional gifts from Uncle Contarine, by petty loans from Bryanton and Beatty, and by the desperate pawning of his books. He writes street ballads to save himself from actual starvation, sells them at the Reindeer repository in Mountrath Court for five shillings a piece, and steals out of the college at night to hear them sung.

Hidden by some dusky wall or creeping within the dark shadows of the ill-lighted streets, the poor neglected sizar watches and listens. Under the glow of an oil lamp, a large red faced Irishman with head thrown back, hands outstretched, and body swaying from side to side is singing his newly gotten ballads. A few beggars stand about, then some old men pause to listen, and finally an eager throng of lads and lasses crowd around, venturing a purchase with their last farthing.

The voice is cracked, harsh, discordant, but to Goldsmith it is sweet music, and with a light heart and a jaunty step, he makes his way, no longer in the dark shadows of the street, but where the glow is brightest, to the Rose and Bottle in Dame Street, or the Dog and Duck near Pudding Row. And as he goes, a ballad tune floats in the air, then softly dies in the distance.

I am a youthful damsel, I love my laddy well,
I thought his heart was true to me more than tongue can tell,
It's in my father's castle he won this heart of mine,
But he's left me to wander on the lovely Banks of Boyne.

His hair it flowed in ringlets, his cheeks were like the rose,
His teeth as white as ivory, his eyes as black as sloes,
His promises they seem'd sincere and his aspect bold and fine,
He left me here to wander on the lovely Banks of Boyne.

He courted me a year or two, he promised me to wed,
First he gain'd my favour and then from me he fled,
His love it flew like morning dew when the sun begins to shine,
And he quite forgot young Flora on. . . .

The next morning, Goldsmith having an appointment with a college friend, fails to make his appearance. The friend repairs to his room, knocks on the door, and is bidden to enter. To his surprise he finds Goldsmith in bed immersed to the chin in feathers. Goldsmith explains the circumstance.

In the course of the preceding evening's stroll, he met a woman with five children who was begging for charity. Her husband was in the hospital; she was just from the country, a stranger and destitute, and without food and shelter for her children. He brought her to the college gate, gave her the blankets from his bed to cover her children and part of his clothes for her to sell and purchase food. Finding himself cold during the night, he cut open the bed and buried himself among the feathers.

(The members of the Goldsmith clan have always a wealth of compassion but a paltry purse. Yet in their plenty they never turn a beggar away from the door—and there are an estimated 35,000 roaming the highways of Ireland. They accept the prevailing system: God made rich and poor, and each is to accept his lot meekly and unquestioningly. "Let us draw upon content for the deficiencies of fortune," says the Vicar. The good Lord will reward His (poor) children is His own good time.)

A report is brought to the college that a student is in the hands of the bailiff. A number of scholars fly to arms and sally forth to battle. They are headed by a hair-brained fellow nicknamed Gallows Welch, noted for his fondness for drink and riot. The stronghold of the bailiffs is carried by storm, the scholar set at liberty, and the offending catchpole borne off naked to the college pump where his delinquency is thoroughly washed out of him. Flushed with this signal victory, Gallows Welch now harangues his followers—"On to Newgate. Break open the Black Dog and free the prisoners." Cries and shouts of approval. And away go the madcap youngsters fully bent upon putting an end to the tyranny of justice. They are joined by a mob from the city, and together they make an attack upon the prison with true Irish precipitation and thoughtlessness. The Black Dog stands on the feeblest of legs, but it has a small piece of artillery. A few shots from the prison walls bring the mob to its senses. There is a hasty retreat. Two of the townsmen are killed, several wounded.

A severe scrutiny of the affair takes place at the University. Four of the ringleaders are discovered and expelled. Four others, prominent in the affray, are publicly admonished. Among the latter is the unlucky Oliver Goldsmith.

To counteract the disgrace he tries in the next month for a scholarship. He loses the scholarship but gains an exhibition, a small exhibition truly, worth some thirty shillings. There are nineteen such prizes—and his is the seventeenth on the list. This turn of fortune is too much for poor Goldy. The sudden influx of wealth goes to his head. He gives a supper and dance at his chamber to a number of young persons of both sexes from the city—in direct violation of the college rules.

Theaker Wilder is poring over his book on mathematics when the sounds of a fiddle and the stamping of feet reach his ears. He rushes into the banquet room, flaming fire and breathing vengeance, knocks down the father of the feast, and turns the astonished guests neck and heels out of doors.

This fills the measure of Goldsmith's humiliations. He feels degraded both within college and without. He dreads the ridicule of his fellow students for the ludicrous termination of his orgy, and he is ashamed to meet his city acquaintances after the degrading chastisement he received in their presence and after their ignominious expulsion. Above all, he refuses to submit any longer to the insulting tyranny of Wilder. He determines, therefore, to leave not merely the college, but also his native land, and to bury his disgrace in some distant country. Accordingly he sells his books and clothes, and with the proceeds, a few golden sovereigns jingling in his pocket, he sallies forth from the college gate the very next day, intending to embark at Cork for—any part beyond the sea—oh, well, America. But he loiters about Dublin, alternates between the Rose and Bottle and the Golden Sugar Loaf in Abbey Street, and reduces his finances to a shilling. With this amount he sets out on his journey.

For three days he subsists on the shilling. When that is

spent, he parts by degrees with some of the clothes on his back. Of all the exquisite meals he has tasted, the most delicious is a handful of grey peas given him by a girl at a wake after twenty-four hours fasting. Visions of America fade; hunger and fatigue calm his anger, and with feeble steps he turns to Lissoy. His brother Henry hears of his distress, goes to him, clothes him, and accompanies him back to college—and something of a reconciliation is affected between him and Wilder. But the latter at times cannot resist the temptation to taunt the scapegrace. Once, when discussing the center of gravity, Wilder asks, "Now, blockhead, where is your center of gravity?" and Goldsmith gives an obscene retort which sends him to the foot of the class.

The passing days witness, however, greater submission of the victim which marks an unsuccessful rebellion. He offers no resistance, makes no effort of any kind, and sits for the most part indulging in day dreams. One half of the day he is with Steele and Addison; the other half with Collins or Fielding.

On the twenty-seventh of February, 1749, he takes his degree of Bachelor of Arts. He is lowest in the list of the graduates who pass on the same day and become thereby entitled to use the college library.

His tutors are pleased to observe that they believe he is tolerably good natured and has not the least harm in him.

~~~~~~

CHAPTER 4

THREE JOLLY PIGEONS

IN HER STRAITENED CIRCUMSTANCES, Mrs.
Goldsmith has moved to a small cottage in Ballymahon to
which her son Oliver returns after his college career. He is
now in his twenty-first year. It is necessary that he should
do something—and his education has fitted him to do nothing but dress himself in gaudy colors, of which he is fond
as a magpie, take a hand at cards, sing Irish airs, play the
flute, angle in summer, and tell ghost stories by the fire in
winter.

His relatives urge him to prepare for holy orders. But
Goldsmith has both a settled repugnance to clerical life
and roving propensities. To be obliged to wear a long wig
when he likes a short one, or a black coat when he generally dresses in brown, he thinks such a restraint upon
his liberty that he absolutely rejects the proposal. But his
scruples are overruled by Uncle Contarine and he agrees
to qualify for the office. However, he is only twenty-one
and must pass two years of probation.

Ireland for centuries has been the field of the vagrant,
the home of the thriftless, the paradise of the lazy. There
the inhabitants can go on doing nothing for ever and ever.
It is the custom of the country to give every idler a chance
of pursuing a career of idleness. Only very rarely does such

a one fail to take advantage of the laxity of his friends.

Oliver Goldsmith occupies himself agreeably enough. From Ballymahon he wanders to Lissoy, from Lissoy to Pallas, and from Pallas to Uncle Contarine's at Roscommon, leading the life of a buckeen. His days are made up of journeyings from one house to another, of friendly fetching and carrying, of fishing and otter hunting in the isleted river of Inny, of flute playing with cousin Jane Contarine, and of throwing the hammer at the country fair. And on the roads at fair time, what opportunities for laughing, ogling, kissing, and sighing! Barefoot girls with cheeks like ripe pippins, laughing eyes with long dark, wicked lashes, teeth like ivory, necks of perfect poise, and waists that, never having known a corset, are pure Greek. There is beauty in Ireland—beauty of a rare and radiant type!

And lastly in the evenings, he presides over his merry companions at George Conway's Inn in Ballymahon. Here he is a triton among the minnows, the delight of horse doctors and bagmen and the idol of cousin Bob Bryanton, now of Ballymulvey—the triton, for has he not wit, is he not great at Latin quotations, and has not Cousin Bob seen his disgrace in college?

There is Dick Muggins, the exciseman, Jack Slang, the horse doctor, little Aminadab that grinds the music box, Tom Twist that spins the pewter platter, and Bill Bullet who picks up countesses at masquerades and walks around with lords and peers who admire his lounging gait and talk to him as to the Lords of State. And on Wednesdays and holidays, the Squire drops in, a thick merry wight in tight breeches, red coat, and a number six hat.

They dance a jig, step a minuet, lay cards, swap stories, and drive round the flowing bowl.

Omnes. "Hurrea! hurrea! hurrea! bravo!"

Bullet. "Well, but you must allow her a little beauty. Yes, you must allow her some beauty."

Muggins. "Order, gentlemen, order!"

Squire. "Ay! A pretty creature. I always loved Cousin

Con's hazel eyes, and her pretty long fingers, that she twists this way and that over the haspicholls, like a parcel of bobbins. But she's a bandbox!"

Jack Slang. "Oh, his father kept the best horses, dogs, and girls in the whole county."

Squire. "She's all a made up thing, mun. Ah! Could you but see Bet Bouncer of these parts, you might then talk of beauty. Ecod, she has two eyes as black as sloes, and cheeks as broad and red as a pulpit cushion. She'd make two of she." . . .

Tom Twist. "Now, gentlemen, silence for a song. Goldy is going to knock himself down for a song."

Omnes. "Ay, a song, a song!"

Aminadab. "I loves to hear him sing, bekcays he never gives us nothing that's low."

Jack Slang. "O damn anything that's low, I cannot bear it."

Goldsmith. "Then I'll sing you, gentlemen, a song I made upon this alehouse, the Three Pigeons."

> Let schoolmasters puzzle their brain
> With grammar, and nonsense, and learning,
> Good liquor, I stoutly maintain,
> Gives *genus* a better discerning.
> Let them brag of their heathenish gods,
> Their Lethes, their Styxes, and Stygians,
> Their Quis, and the Quaes, and their Quods,
> They're all but a parcel of Pigeons.
> Toroddle, toroddle, toroll.

> When Methodist preachers come down,
> A-preaching that drinking is sinful,
> I'll wager the rascals a crown,
> They always preach best with a skinful.
> But when you come down with your pence,
> For a slice of their scurvy religion,
> I'll leave it to all men of sense,
> But you, my good friend, are the Pigeon.
> Toroddle, toroddle, toroll.

Then come, put the jorum about,
    And let us be merry and clever,
Our hearts and our liquors are stout,
    Here's the Three Jolly Pigeons forever.
Let some cry up woodcock or hare,
    Your bustards, your ducks, and your widgeons;
But of all the *gay* birds in the air,
    Here's a health to the Three Jolly Pigeons.
                    Toroddle, toroddle, toroll.

Omnes. "Hurrea! Bravo! Bravo!"

Local tradition has it that Goldy is caught robbing Lord Annaly's orchard with another ne'er-do-well and is saved from prosecution because of his family's prominence.

So he spends his time idling. And when the two years are up, he dons his best scarlet breeches and makes his way to the Bishop of Elphin. The Bishop sends him back as he went, in short, plucked. And his friends are now perfectly satisfied he is undone, and yet they think it a pity, for one that has not the least harm in him and is so very good natured.

Uncle Contarine is still unwavering in his kindness, though he is much less sanguine in his expectations. He finds a gentleman of his county, a Mr. Flinn in want of a tutor, and he recommends Oliver. The situation is respectable—he has his seat at the table and he joins the family in their evening game at cards. But his deference for the family does not increase upon familiar intercourse. He charges a member of it with cheating at cards. A violent argument follows, and Oliver throws up his situation as tutor. Perhaps he has the Flinns in mind when he afterwards complains that "men of a thousand pound a year in Ireland spend their whole lives in running after a hare, drinking to be drunk, and getting every girl with child that will let them." On being paid he is in possession of an unheard of amount of money. He desires to see the world. He procures a good plump horse, and with thirty pounds in his pocket, makes a second sally into the world.

Weeks elapse. Nothing is seen or heard of him. It is feared he has left the country on one of his wandering freaks, and his poor mother is reduced almost to despair. But one day, Oliver rides up to the gate—with nothing in his pocket and on a lean beast Fiddleback. "And now my dear mother, after having struggled so hard to come home to you, I wonder you are not more rejoiced to see me."

His mother rates him soundly—calls him "an ungrateful savage, a monster in short." But his brothers and sisters interfere and succeed in cooling her ire. Gathering the family around him, he tells a whimsical story:

"My dear mother, if you will sit down and calmly listen to what I say, you shall be fully resolved in every one of those many questions you have asked me. I went to Cork and converted my horse, which you prize so much higher than Fiddleback, into cash, took my passage in a ship bound for America, and, at the same time, paid the captain for my freight and all the other expenses of my voyage. But it so happened that the wind did not answer for three weeks, and you know, mother, that I could not command the elements. My misfortune was that, when the wind served, I happened to be with a party in the country, and my friend the captain never inquired after me, but set sail with as much indifference as if I had been on board. The remainder of my time I employed in the city and its environs, viewing everything curious, and you know no one can starve while he has money in his pocket." (Maurice and Charles shake their heads. Mrs. Goldsmith glowers.) He continues:

"Reduced, however, to my last two guineas, I began to think of my dear mother and friends whom I had left behind me, and so bought that generous beast Fiddleback and bade adieu to Cork with only five shillings in my pocket." (Oliver waits until Uncle Contarine has stopped laughing.) "This, to be sure, was but a scanty allowance for man and horse toward a journey of above a hundred miles, but I did not despair, for I knew I must find friends on the road.

"I recollected particularly an old and faithful acquaintance I made at college, who had often and earnestly pressed me to spend a summer with him, and he lived but eight miles from Cork. This circumstance of vicinity he would expatiate on me with peculiar emphasis. 'We shall,' said he, 'enjoy the delights of both city and country, and you shall command my stable and my purse.'

"However, upon the way I met a poor woman all in tears, who told me her husband had been arrested for a debt he was not able to pay, and that his eight children must now starve, bereaved as they were of his industry, which had been their only support. I thought myself at home, being not far from my friend's house, and therefore parted with a moiety of all my store. And pray, mother, ought I not to have given her the other half crown, for what she got would be of little use to her?" ("Surely, surely," cries brother Henry. "Go on," remarks Mrs. Goldsmith.) "However, I soon arrived at the mansion of my affectionate friend, guarded by the vigilance of a huge mastiff, who flew at me and would have torn me to pieces but for the assistance of a woman, whose countenance was not less grim than that of the dog. Yet she with great humanity relieved me from the jaws of this Cerberus, and was prevailed on to carry up my name to her master."

("I hope your father's jacket is in good conditon."— "Why, yes, mother.")

"Without suffering me to wait long, my old friend, who was then recovering from a severe fit of sickness, came down in his nightcap, nightgown, and slippers, and embraced me with the most cordial welcome, showed me in, and, after giving me a history of his indisposition, assured me that he considered himself peculiarly fortunate in having under his roof the man he most loved on earth, and whose stay with him must, above all things, contribute to perfect his recovery. I now repented sorely I had not given the poor woman the other half crown, as I thought all my bills of humanity would be punctually answered by this worthy man. I revealed to him my whole soul. I opened to him all my distresses, and freely owned that I had but one half crown in my pocket; but that now, like a ship after weathering out the storm, I considered myself secure in a safe and hospitable harbor. He made no answer, but walked about the room, rubbing his hands as one in deep study. This I imputed to the sympathetic feelings of a tender heart, which increased my esteem for him, and, as that increased, I gave the most favorable interpretation to his silence. I construed it into delicacy of sentiment, as if he dreaded to wound my pride by expressing his commiseration in words, leaving his generous conduct to speak for itself.

"It now approached six o'clock in the evening, and as I had eaten no breakfast, and as my spirits were raised, my appetite for dinner grew uncommonly keen. At length the old woman came into the room with two plates, one spoon, and a dirty cloth, which she laid upon the table. This appearance, without increasing my spirits, did not diminish my appetite. My protectress soon returned with a small bowl of sago, a small porringer of sour milk, a loaf of stale brown bread, and the heel of an old cheese all over crawling with mites. My friend apologized that his illness obliged him to live on slops, and that better fare was not in the house, observing at the same time, that a milk diet was certainly the most healthful; and at eight o'clock he again recommended a regular life, declaring that for his part he would lie down with the lamb and rise with the lark. My hunger was at this time so exceedingly sharp that I wished for another slice of the loaf, but was obliged to go to bed without even that refreshment.

"This lenten entertainment I had received made me resolve to depart as soon as possible. Accordingly, next morning, when I spoke of going, he did not oppose my resolution; he rather commended my design, adding some very sage counsel upon the occasion. 'To be sure,' said he, 'the longer you stay away from your mother, the more you will grieve her and your other friends; and possibly they are already afflicted at hearing of this foolish expedition you have made.' Notwithstanding all this, and without any hope of softening such a sordid heart, I again renewed the tale of my distress, and asking how he thought I could travel above a hundred miles upon one half crown, I begged to borrow a single guinea, which I assured him should be repaid with thanks. 'And you know, sir,' said I, 'it is no more than I have done for you.' To which he firmly answered, 'Why, look you, Mr. Goldsmith, that is neither here nor there. I have paid you all you ever lent me, and this sickness of mine has left me bare of cash. But I have bethought myself of a conveyance for you. Sell your horse and I will furnish you a much better one to ride on.' I readily grasped at his proposal, and begged to see the nag, on which he led me to his bedchamber, and from under the bed he pulled out a stout oak stick. 'Here it is,' said he, 'take this in your hand, and it will carry you to your mother's with more safety than such a horse as you ride.' I was in doubt, when I got it into my hand, whether I should not, in the first place, apply it to his pate, but a rap at the street door made the wretch fly to it, and when I returned to the parlor, he introduced me, as if nothing of the kind had happened, to the gentleman who entered, as Mr. Goldsmith, his most ingenious and worthy friend, of whom he had so often heard him speak with rapture. I could scarcely compose myself, and must have betrayed indignation in my mien to the stranger, who was a counselor-at-law in the neighborhood, a man of engaging aspect and political address.

"After spending an hour, he asked my friend and me to dine with him at his house. This I declined at first, as I wished to have no further communication with my hospitable friend, but at the solicitation of both, I at last consented, determined as I was by two motives: one that I was prejudiced in favor of the looks and manner of the counselor; and the other that I stood in need of a comfortable dinner. And there, indeed, I found everything that I could wish, abundance without profusion and elegance without affectation. In the evening, when my old friend, who had eaten very plentifully at his neighbor's table, but talked again of lying down with the lamb, made a motion to me for retiring, our generous host requested I should take a bed with him, upon which I plainly told my old friend that he might go home and take care of the horse he had given me, but that I should never reenter his doors. He went away with a laugh, leaving me to add this to the other little things the counselor already knew of his plausible neighbor.

"And now, my dear mother, I found sufficient to reconcile me to all my follies, for here I spent three whole days. The counselor had two sweet girls for daughters, who played enchantingly on the harpsichord; and yet it was but a melancholy pleasure I felt the first time I heard them, for that being the first time also that either of them had touched the instrument since their mother's death, I saw the tears in silence trickle down their father's cheeks. I every day endeavored to go away, but every day was pressed and obliged to stay. On my going, the counselor offered me his purse, with a horse and servant to convey me home, but the latter I declined, and only took a guinea to bear my necessary expenses on the road. . . ."

A new consultation is held among the family and it is determined Oliver shall try law. Good Uncle Contarine comes forward with fifty pounds, and Goldy sets off for London to enter on his studies at the Temple. In Dublin a Roscommon acquaintance lays hold of him, shakes him by the hand, proposes adjourning to a public house and taking a glass of whatever they can get. Goldy readily closes with the offer, and entering an alehouse, they are shown into a little back room where there is only a venerable old man, who sits wholly intent over a large book, which he is reading. The friends never in their lives have seen a figure that prepossesses them more favorably. His locks of silver grey venerably shade his temples, and his green old age seems to be the result of health and benevolence. However, his

presence does not interrupt their conversation, and they
discourse on the various turns of fortune they have met.
But their attention is in a short time diverted by the appearance of a youth, who, entering the room, respectfully
says something softly to the stranger.

"Make no apologies, my child," says the old man, "to do
good is a duty we owe to all our fellow creatures. Take this,
I wish it were more, but five pounds will relieve your distress and you are welcome."

The modest youth sheds tears of gratitude and yet his
gratitude is scarce equal to theirs. They can hug the good
old man, his benevolence pleases them so. He continues
to read and they resume their conversation, referring by
the way to the late Reverend Charles Goldsmith. The old
gentleman, hearing the name mentioned, seems to look at
Goldy for some time, and then respectfully demands if he
is in any way related to the great Doctor Goldsmith, that
courageous monogamist, who has been the bulwark of the
Church. Never does Goldy's heart feel sincerer rapture than
at that moment.

"Sir," says the stranger, "I fear I have been too familiar,
but you'll forgive my curiosity, sir. I beg pardon."

"Sir," cries Goldy, grasping his hand, "you are so far
from displeasing me by your familiarity that I must beg
you'll accept my friendship, as you already have my esteem."

"Then with gratitude, young sir, I accept the offer,"
squeezing Goldy by the hand. No lovers in romance ever
cemented a more instantaneous friendship.

They talk upon several subjects and take occasion to
observe that the world in general is beginning to be blam-
ably indifferent as to doctrinal matters and follow human
speculations too much.

"Ay, sirs," replies he, as if he reserved all his learning to
that moment. "Ay, sirs, the world is in its dotage, and yet
the cosmogony, or creation of the world, has puzzled philosophers of all ages. What a medley of opinions have they
not broached upon the creation of the world! Sanchoniathon,

Manetho, Berosus, and Ocellus Lucanus, have all attempted it in vain. The latter has these words, *Anarchon ara kai ate-lutaion to pan,* which imply that all things have neither beginning nor end. Manetho also, who lived about the time of Nebuchadon-Asser-Asser, being a Syriac word, usually applied as a surname to the kings of that country, as Teglat Pháel-Asser, Nabon-Asser—he, I say, formed a conjecture equally absurd, for as we usually say, *ek to biblion kuber-netes,* which implies that books will never teach the world, so he attempted to investigate—But, sirs, I ask pardon, I am straying from the question."

That he actually is, nor can the friends for their lives, see how the creation of the world has anything to do with the business they are talking of. But it is sufficient to show them that he is a man of letters, and they now reverence him the more. They are resolved, therefore, to bring him to the touchstone, but he is too mild and gentle to contend for victory. Whenever they make an observation that looks like a challenge to controversy, he smiles, shakes his head, and says nothing. By which the friends understand he can say much, if he thinks proper. Subjects are thus changed quickly, and Goldy is about to launch on the wide seas of politics when a loutish young fellow enters the room, throws a pack of cards on the table, and asks if there are any real *honest* gentlemen to join him. The Roscommon lad jumps at the proposition. Goldy looks doubtful. Then their vene-rable friend screwing up his face and looking quizzically at him, says, "What say you, lad, shall we not join them?" . . . A bottle of wine is poured and the cards are dealt. And Ephraim Jenkinson, for that is the good man's name, slowly closes his book, takes a large pinch of snuff, and rubs his hands. . . .

The fifty pounds are reduced to fifty pence. In bitter shame, Goldsmith writes to Uncle Contarine, confesses, and is forgiven. On his return to Ballymahon, his mother objects to receiving him; his brother Henry loses patience, and quarrels with him. And so he is welcomed at the parsonage of his affectionate, forgiving, generous Uncle Contarine.

Uncle Contarine is a disciple of Bacon, who compares money to manure. "If gathered in heaps," he says, "it does no good; on the contrary, it becomes offensive. But being spread, though never so thinly, over the surface of the earth, it enriches the whole country."

With Uncle Contarine's influence, Oliver is invited to a visitation dinner. To understand this term, you must know that it was formerly the custom for the bishops to go about the country once a year, and examine upon the spot whether those of subordinate orders did their duty or were qualified for the task; whether their temples were kept in proper repair, or the laity pleased with their administration. Though a visitation of this nature was extremely useful, yet it was found to be exceedingly troublesome, and for many reasons utterly inconvenient; for as the bishops were obliged to attend at court in order to solicit preferment, it was impossible that they could at the same time attend in the country, which was quite out of the road to promotion. If we add to this the gout, a clerical disorder, together with the bad wine and ill-dressed provisions that must infallibly be served up by the way, it is not strange that the custom has been long discontinued. At present, therefore, every head of the Church, instead of going about to visit his priests, is satisfied if his priests come in a body once a year to visit him. By this means the duty of half a year is dispatched in a day. When assembled, he asks each in turn how they have behaved, and are liked, upon which those who have neglected their duty or are disagreeable to their congregation, no doubt accuse themselves, and tell him all their faults, for which he reprimands them most severely.

The thought of being introduced into a company of philosophers and learned men (for as such he conceives them) gives Oliver no small pleasure. He expects the entertainment to resemble those sentimental banquets so finely described by Xenophon and Plato. He is hoping some Socrates will be brought in from the door, in order to harangue upon divine love. As for eating and drinking, he has prepared himself to be disappointed in that particular—so that he expects an entertainment where there will be much reasoning and little meat.

Upon being introduced he finds no great signs of frugality in the faces or persons of the company. However, he imputes their florid looks to temperance, and their corpulency to a sedentary way of living. He sees several preparations, indeed, for dinner, but none for philosophy. The company seems to gaze upon the table with silent expectation, but this he easily excuses. Men of wisdom, thinks he, are ever slow of speech. They deliver nothing inadvisedly. "Silence," says Confucius, "is a friend that will never betray."

Oliver's curiosity is now wrought up to the highest pitch. He impatiently looks around to see if any are going to interrupt the mighty pause, when at last one of the company declares that there is a sow in his neighborhood that farrows fifteen pigs at a litter. This, Oliver thinks, a very preposterous beginning, but just as another is going to second the remark, dinner is served, which interrupts the conversation for that time.

The appearance of dinner, which consists of a variety of dishes, seems to diffuse new cheerfulness upon every face, so that he now expects the philosophical conversation to begin, as they improve in good humor. The principal priest, however, opens his mouth with only observing that the venison has not been kept enough, though he has given strict orders for having it killed ten days before. "I fear," continues he, "it will be found to want the true healthy flavor. You will find nothing of the original wildness in it."

A priest who sits next him, having smelled it and wiped his nose, "Ah, my good lord," cries he, "you are too modest. It is perfectly fine. Everybody knows that nobody understands keeping venison with your lordship."

"Ay, and partridges, too," interrupts another. "I never find them right anywhere else."

His lordship is going to reply when a third takes off the attention of the company, by recommending the pig as inimitable. "I fancy, my lord," continues he, "it has been smothered in its own blood."

"If it has been smothered in its blood," cries a facetious member, helping himself, "we'll now smother it in egg sauce."

This poignant piece of humor produces a long, loud laugh, and the facetious brother, now that he is in luck, willing to second the blow, assures the company he will tell them a good story. "As good a story," cries he, bursting into a violent fit of laughter himself, "as ever you heard in your lives. There was a farmer in my parish who used to sup upon wild ducks and flummery, so this farmer——"

"Doctor Marrowfat," cries his lordship, interrupting him, "give me leave to drink your health."

"So being fond of wild ducks and flummery——"

"Doctor," adds a gentleman who sits next to him, "let me advise you to a wing of this turkey."

"So this farmer being fond——"

"Hob and nob, Doctor. Which do you choose, white or red?"

"So being fond of wild ducks and flummery——"

"Take care of your band, sir, it may dip in the gravy."

The Doctor, now looking round, finds not a single eye disposed to listen. Wherefore, calling for a glass of wine, he gulps down the disappointment and the tale in a bumper.

The conversation now begins to be little more than a rhapsody of exclamations. As each has pretty well satisfied his own appetite, he now finds sufficient time to press others. "Excellent! the very thing! let me recommend the pig. Do but taste the bacon! never ate a better thing in my life. Exquisite! Delicious!" This edifying discourse continues through three courses, which lasts as many hours, till every one of the company is unable to swallow or utter anything more.

Then Oliver gets up and returns again to Uncle Contarine's fireside, talking literature to the good natured man, writing new verses to please him, and joining his flute to Miss Jane Contarine's harpsichord.

CHAPTER 5

OATCAKES AND PREJUDICES

DEAN GOLDSMITH of Cloyne pays a visit. A cold grandee and arbiter elegantiarum of the Goldsmith family. Oliver makes a remark which shows him to be no fool, and the Dean suggests that as he has attempted divinity and law without success, he should now try physic. The Dean having given the advice, adds to it his blessing, but no money. That is furnished by Henry, Mrs. Hodson, and Uncle Contarine. And so in the autumn of 1752 Oliver Goldsmith starts for Edinburgh as a medical student.

On the day of his arrival, after leaving his baggage at his hired lodgings, he sallies forth to see the town. At a late hour, when he thinks of returning home, he finds to his confusion that he has forgotten to inquire the name either of his landlady or the street in which she lives. Fortunately, in the height of his perplexity, he meets the porter who has carried his trunk and who now acts as his guide.

He does not remain long in the lodgings in which he has put up. His hostess is too adroit at that hocus pocus of the table often practised in cheap boarding houses. No one can conjure a single loin of mutton through a greater variety of forms—a brandered chop one day, a fried steak another, chops with onion sauce, a third, and so on till the fleshy parts are quite consumed. Then finally, on the seventh day, a dish of broth manufactured from the bones appears, and

[51]

the ingenious landlady rests from her labors. Falling in with some fellow students from his own country, Oliver joins them at more eligible quarters.

He finds the faculty of the college disappointing. The professors speak but little to the purpose, or say nothing but what may be found in books laid before the students, or lecture in so droning and heavy a manner that their hearers are not many degrees in a better state than their patients. But, happily, there are no residence requirements, no supervision of the students' conduct outside of class, and a young man can present himself for examination whenever he feels prepared to do so.

Any learned renown Oliver gets in the schools pales before his amazing social repute. He is the inimitable story teller, the capital singer of Irish songs, the rallying point of good fellowship. He becomes a member of the Medical Society and on his admission is exempted from the usual condition of reading a paper on a medical subject.

Once, in company with several fellows on the first night of a new play, he suddenly proposes to draw lots with any one present which of the two shall treat the whole party to the theater. The moment the proposition bolts from his lips, his heart is in his throat. But the Scotsmen shake their hands and decline the challenge. They are ready to carry the evening's orgy a certain distance, but they know where to stop. "Had the challenge been accepted," Oliver says, "and had I proved the loser, a part of my wardrobe must have been pledged in order to raise the money."

One of his friends, Honmer, introduces him at the beginning of the year to a merchant tailor with whom he deals for sundry items of hose, hats, silver lace, satin, allapeen, fustian, durant, shalloon cloth, and velvet. These materials are charged to him from January to December of the year in the not very immoderate sum of £9, 11s, 2¼d. Among the items listed are sky-blew satten," fine sky-blue shalloon with superfine silver laced small hat, rich black "Genoa velvett," and, of course, that best superfine "clarett-colour'd" cloth in which this odd little clumsy figure thus early arrays itself.

His convivial talents gain him attention in a high quarter. Every second day, for more than a fortnight, he is at the Duke of Hamilton's. But it seems they like him more as a jester than as a companion, so he disdains so servile an employment as unworthy his calling as a physician.

At first there is no great trouble in listening attentively when his lordship speaks, and laughing when he looks round for applause. This even good manners oblige him to perform. He finds, however, too soon, that his lordship is a greater dunce than himself and from that moment flattery is at an end. He now rather aims at setting his lordship right than at receiving his absurdities with submission. (To flatter those we do not know is an easy task, but to flatter our intimate acquaintances, whose foibles are strongly in our eyes, is drudgery insupportable.) Every time he now opens his lips in praise, his falsehood goes to his conscience. His lordship soon perceives him to be very unfit for his service, and he is therefore discharged—his patron at the same time being graciously pleased to observe that he believes he is tolerably good natured and has not the least harm in him.

He takes, on one occasion, a month's excursion to the Highlands. He sets out the first day on foot, but an ill-natured corn on his toe for the future prevents that cheap mode of travelling. So the second day he hires a horse about the size of a ram, and the horse walks away (trot he cannot) as pensive as his master.

To Robert Bryanton of Ballymahon, Ireland. "MY DEAR BOB—How many good excuses (and you know I was ever good at an excuse) might I call up to vindicate my past shameful silence. I might tell how I wrote a long letter on my first coming hither, and seem vastly angry at my not receiving an answer. I might allege that business (with business you know I was always pestered) had never given

me time to finger a pen. But I suppress those and twenty
more as plausible, and as easily invented, since they might
be attended with a slight inconvenience of being known to
be lies. Let me then speak truth. An hereditary indolence
(I have it from the mother's side) has hitherto prevented
my writing to you, and still prevents my writing at least
twenty-five letters more, due to my friends in Ireland. No
turn spit dog gets up into his wheel with more reluctance
than I sit down to write, yet no dog ever loved the roast
meat he turns better than I do him I now address.

"Yet what shall I say now I am entered? Shall I tire you
with a description of this unfruitful country, where I must
lead you over their hills all brown with heath, or their
valleys scarcely able to feed a rabbit? Man alone seems to
be the only creature who has arrived to the natural size in
this poor soil. Every part of the country presents the same
dismal landscape. No grove, nor brook lend their music to
cheer the stranger or make the inhabitants forget their poverty. Yet with all these disadvantages to call him down to
humility, a Scotchman is one of the proudest things alive.
The poor have pride ever ready to relieve them. If mankind should happen to despise them, they are masters of
their own admiration, and that they can plentifully bestow
upon themselves.

"From their pride and poverty, as I take it, results one
advantage this country enjoys—namely, the gentlemen here
are much better bred than among us. No such character
here as our fox-hunters; and they have expressed great surprise when I informed them that some men in Ireland of
one thousand pounds a year spend their whole lives in
running after a hare, and drinking to be drunk. Truly if
such a being, equipped in his hunting dress, came among
a circle of Scotch gentry, they would behold him with the
same astonishment that a countryman does King George
on horseback.

"The men here have generally high cheek bones, and
are lean and swarthy, fond of action, dancing in particular.

Now that I have mentioned dancing, let me say something of their balls, which are very frequent here. When a stranger enters the dancing hall, he sees one end of the room taken up by the ladies, who sit dismally in a group by themselves; in the other end stand their pensive partners that are to be; but no intercourse between the sexes than there is between two countries at war. The ladies indeed may ogle, and the gentlemen sigh, but an embargo is laid on any closer commerce. At length, to interrupt hostilities, the lady directress, or intendant, or what you will, pitches upon a lady and gentleman to walk a minuet, which they perform with a formality that approaches to despondence. After five or six couples have thus walked the gantlet, all stand up to country dances, each gentleman furnished with a partner from the aforesaid lady directress. So they dance much, say nothing, and thus concludes our assembly. I told a Scotch gentleman that such profound silence resembled the ancient procession of the Roman matrons in honor of Ceres, and the Scotch gentleman told me (and faith, I believe he was right) that I was a very great pedant for my pains.

"Now I am come to the ladies, and to show that I love Scotland, and everything that belongs to so charming a country, I insist on it, and will give him leave to break my head that denies it—that the Scotch ladies are ten thousand times finer and handsomer than the Irish. To be sure, now, I see your sisters Betty and Peggy vastly surprised at my partiality—but tell them flatly, I don't value them—or their fine skins, or eyes, or good sense a potato—for I say it and will maintain it; and as a convincing proof (I am in a great passion) of what I assert, the Scotch ladies say it themselves. But to be less serious. Where will you find a language so prettily become a pretty mouth as the broad Scotch? And the women here speak it in its highest purity. For instance, teach one of your young ladies at home to pronounce the 'Whoar wull I gong?' with a becoming widening of mouth, and I'll lay my life they'll wound every hearer.

"We have no such character here as a coquette, but alas!

how many envious prudes! Some days ago I walked into my Lord Kilcoubry's (don't be surprised, my lord is but a glover), when the Duchess of Hamilton (that fair who sacrificed her beauty to her ambition, and her inward peace to a title and gilt equipage) passed by in her chariot. Her battered husband, or more properly the guardian of her charms, sat by her side. Straight envy began, in the shape of no less than three ladies who sat with me, to find faults in her faultless form. 'For my part,' says the first, 'I think what I always thought, that the Duchess has too much of the red in her complexion.' 'Madame, I am of your opinion,' says the second. 'I think her face has a palish cast too much on the delicate order.' 'And let me tell you,' added the third lady, whose mouth was puckered up to the size of an issue, 'that the duchess has fine lips, but she wants a mouth.' At this every lady drew up her mouth as if going to pronounce the letter P.

"But how ill, my Bob, does it become me to ridicule women with whom I have scarcely any correspondence! There are, 'tis certain, handsome women here, and 'tis certain they have handsome men to keep them company. An ugly and poor man is society only for himself, and such society the world lets me enjoy in great abundance. Fortune has given you circumstances, and nature a person to look charming in the eyes of the fair. Nor do I envy my dear Bob such blessings, while I may sit down and laugh at the world and at myself—the most ridiculous object in it. But you see I am grown downright splenetic, and perhaps the fit may continue till I receive an answer to this. I know you cannot send me much news from Ballymahon, but such as it is, send it all. Everything you send will be agreeable to me.

"Has George Conway put up a sign yet, or John Binley left off drinking drams, or Tom Allen got a new wig? But I leave you to your own choice what to write. While I live, know you have a true friend in yours, etc., etc.

"OLIVER GOLDSMITH

"P.S.—Give my sincere respects (not compliments, do you mind) to your agreeable family, and give my service to my mother, if you see her, for, as you express it in Ireland, I have a sneaking kindness for her still. Direct to me,——, Student in Physic, in Edinburgh."

After spending two winters at Edinburgh, Goldsmith expresses a desire to finish his medical studies on the continent, and Uncle Contarine agrees to furnish the funds. The wastrel has now persuaded himself of what he has sought to persuade his uncle—that nothing gathers more moss than a rolling stone. "I intend," says he, in a letter to his uncle, "to visit Paris, where the great Farheim, Petit, and Du Hammel de Monceau instruct their pupils in all the branches of medicine. They speak French and consequently I shall have much the advantage of most of my countrymen, as I am perfectly acquainted with that language, and few who leave Ireland are so." (A considerable body of French Huguenots live in Dublin and perhaps Goldy has become familiar with some of them.) "I shall spend the spring and summer in Paris, and the beginning of next winter go to Leyden. The great Albinus is still alive there and 'twill be proper to go, though only to have it said that we have studied in so famous a university."

His usual indiscretion attends him at the outset. He is bound for Leyden, but on arriving at Leith, he finds a ship about to sail for Bordeaux with six agreeable passengers whose acquaintance he has made at an inn. And so, instead of embarking for Leyden, he finds himself plowing the seas on his way to the other side of the Continent. Scarcely has the ship been two days out at sea than she is driven by a storm to Newcastle-on-Tyne. Here, of course, Goldy and his agreeable companions find it expedient to go on shore and refresh themselves after the fatigues of the voyage. And, of course, they frolic and make merry until a late hour of the evening. Then, suddenly, in the midst of their hilarity, the door is burst open—a sergeant and twelve grenadiers enter with fixed bayonets—and the whole convivial party are taken prisoners.

Our greenhorn now discovers that the agreeable companions, with whom he has struck up such a sudden intimacy, are Scotsmen in the French service who have been in Scotland enlisting recruits for the French army.

In vain he protests his innocence. He is marched off with his fellow revelers to prison, and only at the end of a fortnight does he succeed in obtaining his freedom.

But everything has turned out for the best, for during his detention the ship sails without him and sinks at the mouth of the Garonne.

At last he gets to Leyden—and looks around. To Uncle Contarine: "The modern Dutchman is quite a different creature from him of former times. He in everything imitates a Frenchman but in his easy, disengaged air. He is vastly ceremonious, and is, perhaps, exactly what a Frenchman might have been in the reign of Louis XIV. Such are the better bred. But the downright Hollander is one of the oddest figures in nature. Upon a lank head of hair he wears a half-cocked narrow hat, laced with black ribbon; no coat but seven waistcoats and nine pair of breeches, so that his hips reach up almost to his armpits. This well clothed vegetable is now fit to see company or make love. But what a pleasing creature is the object of his appetite! Why she wears a large fur cap, with a deal of Flanders lace, and for every pair of breeches he carries, she puts on two petticoats.

"A Dutch lady burns nothing about her phlegmatic admirer but his tobacco. You must know, sir, every woman carries in her hand a stove of coals, which, when she sits, she snugs under her petticoats, and at this chimney dozing Strephon lights his pipe."

He contrasts Scotland and Holland. "There hills and rocks intercept every prospect; here it is all a continued plain. There you might see a well dressed duchess issuing from a dirty close, and here a dirty Dutchman inhabiting a palace. The Scotch may be compared to a tulip, planted in dung, but I can never see a Dutchman in his own house but I think of a magnificent Egyptian temple dedicated to an ox."

He remains about a year at the learned city, attends the lectures of Gaubius on chemistry and Albinus on anatomy, and makes the acquaintance of our Chinese philosopher, Lien Chi Altangi, on the way to London town. He wears a sword like the regularly enrolled students, frequents the Indian cabinet and the gallery of the famous physic garden where he observes such oddities as a hippopotamus, a winged cat, and a mermaid's hand. Perhaps his extreme poverty prevents him from becoming a regular student.

The thirty-three pounds with which he has set out on his journey are soon consumed, and he is put to many a shift to meet his expenses. Sometimes, when pinched, he borrows from his fellow student and countryman, Ellis; sometimes, when flush, he resorts to the gaming tables which abound in Holland. And sometimes he undertakes teaching. He addresses himself to two or three of those he meets whose appearance seems most promising, but it is impossible to make themselves mutually understood. It is not till this moment he recollects, that in order to teach the Dutchman English, it is necessary that they should first teach him Dutch. How he comes to overlook so obvious an objection is to him amazing, but certain it is, he overlooks it.

The gaming tables strip him of every shilling. Ellis again steps in with true Irish generosity and offers to aid him if he quits Holland. Goldsmith gladly consents, speaks of Paris, and is furnished by his friend with a trifling sum for the journey. But before quitting Leyden, he happens to pass a tulip garden, and seeing some rare and high priced flowers which his Uncle Contarine, a tulip fancier, has long been in search of, he runs in, buys a parcel of the roots, and sends them off to Ireland. Then he bethinks himself that he has spent all the money borrowed for his travelling expenses. Too proud, however, to give up his journey, and too shamefaced to make another appeal to Ellis, he determines to travel on foot. And so, the next day, he leaves Leyden with a guinea in his pocket, one shirt to his back, and a flute in his hand.

CHAPTER 6

A PHILOSOPHIC VAGABOND

1.

BLESSED WITH A GOOD CONSTITUTION, an adventurous spirit, and a thoughtless disposition, Goldsmith continues his travels for a long time in spite of innumerable privations. He has some knowledge of music, a tolerable voice, and now turns what is his amusement into a present means of subsistence. He passes among the harmless peasants of Flanders, and among such of the French as are poor enough to be very merry, for he ever finds them sprightly in proportion to their wants. Whenever he approaches a peasant's house towards nightfall, he plays one of his most merry tunes, and that procures him not only a lodging, but subsistence for the next day. He once or twice attempts to play for people of fashion, but they always think his performance odious and never reward him even with a trifle. This is to him the more extraordinary, as, whenever he used, in better days, to play for company, when playing was his amusement, his music never failed to throw them into raptures, and the ladies especially. But as it is now his only means, it is received with contempt.

And so he wanders on, sleeping in barns, begging, bear

leading, and disputing his passage through Europe. And he
lives on hope, which, as Bacon says, is a good breakfast
but a bad supper.

Louvain attracts him as he passes through Flanders, but
despite later reports he does not take a degree of bachelor
of medicine. At Antwerp he lets no time pass till he has
seen the great paintings—Rubens, Vander Meuylen, Van
Dyke, and Wouverman. From these he goes to view the
cardinal's statues, which are really very fine, and is puz-
zling before a torso when a guide informs him that it is
a Hercules spinning and not a Cleopatra bathing as has
been conjectured. There has been a treatise written to
prove it.

He proceeds to Paris with no design but just to look
about him and then to go forward. The people of Paris
are much fonder of strangers that have money than those
that have wit. As he cannot boast much of either, he is
no great favorite. After walking about the town four or five
days, and seeing the outsides of the best houses, he is preparing to leave, when passing through one of the principal
streets, he meets a friend and fellow countryman. The
friend inquires into the nature of his journey to Paris, and
informs him of his own business there, which is to collect
pictures, medals, intaglios, and antiques of all kinds for a
gentleman in London who has just stepped into taste and
a large fortune. Goldsmith is the more surprised at seeing
his friend pitched upon for this office, as he himself has
often told him that he knows nothing of the matter. Upon
asking how he has been taught the art of *cognoscento* so
very suddenly, he assures Goldsmith that nothing is easier.
The whole secret consists in a strict adherence to two
rules: the one, always to observe the picture might have
been better if the painter had taken more pains, and the
other, to praise the works of Pietro Perugino. "But," says
he, "I'll now undertake to instruct you in the art of picture buying at Paris."

With this proposal Goldsmith very readily closes, as it

is a living, and now all his ambition is to live. He goes therefore to his lodgings, improves his dress, and after some time, accompanies his friend to auctions of pictures, where the English gentry are expected to be purchasers. He is not a little surprised at his friend's intimacy with people of the best of fashion, who refer themselves to his judgment upon every picture or medal, as to an unerring standard of taste. He makes very good use of Goldsmith's assistance upon these occasions, for when asked his opinion, he gravely takes our physician aside and asks his, shrugs, looks wise, returns, and assures the company that he can give no opinion upon an affair of so much importance. Yet there is sometimes an occasion for a more important assurance. Once after giving his opinion that the coloring of a picture is not mellow enough, he deliberately takes a brush with brown varnish that is accidentally lying by and rubs it over the piece with great composure before all the company. He then asks if he has not improved the tints. . . .

There is a sensible improvement to be observed in Goldsmith's resources. He is a student at the fashionable chemical lectures of Rouelle—as bright a circle of beauty as graces the court of Versailles—and he goes often to see and admire the celebrated actress Mademoiselle Clairon of the silver voice.

In his rambles about the environs of Paris he is struck with the immense quantities of game running about on every side of him; and he sees in those costly preserves for the amusement of the privileged few a sure "badge of the slavery of the people." But he notes down the following: "As the Swedes are making concealed approaches to despotism, the French on the other hand, are imperceptibly vindicating themselves into freedom. . . . When I consider that these parliaments, the members of which are all created by the court, and the presidents of which can only act by immediate direction, presume even to mention privileges and freedom, when this is considered, I cannot help fancying that the genius of Freedom has entered that kingdom in disguise. If they have but three weak monarchs more successively on the throne, the mask will be laid aside and the country will certainly once more be free."

From Oliver Goldsmith to Lien Chi Altangi, the Discontented Wanderer: "I may upon another occasion point out what is most strikingly absurd in other countries. I shall at present confine myself only to France. The first national peculiarity a traveller meets upon entering that kingdom is an odd sort of staring vivacity in every eye, not excepting even the children. The people, it seems, have got it into their heads that they have more wit than others, and so stare in order to look smart.

"I know not how it happens, but there appears a sickly delicacy in the faces of their finest women. This may have introduced the use of paint, and paint produces wrinkles, so that a fine lady shall look like a hag at twenty-three. But as, in some measure, they never appear young, so it may be equally asserted, that they actually think themselves never old. A gentle miss shall prepare for new conquests at sixty, shall hobble a rigadoon when she can scarce walk out without a crutch. She shall affect the girl, play her fan and her eyes, and talk of sentiments, bleeding hearts, and expiring for love, when actually dying with age. Like a departing philosopher, she attempts to make her last moments the most brilliant of her life.

"Their civility to strangers is what they are chiefly proud of; and, to confess sincerely, their beggars are the very politest beggars I know. In other places a traveller is addressed with a piteous whine, or a sturdy solemnity, but a French beggar shall ask your charity with a very genteel bow, and thank you for it with a smile and shrug.

"Another instance of this people's breeding I must not forget. An Englishman would not speak his native language in a company of foreigners, where he was sure that none understood him. A travelling Hottentot himself would be silent if acquainted only with the language of his country, but a Frenchman shall talk to you whether you understand his language or not. Never troubling his head whether you have learned French, still he keeps up the conversation, fixes his eye full in your face, and asks a thousand questions, which he answers himself for want of a more satisfactory reply.

"But their civility to foreigners is not half so great as their admiration of themselves. Everything that belongs to them and their nation is great, magnificent beyond expression, quite romantic! Every garden is a paradise, every hovel a palace, and every woman an angel. They shut their eyes close, throw their mouths wide open and cry out in a rapture, '*Sacré!* What beauty! *O Ciel!* What taste! *Mort de ma vie!* What grandeur! Was ever any people like ourselves? We are the nation of men, and all the rest no better than two-legged barbarians.'

"I fancy the French would make the best cooks in the world if they had but meat. As it is they can dress you out five different dishes from a nettle top, seven from a dock leaf, and twice as many from a frog's haunches. These eat prettily enough when one is used to them, are easy of digestion, and seldom overload the stomach with crudities . . .

"Even religion loses its solemnity among them. Upon their roads, at about every five miles distance, you see an image of the Virgin Mary, dressed up in grim head-cloths, painted cheeks, and an old red petticoat. Before her a lamp is often kept burning, at which, with the saint's permission, I have frequently lighted my pipe. Instead of the Virgin, you are sometimes presented with a crucifix, at other times with a wooden Saviour, fitted out in complete garniture, with sponge, spear, nails, pincers, hammer, bees' wax, and vinegar bottle. Some of these images, I have been told, came down from heaven. If so, in heaven they have but bungling workmen. . . .

"But I begin to think you may find this description pert and dull enough. Perhaps it is so, yet in general it is the manner in which the French usually describe foreigners, and it is but just to force a part of that ridicule back upon them, which they attempt to lavish upon others. Adieu."

2.

A parchment figure of skin and bones and bright eyes in white woolen stockings and red breeches, with a waistcoat of blue linen, flowered and lined with yellow, is entertaining his guests at his home, Les Délices, near Geneva. He has on a grizzled wig with three ties and over it a silk night cap embroidered with gold and silver.

Les Délices is the abode of a man whom governments regard with an unfriendly eye. On his plateau he is in the republic of Geneva. He has only to walk ten minutes and cross a short bridge to get into the kingdom of Sardinia. Thirty minutes easy riding will put him in France, and in an hour he can be in the Swiss canton of Vaud. But he is forgetful of danger and lives like a provincial lord. He has his coach, his lackeys, his cook from Paris, his secretary, and a succession of dramas on his little private stage where the nobility also perform. Then there are his beautiful gardens and processions of people who come from Lyons, Geneva, London, Savoy, Switzerland, and even from Paris.

He is president of the intellectual republic of Europe and from his president's chair is laughing quietly at his own follies, heartily at the kings of his acquaintance, and particularly at Frederick and his "Oeuvres des poeshies." Now past sixty, it is the time when he is resolved to have on every occasion "the society of agreeable and clever people."

Monsieur is a haunted castle falling into ruins, but his guests can readily see it is still inhabited by a magician. He is clever, but he lacks one very necessary talent—dialogue.

A large party is present. There is Diderot with his hooked nose, flashing eyes, and quivering face. Full of

bonhommie and *joie de vivre,* laughing one minute, crying
the next, quick to be irritated or appeased, pouring out
torrents of splendid ideas and then of grossest liberty, his
mouth speaking always from the fulness of his heart,
utterly indiscreet, brilliant, ingenuous, delightful. All etiquette flees before his breezy, impulsive personality. He
says what he likes and as much as he likes. No subject that
is started finds him cool or neutral. He is too hot an oven.
Everything gets burnt in him.

Then there is Fontenelle, all mind, the daintiest pedant
in the world. No one is so sparkling in epigram, no one
talks so beautifully of love of which he knows nothing,
and no one talks so delightfully of science of which he
knows a great deal.

The conversation turns upon the English. At the battle
of Dettingen they exhibited prodigies of valour, but less-
ened their well-earned victory by lessening the merit of
those they had conquered. Diderot and Fontenelle enter
into the argument. The latter reviles the English in everything; the first, with unequal ability, defends them. In the
heat and excitement of the debate, Diderot hammers the
old gentleman's knees till he is forced to put a table in
front of him for safety. To the surprise of all, the host
remains silent. At last he is roused from his reverie, a
new life pervades his frame, and he flings himself into
an animated defense of England. Strokes of the finest rail-
lery fall thick and fast on his antagonist and he speaks
without intermission—for three hours.

Oliver Goldsmith, a hero worshipper, is at the foot-
stool; M. Voltaire is on the throne.

(Ah! What a picture is here painted by the imagination of our hero! For he never meets the above mentioned
gentleman in Paris or elsewhere! But may not the pupil
of Paddy Byrne let his fancy roam?)

Goldsmith now rambles on through Germany, attending the dull lectures at universities and the student disputes at graduation. On this occasion, the pupils often dis-

pense with their gravity and seem really all alive. The disputes are managed between the followers of Cartesius, whose exploded system they continue to call the new philosophy, and those of Aristotle. Though both parties are in the wrong, they argue with an obstinacy worthy the cause of truth. Nego, Probo, and Distinguo grow loud; the disputants become warm; the moderator cannot be heard; the audience takes part in the debate, till at last the whole hall buzzes with sophistry and error.

Passing into Switzerland, he sees Schaffhausen frozen quite across and the water standing in columns where the cataract has frozen. He eats a savory dinner on top of the Alps, flushes woodcocks on Mt. Jura, and wonders to see sheep in the valleys following the sound of the shepherd's pipe of reed. Then he sends off a sketch contrasting the sturdy enjoyment of the Swiss with the weak luxuriance of Italy.

At this time he becomes travelling tutor to a mongrel young gentleman, son of a London pawnbroker, who has suddenly been elevated into fortune and absurdity. He is to be the young gentleman's governor, but with a proviso, that he shall always be permitted to govern himself. His pupil, in fact, understands the art of guiding in money concerns much better than himself. He is heir to a fortune of about two hundred thousands pounds, left him by an uncle in the West Indies, and his guardians, to qualify him for the management of it, have bound him an apprentice to an attorney. Thus avarice is the young gentleman's prevailing passion. All his questions on the road are, how money may be saved—which is the least expensive course of travel—whether anything can be bought that will turn to account when disposed of again in London? Such curiosities on the way as can be seen for nothing, he is ready enough to look at, but if the sight of them is to be paid for, he usually asserts that he has been told they are not worth seeing. He never pays a bill without observing how amazingly expensive travelling is—and all this though he is not yet twenty-one. When arrived at Marseilles, as they take a walk to look at the port and shipping, he inquires the expense of the passage by sea home to England. This he is informed by Goldsmith is but a trifle compared to his returning by land. He is therefore unable to withstand the temptation, so paying Goldsmith the small part of his salary that is due, he takes leave and embarks with only one attendant for London.

From our travelling philosopher, Lien Chi Altangi, a letter from London, filled with dashes ———, blanks   , and stars *** of great importance: "Think not, O kind sir, that absence can impair my respect or blot your figure from my memory. The farther I travel I feel the pain of separation with stronger force. Those ties that bind me to you are still unbroken. By every remove I only drag a greater length of chain. . . .

"Behold me in London, gazing at your countrymen, and they at me. It seems they find me somewhat absurd in my figure, and had I never been from home, it is possible I might find an infinite fund of ridicule in theirs; but by long travelling I am taught to laugh at folly alone, and to find nothing truly ridiculous but villainy and vice. . . .

"Judge my disappointment on entering your renowned city to see no signs of that opulence so much talked of abroad. . . . Your houses borrow very few ornaments from architecture. Their chief decoration seems to be a paltry piece of painting hung out at their doors or windows, at once a proof of your countryman's indigence and vanity— their vanity, in each having one of those pictures exposed to public view; and their indigence, in being unable to get them better painted. In this respect the fancy of your painters is also deplorable. Could you believe it? I have seen five black lions and three blue boars in less than the circuits of half a mile, and yet you know that animals of these colors are nowhere to be found, except in the wild imaginations of Europe . . .

GOLDY

"To speak my secret sentiments, most kind sir, the ladies here are horribly ugly. I can hardly endure the sight of them. They no way resemble the beauties of China. When I reflect on the small-footed perfections of an Eastern beauty, how is it possible I should have eyes for a woman whose feet are ten inches long? Dutch and Chinese beauties, indeed, have some resemblance, but your English women are entirely different. Red cheeks, big eyes, and teeth of a most odious whitness, are not only seen here, but wished for; and then they have such masculine feet, as actually serve *some* for walking! . . .

"Yet what though your English women want black teeth, or are deprived of the allurements of feet no bigger than their thumbs, still they have souls, my friend—such souls—so free, so pressing, so hospitable, and so engaging! I have received more invitations in the streets of London from the sex in one night, than I have met with at Pekin in twelve revolutions of the moon. . . .

"But perhaps you may find more satisfaction in a newspaper than in my talk. I therefore send a specimen." Here Goldy unfolds the gazette and reads:

"*Spain.* The queen is more beautiful than the rising sun, and reckoned one of the first wits in Europe. She had a glorious opportunity of displaying the readiness of her invention and her skill in repartee lately at court. The Duke of Lerma coming up to her with a low bow and a smile, and presenting a nosegay set with diamonds, 'Madam,' cries he, 'I am your most obedient humble servant.'

"'O Sir,' replies the queen, without any prompter, or the least hesitation, 'I'm very proud of the very great honor you do me.' upon which she made a low courtesy, and all the courtiers fell a-laughing at the readiness and the smartness of her reply.

"*Lisbon.* Yesterday we had an *auto da fé*, at which were burned three young women accused of heresy, one of them of exquisite beauty, two Jews, and an old woman, convicted of being a witch. One of the friars who attended this last reports that he saw the devil fly out of her at the stake in the shape of a flame of fire. The populace behaved on this occasion with great good humor, joy, and sincere devotion.

"*Vienna.* We have received certain advices that a party of twenty thousand Austrians, having attacked a much superior body of Prussians, put them all to flight and took the rest prisoners of war.

.."*Berlin.* We have received certain advices that a party of twenty thousand Prussians, having attacked a much superior body of Austrians, put them to flight and took a great number of prisoners with their military chest, cannon, and baggage.

"*Paris.* Our distresses are great, but Madame Pompadour continues to supply our king, who is now growing old, with a fresh lady every night. His health, thank Heaven, is still pretty well; nor is he in the least unfit, as was reported, for any kind of royal exercitation. He was so frightened at the affair of Damiens that his physicians were apprehensive lest his reason should suffer, but that wretch's tortures soon composed the kingly terrors of his breast.

"*Dublin.* We hear from Germany that Prince Ferdinand has gained a complete victory, and taken twelve kettle drums, five standards, and four waggons of ammunition, prisoners of war.

"*Edinburgh.* We are positive when we say that Saunder M' Gregor, who was lately executed for horse stealing, is not a Scotsman, but born in Carrickfergus. . . .

"Farewell."

Descending into Piedmont, Goldsmith observes the floating bee houses, and then passes along to Florence, Verona, Mantua, Milan, and Padua. He is a forlorn beggar in tattered garments, unkempt, unwashed, and ungainly. He must not be painted as one of those merry pipers beneath the trellised vines of the Sorrento roadway who appear in brilliant colors on the familiar curtains of the theater; nor as one of a careless group in velvet jackets, glazed leather pumps, and white stockings, who give some action to a scene in an old Italian opera. Every evening after doing eight or ten miles, he arrives at his destination, worn out, dusty, and caked over with mud.

His skill in music can avail him nothing in a country where every peasant is a better musician than he. But by this time he has acquired another talent, which answers his purpose as well, and this is a skill in disputation. In all the foreign universities and convents there are, upon certain days, philosophical theses maintained against every adventitious disputant; for which, if the champion opposes with any dexterity, he can claim a gratuity in money, a dinner, and a bed for one night.

With the members of these places, he can converse on topics of literature, and then he always forgets the meanness of his circumstances.

At Padua he is brought to a pause on being informed that his Uncle Contarine has lapsed into imbecility—and shortly afterwards remittances are stopped. He then makes known his destitution to his own family, and Dan Hodson levies a contribution on all his friends to help him. But the money fails to reach him, nor does he know of the attempt. Thus left to his own precarious resources, he gives up all further wandering in Italy, and once more resuming his pilgrim staff, makes his way to England, walking along from city to city, examining mankind more nearly, and, if I may so express it, seeing both sides of the picture.

CHAPTER 7

A PEDAGOGUE

AFTER TWO YEARS spent in roving about
the Continent, "pursuing novelty and losing content," Goldsmith lands at Dover early in 1756. His only thought is to
get to London, but how is he to get there? His purse is
empty—England is as completely a foreign land to him as
any part of the continent—and where on earth is the penniless stranger more destitute? His flute and his philosophy
are of no avail. The English care nothing for music, and
there are no convents. As to the learned and the clergy, not
one of them would give a vagrant scholar a supper and a
night's lodging for the best thesis ever argued.

He is therefore forced to resort to a series of desperate
expedients. He joins a company of strolling players and
plays his flute to barnstormers for supper and a bed of
hay; he assists the ostlers of inns around Canterbury; and
he pounds drugs in some chemist's shop in one of the
small towns on the way. At length, in the middle of February, he is wandering through the gloom of the London
streets, joining the swarm of thieves, beggars, street walk-
ers, and merry andrews, which makes its nest in Axe Lane.
He applies to the London apothecaries, asks them to let
him spread plasters, pound in their mortars, run with their
medicines, but they want references, and he has none to

give. His threadbare coat, uncouth figure, and Irish brogue cause him to meet with repeated refusals.

For a time he is employed under an assumed name as usher at a country school. His next shift is as assistant to one chemist Jacob of Fish Street Hill. After remaining with Jacob a few months, he hears that Dr. Sleigh, an old fellow student at Edinburgh, is in London, and he resolves to visit him. It is Sunday and he calls in his best clothes, but Sleigh does not know him. However, when he does recollect him, Goldsmith finds his heart as warm as ever, and he shares his purse with him during his stay in London.

With the help of Sleigh and Jacob, Goldsmith now rises from apothecary's drudge to be a physician in a humble way in Bankside, Southwark.

His old Irish acquaintance and schoolfellow, Beatty, meets him at this time in the streets. He is in an old suit of tarnished green and gold with a shirt and neckcloth that appear to have been worn at least a fortnight—but he says he is practising physic and doing very well.

Our next glimpse, though not more satisfactory, is more professional. The green and gold have faded out into a rusty full trimmed black suit, the pockets of which overflow with papers. The coat is second hand velvet, a cast off legacy of a more successful brother of the craft; the cane and wig have served more fortunate owners. And the humble practitioner of Bankside is feeling the pulse of a patient humbler than himself whose courteous entreaties to relieve him of the hat he keeps pressed over his heart, he more courteously, but firmly, declines. Beneath the hat is a large patch in the rusty velvet.

But he cannot conceal his starvation. Even the poor printer whom he attends can see how badly it goes with him—and finds courage one day to suggest that his master has been kind to clever men before now—has visited Mr. Johnson in the sponging house, and might be serviceable to a poor physician. For his master is no less than Samuel

Richardson, of Salisbury Court and Parson's Green, printer and author of *Clarissa Harlowe*.

The hint is successful, and Goldsmith is appointed reader and corrector to the press in Salisbury court. He is admitted now and then to the parlor and is grimly smiled upon by its chief literary ornament, the great poet of the day, the author of "Night Thoughts"—Edward Young. And in the corner, is the short, plump, smoothish faced and ruddy cheeked moralist and printer, Samuel Richardson—in a lightish coat, all black besides, one hand in his bosom, the other with a cane in it to support him when attacked by sudden tremors or dizziness. Surrounding him is a bevy of fair ladies.

Though it is considered beneath their dignity for ladies of the West End of the town to pass Temple Bar, yet they are so daring in their disregard of conventionalities as to seek this elegant author in his house in Salisbury Court off Fleet Street. Here these languishing women are received by the plumpbodied, much honored little man, who welcomes them to his well-ordered library, offers them chocolate, and begs them to partake of fruit with a simplicity that enables them to see the sublime elevation of his soul. Here they gaze with amazement and adoration on this divine man, as they term him, kiss his ink bottle, and speak to him touchingly of the sensibilities of the human heart. In return they hear from him personal details concerning the tremors that shook him on writing certain passages in his books, his general state of nervousness that prevents him from mixing with crowds, the exact quantity of tar water which he drinks as a cure, the amount of exercise he takes daily on a chamber horse, and the causes that hinder him from eating flesh and fish or from drinking wine. Then three young ladies inform him that they dream of him by night. And a mistress tells him that while her hair was being curled, her friend read aloud the seventh volume of *Clarissa*, and the maid let fall such a shower of tears upon her head that she was forced to send her out of the room . . .

The corrector of the press now writes a tragedy, but before it is finished, casts it aside. He then thinks of deciphering the Aramaic inscriptions on the rocks of Mount Sinai. Though he knows nothing of the language they are written in, the salary of three hundred pounds is the temptation. But before he can proceed with this quixotic project, a friend and former fellow student of his, Dr. Milner, offers him a position as assistant in his father's academy at Peckham in Surrey.

A hurried seeking of advice from a cousin. The cousin receives the proposal with a true sardonic grin. "Ay," cries he, "this is indeed a very pretty career that has been chalked out for you. I have been an usher at a boarding school myself, and may I die by an anodyne necklace, but I had rather be an under turnkey in Newgate. I was up early and late. I was browbeat by the master, hated for my ugly face by the mistress, worried by the boys within, and never permitted to stir out to meet civility abroad. But are you sure you are fit for a school? Let me examine you a little. Have you been bred apprentice to the business?"

"No."

"Then you won't do for a school. Can you dress the boys' hair?"

"No."

"Then you won't do for a school. Can you lie three in a bed?"

"No."

"Then you will never do for a school. Have you got a good stomach?"

"Yes."

"Then you will by no means do for a school. No, sir, if you are for a genteel, easy profession, bind yourself seven years an apprentice to turn a cutler's wheel, but avoid a school by any means."

But Goldy has sown his wild oats broadly enough, and

it is time to grow wheat for penny loaves. In other words, he seeks no longer either knowledge or amusement, but sets himself about earning his daily bread. "All my ambition now is to live." And so the beginning of 1757 finds him installed at Peckham Academy, Surrey.

He soon becomes famous among the boys for singing them ballads, telling them stories, and playing for them on his flute. The greater part of his salary goes in sweetmeats for the younger class. He seldom comes into the room without something in his pockets for them—a piece of gingerbread or a half penny whistle. And as usual he is fleeced by every sturdy beggar. So that between his charity and his munificence, he is generally in advance of his salary.

"You had better, Mr. Goldsmith, let me take care of your money," says Mrs. Milner one day, "as I do for some of the young gentlemen."

"In truth, madam, there is equal need," is the good humored reply.

The routine at Peckham school is deadly and monotonous, and the life of an usher a degrading one. He is the laughing stock of the school. Every trick is played upon him. The oddity of his manner, his dress and his brogue, are a fund of eternal ridicule. Besides he is obliged to sleep in the same bed with the French teacher, who disturbs him for an hour every night in papering and filleting his hair and stinks worse than a carrion with his rancid pomatums when he lays his head beside him on the bolster.

Once after playing for hours upon his flute, he speaks with enthusiasm of music as delightful in itself and as a valuable accomplishment for a gentleman. Whereupon a pert youngster, with a glance at his ungainly person, wishes to know if he considers himself a gentleman.

He has his boyish pranks and practical jokes. There is William, the schoolmaster's servant, whose duty it is to wait on the young gentlemen at table, clean their shoes,

comb their hair, etc.—a social position not very far removed from that of the usher. And so they are very
friendly. William is vain and obstinate and believes he can
do astonishing things in eating and drinking. The whole
kitchen laughs at him but refuses to accept his challenge
for a trial at some poisonous draught or fare unfit for a
Christian. At last they enlist Goldsmith. He procures a
piece of uncolored Cheshire cheese, rolls it up in the form
of a candle about an inch in length, and twisting a bit
of white paper to the size of a wick and blacking its
extreme end, thrusts it into one of the ends of the cheese.
He then puts it into a candlestick over the kitchen fireplace, taking care that in another by the side of it, there
is placed the end of a real candle, exactly the same in size
and appearance. Everything thus ready, in comes William
and is straightway challenged by the usher.

"You eat yonder piece of candle," says Goldsmith, taking down the cheese, "and I will eat this."

William assents rather drily.

"I have no objection to begin, but both must finish at
the same time."

William nods, takes his portion of candle, and, still
reluctant, looks ruefully on while Goldsmith gnaws away
at his supposed share, making terrible, wry faces. He beholds with amazement the progress made, and not till
Goldsmith has devoured all but the very last morsel does
he take sudden courage, open his mouth, and fling his
own piece down his throat in a moment. The kitchen rings
with laughter. William now expresses his sympathy for the
defeated usher and really wonders why he did not like
himself swallow the nauseous morsel all at once.

"Why, truly," replies the usher, with a straight face,
"my bit of candle, William, was no other than a bit of
very nice Cheshire cheese and therefore, William, I was
unwilling to lose the relish of it."

One day, a portly gentleman, Ralph Griffiths, the bookseller, who owns the *Monthly Review*, dines at Dr. Milner's. The Doctor is one of his contributors, and the talk of the table turns upon the opposition in the field. The *Monthly Review*, an advocate of Whig principles, was started eight years before, and has had a prosperous existence. Now a formidable Tory rival has bobbed up in the *Critical Review*, published by Archibald Hamilton, and aided by the powerful and popular pen of Doctor Smollett.

Some remarks are made by the humble usher which attract the attention of Griffiths, and he takes him aside. "I see you are a lad of spirit and some learning. What do you think of commencing author, like me? You have read in books, no doubt, of men of genius starving at the trade. At present I'll show you forty very dull fellows about town that live by it in opulence—all honest jog trot men, who go on smoothly and dully, and write history and politics, and are praised—men, sir, who, had they been bred cobblers, would all their lives have only mended shoes, but never made them."

Finding that there is no great degree of gentility affixed to the character of an usher, Goldsmith resolves to accept the proposal, and having the highest respect for literature, hails the *antiqua mater* of Grub Street with reverence. He thinks it a glory to pursue a track which Dryden and Otway trod before him. He considers the goddess of this region as the parent of excellence, and though an intercourse with the world may give us good sense, the poverty she entails he supposes to be the nurse of genius.

A few specimens of criticism are submitted to Griffiths, which prove satisfactory, and before the close of April, 1757, Goldsmith is bound in an agreement for one year. He is to leave Dr. Milner's, to board and lodge with the bookseller, to have a small regular salary, and to devote himself to the *Monthly Review*.

The gloomy prospect of a bookseller's hack fails to dampen the ardor of our cheerful adventurer. Fielding has died in shattered hopes and fortune, at what should have been his prime of life, three years before. Within the next two years, poor and mad Collins is fated to descend to an early grave. Smollett is toughly fighting for his every-day's existence. And Johnson has but the other day been a tenant of a sponging house. Only a few months before, on the author of the English Dictionary presenting himself to the bookseller Wilcox with a plan for obtaining his livelihood as a writer, the other eyeing his powerful frame, with a significant shrug has told him he had better buy a porter's knot. No man thrives that is connected with letters unless he is also connected with their trade and merchandise, and like Richardson is able to print books as well as write them. "Had some of these," cries Smollett in his bitterness, "who were pleased to call themselves my friends, been at any pains to deserve the character, and told me ingenuously what I had to expect in the capacity of an author, when I first professed myself of that venerable fraternity, I should in all probability have spared myself the incredible labor and chagrin I have since undergone."

The patron has gone but the reading public is growing lustily. The seller of books sits crosslegged over the destiny of those who write them. He is shrewd and kindly, but difficult of access and hard to move.

Flat apostasy lifts literature into rank—unpurchasable independence depresses it into ruin. The sum of £50,000 is expended by Walpole's ministry on scribblers for their daily bread; all flows into the pockets of the Guthries, the Amhursts, the Arnalls, the Ralphs, and the Oldmixons. While a Mr. Cook is pensioned, a Harry Fielding (before he needs money to care for a sick wife and dying child and changes his political tune) solicits Walpole in vain.

Pens are as venal as the votes of the House of Commons. Like the daggers of Italian bravoes, they are on hire to anyone who wishes to stab an enemy anonymously in the press.

To become an author is to be treated as an adventurer. A man has only to write to be classed with what Mr. Johnson calls, the lowest of all human beings, the scribblers for party. It is sufficient to throw doubt upon the career of Edmund Burke that in this very year he has opened it with the writing of a book. It is Horace Walpole's vast surprise four years later that so sensible a man as young Mr. Burke should not have "worn off his authorism yet. He thinks there is nothing so charming as writers, and to to be one. He will know better one of these days."

Periodicals are the fashion of the day. Scarcely a week passes in which some new magazine or paper does not start into life, to perish or survive as may be. Even Fielding has turned from his Tom Jones and Amelia to his *Covent Garden Journal.*

It is the life and soul of a magazine never to be long dull upon one subject. If a magazine be dull upon the Spanish war, it soon has the reader up again with the Ghost in Cock Lane. If he begins to doze upon that, he is quickly roused by an Eastern tale. Tales prepare him for poetry, and poetry for the meteorological history of the weather. The reader, like the sailor's horse, has at least the comfortable refreshment of having the spur often changed.

CHAPTER 8

MALADIE DU PAIS

1.

PRIM, ANTIQUATED MRS. GRIFFITHS in her neat and elevated wire-winged cap peeps in her parlor in Paternoster Row at the sign of the Dunciad to see if her literary drudge is at work. But there he sits at a table, slaving hard from an early hour of the morning.

He has to write daily from nine o'clock until two and often throughout the day—whether in the vein or not, and on subjects dictated by his taskmaster. If he dare dabble in verse or produce the acts of his tragedy, Mr. and Mrs. Griffiths will take council on the expenses of his lodging.

Still worse, the critical supervision of Griffiths and his wife grieve him—the "illiterate, bookselling Griffiths," as Smollett calls them, "who presume to revise, alter, and amend the articles" contributed to their review. "Thank heaven," he crows, "the *Critical Review* is not written under the restraint of a bookseller and his wife. Its principal writers are independent of each other, unconnected with booksellers and unawed by old women."

Excepting Christopher Smart's ninety-nine year lease on a monthly journal and the contract between the Devil and Dr. Faustus, as is satirically remarked, there has never been a harder bargain driven with any literary man.

This literary vassalage, however, does not last long. After five months there is a serious quarrel. Griffiths accuses his hack writer of idleness, says that he affects a tone and independence which do not become his conditon and that he abandons his writing desk at an early hour of the day. Goldsmith in turn charges him with impertinence, his wife with meanness and both with marring his articles as it suited their ignorance or convenience. The engagement is broken off by mutual consent but without any violent rupture.

His reviews express self-assurance. He has little good to say for Home's *Douglas,* finds Burke's *Of the Sublime and Beautiful* sagacious and learned (In his summary he largely borrows Burke's phrasing and relegates his objections to the footnotes. His chief stricture is Burke's division of the sublime and beautiful on the basis of pain and pleasure), and advises Thomas Gray (concerning his "Odes") to "study the people."

When he escapes from Griffiths and his spouse, he trails a string which still attaches him to the firm's counting house, a translation of Jean Marteilhe's *The Memoirs of a Protestant, Condemned to the Galleys of France for his Religion: Written by Himself,* which appears in February, 1758. It is a dull chronicle enlivened by the translator's imagination and intended as propaganda against the alleged cruelties of the Roman Catholic Church.

Goldsmith is again launched on a wide, friendless world. The scantiness of his purse obliges him to take a small room in one of the courts near Salisbury Square, Fleet Street. While he burrows in lodgings suited to his means, he hails from the Temple Exchange Coffee House, near Temple Bar. Here he receives his medical calls, dates his letters, and passes much of his leisure hours conversing with the "geniuses" of the place. "Thirty pounds a year," says a poor Irish painter, who understands the art of shifting, "is enough to enable a man to live in London without being contemptible. Ten pounds will find him in clothes and linen; he can live in a garret on eighteen pence a week; hail from a coffee house, where, by occasionally spending three pence, he may pass some hours each day in good company; he may breakfast on bread and milk for a penny; dine for sixpence; do without supper; and on clean shirt day he may go abroad and pay visits."

2.

A dingy garret, Salisbury Square. Its inmate is sitting over his wretched drudgery when the door opens, and a raw looking country youth of twenty stands doubtfully on the threshold. Goldsmith turns and sees at once his youngest brother Charles.

While lounging in weary idleness round Ballymahon it suddenly occurred to this enterprising Irish lad that as brother Oliver had not been asking for assistance lately, perhaps he had gotten great men for his friends and a kind word to one of them might be the making of his fortune. Full of this he has scrambled to London as best he could.

"All in good time, my dear boy," cries Oliver, joyfully, to check his brother's despair, "all in good time. I shall be richer by and by. Addison, let me tell you, wrote his poem of *The Campaign* in a garret in the Haymarket, three stories high, and you see I am not come to that yet, for I have only got to the second story." Then he makes Charles sit down and answer questions about his Irish friends.

But in a few days Charles suddenly quits London for Ireland and settles at home to the business of cabinet making. Twelve years later he gets restless and departs for Jamaica to seek his fortune. He so far resembles Oliver that at the close of a long life of great vicissitude, he says he has met with no such friend in adversity as his flute.

To his brother-in-law, Daniel Hodson, December 27, 1757: "I suppose you desire to know my present situation.

As there is nothing in it at which I should blush, or which mankind could censure, I see no reason for making it a secret. In short, by a very little practice as a physician, and a very little reputation as a poet, I make a shift to live. Nothing is more apt to introduce us to the gates of the muses than poverty, but it were well if they only left us at the door. The mischief is they sometimes choose to give us their company to the entertainment; and want, instead of being gentleman usher, often turns master of the ceremonies.

"Thus, upon learning I write, no doubt you imagine I starve, and the name of an author naturally reminds you of a garret. In this particular I do not think proper to undeceive my friends. But whether I eat or starve, live in a first floor or four pairs of stairs high, I still remember them with ardor; nay, my very country comes in for a share of my affection. Unaccountable fondness for country, this *maladie du pais,* as the French call it! Unaccountable that he should still have an affection for a place, who never when in it, received above common civility; who never brought anything out of it except his brogue and his blunders. Surely my affection is equally ridiculous with the Scotchman's, who refused to be cured of the itch because it make him unco' thoughtful of his wife and bonny Inverary.

"But now, to be serious. Let me ask myself what gives me a wish to see Ireland again. The country is a fine one, perhaps? No. There are good company in Ireland? No. The conversation there is generally made up of a smutty toast or a bawdy song, the vivacity supported by some humble cousin, who had just folly enough to earn his dinner. Then, perhaps, there's more wit and learning among the Irish? Oh! Lord, no! There has been more money spent in the encouragement of the Padareen mare there one season than given in rewards to learned men since the time of Usher. All their productions in learning amount to perhaps a translation, or a few tracts in divinity, and all their productions in wit to just nothing at all. Why the plague, then, so fond of Ireland? Then, all at once, because you, my dear friend, and a few more who are exceptions to the general picture, have a residence there. This it is that gives me all the pangs I feel in separation. I confess I carry this spirit sometimes to the souring the pleasures I at present possess. If I go to the opera, where Signora Columba pours out all the mazes of melody, I sit and sigh for Lissoy fireside, and Johnny Armstrong's 'Last Good Night' from Peggy Golden. If I climb Hampstead Hill, than where nature never exhibited a more magnificent prospect, I confess it fine, but then I had rather be placed on the little mount before Lissoy gate, and there take in, to me, the most pleasing horizon in nature.

"Before Charles came hither my thoughts sometimes found refuge from severer studies among my friends in Ireland. I fancied strange revolutions at home, but I find it was the rapidity of my own motion that gave an imaginary one to objects really at rest. No alterations there. Some friends, he tells me, are still lean, but very rich; others very fat, but still very poor. Nay, all the news I hear of you is, that you sally out in visits among the neighbors, and sometimes make a migration from the blue bed to the brown. I could from my heart wish that you and she (Mrs. Hodson), and Lissoy and Ballymahon, and all of you, would fairly make a migration into Middlesex, though, upon second thoughts, this might be attended with a few inconveniences. Therefore, as the mountain will not come to Mohammed, why Mohammed shall go to the mountain, or, to speak plain English, as you cannot conveniently pay me a visit, if next summer I can contrive to be absent six weeks from London, I shall spend three of them among my friends in Ireland. But first, believe me, my design is purely to visit, and neither to cut a figure nor levy contributions; neither to excite envy nor solicit favor. In fact, my circumstances are adapted to neither. I am too poor to be gazed at, and too rich to need assistance."

CHAPTER 9

POLITE LEARNING

FOR SOME TIME Goldsmith continues to write miscellaneously for reviews and other periodical publications without making any decided hit. The learned world says nothing of his work, nothing at all. Every man of them is employed in praising his friends and himself or condemning his enemies; and unfortunately as he has neither, he suffers the cruellest mortification—neglect. His essays are buried among the essays upon liberty, Eastern tales, and cures for the bite of a mad dog, while Philautos, Philalethes, Philelutheros, and Philanthropos all write better because they write faster than he.

In a sudden surge of misery he decides to drop literature as a trade and to show his indignation against the public by discontinuing his efforts to please. He is bravely resolved, like Raleigh, to vex them by burning his manuscripts in a passion. Upon reflection, however, he considers what set or body of people will be displeased at his rashness. The sun, after so sad an accident, will shine next morning as bright as usual; men will laugh and sing the next day, and transact business as before, and not a single creature feel any regret but himself. Instead of having Apollo in mourning, or the Muses in a fit of the spleen, perhaps all Grub Street will laugh at his fate, and self approving dignity be unable to shield him from ridicule.

While supping coffee at the Temple Exchange, he unburdens himself to one of the learned lights of the place. "Here," says he, "have I spent part of my youth in attempting to instruct and amuse my fellow creatures, and all my reward has been solitude, poverty, and reproach, while a fellow, possessed of even the smallest share of fiddling merit, or who has perhaps learned to whistle double, is rewarded, applauded, and caressed!"

"Prithee, young man," says the learned sage to Goldsmith, "are you ignorant that in so large a city as this it is better to be an amusing than a useful member of society? Can you leap up, and touch your feet four times before you come to the ground?"

"No, sir."

"Can you pimp for a man of quality?"

"No, sir."

"Can you stand upon two horses at full speed?"

"No, sir."

"Can you swallow a penknife?"

"I can do none of these tricks."

"Why then," cries the sage, "there is no other prudent means of subsistence left, but to apprise the town that you speedily intend to eat up your own nose by subscription."

In despair Goldsmith journeys to Peckham and knocks at Dr. Milner's door. He is again installed as usher, as the Doctor is ill and cannot attend to his school. In return for his timely services, Milner promises to use his influence with a friend, an East India director, to procure him a medical appointment in India.

But how is he to fit himself out for the voyage? In this emergency, he is driven to a more extended exercise of his pen. No longer overawed by an antiquated Sappho sitting in the chair of Aristarchus, such store of literary fruit as he has gathered in his travels he puts into a treatise entitled, *An Inquiry into the Present State of Polite Learning in Europe.* (Who in these days has ever heard of "polite learning"?)

Feeling secure of success in England, he is anxious to forestall the piracy of the Irish press, for as yet the Union has not taken place, and the English law of copyright does not extend to the other side of the Irish channel. He writes, therefore, to his friends in Ireland, urging them to obtain subscriptions for his work, payable in advance.

The requests are unheeded. Dublin is the poorest place in the world for subscriptions to books. It is much easier to get a hundred dinners, with as many dozen bottles of claret, than a single guinea for the best author. Few or no people there care to subscribe; reading is not the prevailing taste.

To Cousin Edward Mills, living at ease on his estate at Roscommon: "You have quitted the plan of life which you once intended to pursue, and given up ambition for domestic tranquility. I cannot avoid feeling some regret that one of my few friends has declined a pursuit in which he had every reason to expect success. I have often let my fancy loose when you were the subject, and have imagined you gracing the bench, or thundering at the bar; while I have taken no small pride to myself, and whispered to all that I could come near, that this was my cousin. Instead of this, it seems you are merely contented to be a happy man, to be esteemed by your acquaintances, to cultivate your paternal acres, to take unmolested a nap under one of your own hawthorns or in Mrs. Mills' bedchamber, which, even a poet must confess, is rather the more comfortable place of the two. But, however your resolutions may be altered with regard to your situation in life, I persuade myself they are unalterable with respect to your friends in it. I cannot think the world has taken such entire possession of that heart (once so susceptible of friendship) as not to have left a corner there for a friend or two, but I flatter myself that even I have a place among the number. . . . You know me too proud to stoop to unnecessary insincerity—I have a request to make, but as I know to whom I am a petitioner, I make it without diffidence or confusion. It is in short, this, I am going to publish a book in London," etc., etc.

Another letter dated from the Temple Exchange Coffee House, is addressed to Robert Bryanton with whom he has long ceased to be in correspondence: "DEAR SIR—I have heard it remarked, I believe by yourself that they who are drunk, or out of their wits, fancy everybody else in the same condition. Mine is a friendship that neither distance nor time can efface, which is probably the reason that, for the soul of me, I can't avoid thinking yours of the same complexion; and yet I have many reasons for being of a contrary opinion, else why, in so long an absence, was I never made a partner in your concerns? . . . However, since you have not let me hear from you, I have in some measure disappointed your neglect by frequently thinking of you. Every day or so I remember the calm anecdotes of your life, from the fireside to the easy chair; recall the various adventures that first cemented our friendship; the school, the college, or the tavern; preside in fancy over your cards; and am displeased at your bad play when the rubber goes against you, though not with all that agony of soul as when I was once your partner.

"Is it not strange that two of such like affections should be so much separated, and so differently employed as we are? You seem placed at the center of fortune's wheel, and, let it revolve ever so fast, are insensible of the motion. I seem to have been tied to the circumference, and turned disagreeably round like a whore in a whirligig.

"I sat down with an intention to chide and yet methinks I have forgot my resentment already. The truth is I am a simpleton with regard to you. I may attempt to bluster, but like the lute of Anacreon, my heart is respondent only to softer affections. And yet now I think on't again I will be angry. God's curse, Sir! Who am I? Eh! What am I? Do you know whom you have offended? A man whose character may one of these days be mentioned with profound respect in a German comment or Dutch dictionary—whose name you will probably hear ushered in by a Doctissimus Doctissimorum or heel-pieced with a long Latin termination. Think how Goldsmithius or Gubblegurchius, or some such sound as rough as a nutmeg grater, will become me? Think of that!—God's curse, Sir! Who am I? I must own my ill natured contemporaries have not hitherto paid me those honours I have had such just reason to expect. I have not yet seen my face reflected in all the lively display of red and white paints on any sign posts in the suburbs. Your handkerchief weavers seem as yet unacquainted with my merit or physiognomy, and the very snuff box makers appear to have forgot their respect. Tell them all from me, they are a set of Gothic, barbarous, ignorant scoundrels. There will come a day, no doubt it will—I beg you may live a couple of hundred years longer only to see the day—when the Scaligers and Daciers will vindicate my character, give learned editions of my labours, and bless the times with copious comments on the text. You shall see how they will fish up the heavy scoundrels who disregard me now, or will then offer to cavil at my productions. How will they bewail the times that suffered so much genius to lie neglected. If ever my works find their way to Tartary or China, I know the consequence. Suppose one of your Chinese Owanowitzers instructing one of your Tartarian Chianobacchi—you see I use Chinese names to show my erudition, as I shall soon make our Chinese talk like an Englishman to show his. This may be the subject of the lecture——

"*Oliver Goldsmith flourished in the eighteenth and nineteenth centuries. He lived to be an hundred and three years old, and in that age may justly be styled the sun of literature and the Confucius of Europe. Many of his earlier writings, to the regret of the learned world, were anonymous, and have probably been lost, because united with those of others. The first avowed piece the world has of his is entitled an 'Essay on the Present State of Taste and Literature in Europe.'*

"But as I choose neither to tire my Chinese Philosopher, nor you, nor myself, I must discontinue the oration, in order to give you a good pause for admiration, and I find myself most violently disposed to admire too. Let me, then, stop my fancy, take a view of my future self, and, as the boys say, light down to see myself on horseback. Well, now, I am down, where the devil *is* I? Oh, Gods! Gods! here in a garret, writing for bread, and expecting to be dunned for a milk score!"

Finally to Mrs. Lawder, the Jane Contarine of happy old Kilmore days. Goldsmith's long silence has been misinterpreted by the Lawders as a token of indifference, and they ever afterwards display a coolness towards him. He writes conciliatory letters to them, but the Lawders do not respond, nor do they trouble to notify him of a legacy of £15 left him by Mr. Contarine at his death.

"If you should ask why, in an interval of so many years, you never heard from me, permit me madam, to ask the same question. I have the best excuse in recrimination. I wrote to Kilmore from Leyden in Holland, from Louvain in Flanders, and Rouen in France, but received no answer. To what could I attribute this silence but to displeasure or forgetfulness? Whether I was right in my conjecture I do not pretend to determine, but this I must ingenuously own that I have a thousand times in my turn endeavored to forget *them* whom I could not but look upon as forgetting *me*. I have attempted to blot their names from my memory, and, I confess it, spent whole days in efforts to tear their image from my heart. Could I have succeeded, you had not now been troubled with this renewal of a discontinued correspondence; but, as every effort the restless make to procure sleep serves but to keep them waking, all my attempts contributed to impress what I would forget deeper on my imagination. But this subject I would willingly turn from, and yet, 'for the soul of me,' I can't till I have said all. I was, madam, when I discontinued writing to Kilmore, in such circumstances that all my endeavors to continue your regard might be attributed to wrong motives. My letters might be looked upon as the petitions of a beggar, and not the offerings of a friend; while all my professions, instead of being considered as the result of disinterested esteem, might be ascribed to venal insincerity. I believe, indeed, you had too much generosity to place them in such a light, but I could not bear even the shadow of such a suspicion. The most delicate friendships are always most sensible of the slightest invasion, and the strongest jealousy is ever attendant on the warmest regard. I could not—I own I could not—continue a correspondence in which every acknowledgment for past favors might be considered as an indirect request for future ones; and where it might be thought I gave my heart from a motive of gratitude alone, when I was conscious of having bestowed it on much more disinterested principles.

"It is true, this conduct might have been simple enough, but yourself must confess it was in character. Those who know me at all, know that I have always been actuated by different principles from the rest of mankind, and while none regarded the interest of his friends more, no man on earth regarded his own less. I have often affected bluntness to avoid the imputation of flattery; have frequently seemed to overlook those merits too obvious to escape notice, and pretended disregard to those instances of good nature and good sense, which I could not fail tacitly to applaud—and all this lest I should be ranked among the grinning tribe, who say 'very true' to all that is said, who fill a vacant chair at a tea table, whose narrow souls never moved in a wider circle than the circumference of a guinea, and who had rather be reckoning the money in your pocket than the virtue in your breast. All this, I say, I have done, and a thousand other very silly, though very disinterested, things in my time, and for all which no soul cares a farthing about me. God's curse, madam! Is it to be wondered that he should once in his life forget you, who has been all his life forgetting himself.

"However, it is probable you may one of these days see me turned into a perfect hunks, and as dark and intricate as a mousehole. I have already given my landlady orders for an entire reform in the state of my finances. I declaim against hot suppers, drink less sugar in my tea, and check my grate with brickbats. Instead of hanging my room with pictures, I intend to adorn it with maxims of frugality. These will make pretty furniture enough, and won't be a bit too expensive, for I will draw them all out with my own hands, and my landlady's daughter shall frame them with the parings of my black waistcoat. Each maxim is to be inscribed on a sheet of clean paper, and wrote with my best pen, of which the following will serve as a specimen——

"Look sharp. Mind the main chance. Money is money now. If you have a thousand pounds you can put your hands by your sides, and say you are worth a thousand pounds every day of the year. Take a farthing from a hundred and it will be a hundred no longer.

"Thus, which way soever I turn my eyes, they are sure to meet one of those friendly monitors; and as we are told of an actor who hung his room round with looking glasses to correct the defects of his person, my apartment shall be furnished in a peculiar manner, to correct the errors of my mind.

"Faith! madam, I heartily wish to be rich, if it were only for this reason, to say without a blush how much I esteem you. But, alas! I have many a fatigue to encounter before that happy time comes, when your poor old simple friend may again give a loose to the luxuriance of his nature; sitting by Kilmore fireside, recount the various adventures of a hard fought life, laugh over the follies of the day, join his flute to your harpsichord, and forget that ever he starved in those streets where Butler and Otway starved before him. And now I mention those great names—my uncle! he is no more that soul of fire as when I once knew him. Newton and Swift grew dim with age as well as he.

But what shall I say? His mind was too active an inhabitant not to disorder the feeble mansion of its abode, for the richest jewels soonest wear their settings. Yet who but the fool would lament his condition! He now forgets the calamities of life. Perhaps indulgent Heaven has given him a foretaste of that tranquility here, which he so well deserves hereafter.

"But I must come to business, for business, as one of my maxims tells me, must be minded or lost. I am going to publish in London a book entitled 'The Present State of Taste and Literature in Europe.' The booksellers in Ireland republish every performance there without making the author any consideration. I would, in this respect, disappoint their avarice and have all the profits of my labor to myself. I must therefore request Mr. Lawder to circulate among his friends and acquaintances a hundred of my proposals which I have given the bookseller, Mr. Bradley, in Dame Street, directions to send to him. If, in pursuance of such circulation, he should receive any subscriptions, I entreat when collected, they may be sent to Mr. Bradley, as aforesaid . . . but if I know Mr. Lawder (and sure I ought to know him), he will accept the employment with pleasure. All I can say—if he writes a book, I will get him two hundred subscribers, and those of the best wits in Europe. Whether this request is complied with or not, I shall not be uneasy, but there is one petition I must make to him and to you, which I solicit with the warmest ardor, and in which I cannot bear a refusal. I mean, dear madam, that I may be always your ever affectionate and obliged kinsman, OLIVER GOLDSMITH. Now you see how I blot and blunder, when I am asking a favor."

CHAPTER 10

SURGEON'S HALL

1.

GOLDSMITH IS APPOINTED physician and surgeon to one of the factories on the coast of Coromandel. The road to fortune is broad and straight before him. But he needs money for his warrant, his passage, his sea stores. Any delay may be fatal. And so he goes to Archibald Hamilton of the *Critical Review,* who makes him a small advance on three articles.

His purse thus slenderly replenished, he pays for the warrant, wipes off the score of the milkmaid, abandons his garret, and moves into a shabby first floor in a forlorn court near the Old Bailey. There he awaits the time for his migration to the magnificent coast of Coromandel.

In April, 1758, the French forces under Count Lally land unexpectedly at Pondicherry with the declared intention of clearing the English from their footholds. News of Lally's attack does not reach the English public until the following March. Previous bulletins report India quiet. Then on March 22, 1759, news burst on England from the Paris papers of the French success. Madras is in imminent danger of falling; the English are about to be thrust out of Southern India entirely—and the French papers accuse the British East India Company of having suppressed intelligence of the French victories.

Events affect poor Goldsmith. The East India Company has assigned a civilian physician to a post, which, sometime in the summer of 1758, they learn they no longer possess. Not wishing to make public the real state of affairs, they simply postpone his sailings, meanwhile fitting out ships of war for Coromandel.

Goldsmith sees a chance of saving fifty pounds of his passage money and tries for the position of hospital mate on one of the ships bound for the coast. Even here poverty stands in his way. It is necessary to appear in a decent garb before the examining committee, but how is he to do it? He is literally out at the elbows as well as out of cash. But again the bedraggled Muse comes to his aid. In consideration of four articles furnished to the *Monthly Review*, Griffiths, his old taskmaster, undertakes to become his security to the tailor for a suit of clothes. This pauper proposal acceded to, Goldsmith returns to his room with four books under his arm—the articles are scribbled off and sent to the bookseller—and the clothes come in due time from the tailor.

A crowd of nervous young fellows is sitting in the outward room at Surgeon's Hall. The door opens, and a young fellow steps out from the place of examination with a pale countenance, quivering lip, and looks as wild as if he has seen a ghost. No sooner does he appear than they all flock eagerly about him. What questions was he asked? What answers did he make? What reception did he meet with? While he is describing his examination, the beadle calls out the name of Oliver Goldsmith, with a voice that makes him tremble as much as if it were the sound of the last trumpet. However, there is no remedy, and Goldsmith is conducted into a large hall where he sees about a dozen grim faces, sitting at a long table, one of whom bids him come forward in such an imperious tone that he is actually for a minute or two bereft of his senses. The first question put to him is, "Where was you born?" To which Goldy replies, "In Ireland, sirs."

"In Ireland," says the gentleman, "I know that very well. We have scarce any other countrymen to examine here. You Irishmen have overspread us of late as the locusts did Egypt. I ask you in what part of Ireland was you born."

Goldy names the place of his birth which has never before been heard of. He is then asked by the examiner if he has ever served as apprentice to a surgeon and he answers no. Then on his venturing the information that he has taken his degree abroad, the same gentleman falls into a violent passion, swears it is a shame and a scandal to take degrees on foreign soil, that it is a great presumption in him and an affront upon the English—and that his friends would have done better if they had made him a weaver or a cobbler. This exordium not at all contributes to a recovery of Goldy's spirits, but on the contrary reduces him to such a situation that he is scarce able to stand. Then the examination begins. . . .

"At a Court of Examiners held at the Theatre, 21st December, 1758, Present." There is a long list of the candidates who have passed, in the midst of which these occur: *"James Bernard, mate to a hospital. Oliver Goldsmith, found not qualified for ditto."*

Four days after his rejection at Surgeon's Hall, on Christmas day, 1758, his landlady, to whom he owes some small arrears of rent, enters his room and tells him a piteous tale of distress. Her husband has been suddenly dragged off by bailiffs the night before, and there is not food enough for the children. Can he not help them? What is to be done? He has no money, it is true, but there hangs the new suit in which he stood his unlucky examination at Surgeon's Hall. He immediately sends it off to the pawnbroker's and raises a sufficient sum to pay off his own debt and release the landlord from prison.

In another week he carries the four books he has recently reviewed for Griffiths to a neighbor and leaves them in pledge for a trifling loan. It is hardly done when a letter from Griffiths is put into his hand, peremptorily demanding the return of the books and the suit of clothes, or the instant payment of both. Goldsmith prays for some delay, but his reply only increases the ire of the bookseller and draws from him another letter still more harsh than the first, denouncing the author as a knave, sharper, villain, and containing threats of prosecution. Goldsmith replies:

"Sir—I know of no misery but a jail to which my imprudences and your letter seem to point. I have seen it inevitable these three or four weeks, and, by heavens! request it as a favor—as a favor that may prevent something more fatal. I have been some years struggling with a wretched being—with all that contempt and indigence brings with it—with all those passions which make contempt insupportable. What, then, has a jail that is formidable? I shall at least have the society of wretches, and such is to me true society. I tell you, again and again, that I am neither able nor willing to pay you a farthing, but I will be punctual to any appointment you or the tailor shall make. Thus far, at least, I do not act the sharper, since, unable to pay my own debts one way, I would generally give some security another. No, sir, had I been a sharper— had I been possessed of less good nature and native generosity, I might surely now have been in better circumstances.

"I am guilty, I own, of meannesses which poverty unavoidably brings with it. My reflections are filled with repentance for my imprudence, but not with any remorse for being a villain. That may be a character you unjustly charge me with. Your books, I assure you, are neither pawned nor sold, but in the custody of a friend, from whom my necessities obliged me to borrow some money. Whatever becomes of my person, you shall have them in a month. It is very possible both the reports you have heard and your own suggestions may have brought you false information with respect to my character. It is very possible that the man whom you now regard with detestation may inwardly burn with grateful resentment. It is very possible that, upon a second perusal of the letter I sent you, you may see the workings of a mind strongly agitated with gratitude and jealousy. If such circumstances should appear, at least spare invective till my book with Mr. Dodsley shall be published, and then, perhaps, you may see the bright side of a mind, when my professions shall not appear the dictates of necessity, but of choice.

"You seem to think Dr. Milner knew me not. Perhaps so, but he was a man I shall ever honor—but I have friendships only with the dead! I ask pardon for taking up so much time, nor shall I add to it by any other professions than that I am, sir, your humble servant,

"OLIVER GOLDSMITH

"P.S.—I shall expect impatiently the result of your resolutions."

The impatient expectation of Griffith's resolutions ends in a contract to write him a life of Voltaire—"there's flesh on his bones yet"—for a translation of the *Henriade* he is about to publish. A mere catchpenny on which Goldsmith spends four weeks.

Portly Griffiths is one of the thriving men of his day. In three years after this, he is able to retire from bookselling and hand over to Becket the publication of the *Review*. As time wears on, he becomes, more and more, a regular attendant at the meeting house, rises higher in the world's esteem, and at last keeps his two carriages and "lives in style." He buys Linden House at Turnham Green in Chiswick—a fine mansion standing in well-timbered gardens which cover four acres of ground and is estimated to have been worth £12,000—where he feasts his friends. The degree of L.L.D. is granted to him—without solicitation—by

Dartmouth College and perhaps by the University of Pennsylvania . . .

2.

Through alleys, courts, and blind passages, traversing Fleet Street and then turning along a narrow street to the bottom of a long steep flight of stone steps, called "Breakneck Steps," Goldsmith makes his way to his lodgings at 12 Green Arbour Court. Tall faded houses, bawling slipshod women, dirty, neglected children. The very intestines of the place seem turned inside out, to judge from the old garments and frippery that flutter from every window. It is a region of washerwomen, and the lines are stretched about the little square, on which clothes are dangling to dry. Just as he enters the square, a scuffle takes place between two viragoes about the disputed right to a wash tub, and immediately the whole community is in a hubbub. Heads in mobcaps pop out of every window—every amazon takes part with one or the other of the disputants, brandishes her arms, dripping with soapsuds, and fires away from her window as from the embrasure of a fortress—while the screams of children, waking with the noise, swell the concert. As Goldsmith ascends to his room he distributes cakes and sweetmeats to the young ones to make them cease their clatter.

Every night he risks his neck at those steep stone steps, and every day, for his clothes are ragged, he keeps within his dirty, naked, unfurnished room with its broken bed, single wooden chair, and window bench.

At the Temple Exchange he is introduced to Thomas Percy, now chaplain to Lord Sussex, afterwards Bishop of Dromore, and already busily engaged in collecting his famous *Reliques*. "He is a man," says Doctor Johnson, "very willing to learn, and very able to teach; a man of whose company I never go without having learned something. It is sure that he vexes me sometimes, but I am afraid it is by making me feel my own ignorance. . . . Percy's attention to poetry has given grace and splendor to his studies of antiquity. A mere antiquarian is a rugged being."

Precise, reserved, stately Thomas Percy, who has a great love of literary men, calls on Goldsmith at his lodgings and finds him writing his *Inquiry* in a miserable, dirty looking room, in which there is but one chair. When from civility Goldsmith offers it to his visitor, he himself is obliged to sit in the window. While they are conversing together, someone taps on the door, and being desired to come in, a poor, ragged little girl enters. Dropping a curtsy, she says, "My mamma sends her compliments and begs the favor of you to lend her a chamber pot full of coals. . . ."

"Speedily will be published," says the *Public Advertiser* of the seventh of February, 1759, "*Memoirs of the life of Monsieur de Voltaire with critical observations on the writings of that celebrated poet, and a new translation of the Henriade. Printed for R. Griffiths in Paternoster Row.*"

However, the publication does not take place. Edward Purdon, the translator, cannot finish his share of the work in time, and some months later, the memoir and translation appear separately in a magazine. Goldsmith describes the *Memoir* as no more than a catchpenny, but though it is poorly proportioned and bewildering in chronology, it is written with his usual verve and is charming in anecdotes and style.

Ned Purdon, Goldsmith's old schoolmate at Dublin, is now a Grub Street writer, starving by the exercise of his pen and often taxing Goldsmith's scanty means to relieve his hunger. His miserable career is summed up by our poet, some years after, on hearing that he has suddenly dropped dead in Smithfield——

> Here lies poor Ned Purdon, from misery freed,
>   Who long was a bookseller's hack;
> He led such a damnable life in this world,
>   I don't think he'll wish to come back.

CHAPTER 11

ENTER DAVID GARRICK

THE *Polite Learning* is now completed and passes through the press of the Dodsleys of Pall Mall. On April 2, 1759, it makes its appearance—a very respectable, well-printed duodecimo, without the author's name on the title page, but with two mottoes in the learned languages. The Greek signifies that the writer esteems philosophers but is no friend to sophists; and the Latin, that those only should destroy buildings who can themselves build. Goldsmith assumes learning is in decline and seeks to point out why. And he confidently remarks, "Write what you think regardless of the critics." Eschew those pedants who judge literature by Latin or Greek rules and who seek knowledge in books rather than in life. He shares the general opinions of his age, but his judgment is guided by common sense, honesty, and courage.

The work is violently attacked in Griffith's *Monthly Review*. Goldsmith is slandered as a man, decried as an author, and accused by innuendo of "laboring under the infamy of having, by the vilest and meanest actions, forfeited all pretensions to honor and honesty," and of practising "those acts which bring the sharper to the cart's tail or the pillory." Griffiths is sensible of the falsehood and extravagance of the attack, and tries to exonerate himself by declaring that the criticism has been written by a person in his employ—Kenrick.

William Kenrick, son of a staymaker, is brought up as a mechanic, but possessing some degree of talent and industry, applies himself to literature as a profession. He tries his hand in every department of prose and poetry—writes plays and satires, philosophical tracts, critical dissertations, and works on philology. Nothing from his pen gains him popularity. Soured by his own want of success, he at length abandons himself to reviewing and becomes one of the Ishmaelites of the press. He has a strong love of notoriety, a jealous and perverse temper, and is often drunk and violent. He becomes the enemy of every decent and successful person, and so notorious a libeller that few condescend to answer him. He lectures at the Devil's Tavern, Temple Bar, on every conceivable subject—from Shakespeare to perpetual motion, which he thinks he has discovered. He seldom writes without a bottle of brandy at his elbow . . . "Sir," says Dr. Johnson, characterizing Kenrick's literary career in one short sentence, "he is one of the many who have made themselves public without making themselves known."

> Dreaming of genius which he never had,
> Half wit, half fool, half critic, and half mad,
> Seizing like Shirley, on the poet's lyre,
> With all his rage, but not one spark of fire;
> Eager for slaughter and resolved to tear
> From other's brows that wreath he must not wear
> Next Kenrick came: all furious and replete
> With brandy, malice, pertness, and conceit;
> Unskill'd in classic lore, through envy blind
> To all that's beauteous, learned, or refined;
> For faults alone behold the savage prowl,
> With reason's offal glut his ravening soul;
> Pleased with his prey, its inmost blood he drinks,
> And mumbles, paws, and turns it—till it stinks.

(In charity we may say: Kenrick is a man of talent deficient in the knowledge of making proper use of it. His examination of Johnson's edition of Shakespeare is a rare amalgam of malice, envy, bad manners and sound, temperate criticism.)

There is a sharp bob for David Garrick in the *Inquiry*. A clamor has been raised against the autocrat of the drama for bringing forward nothing but old plays to the exclusion of new productions. Walpole joins in the charge. "Garrick," says he, "is treating the town as it deserves and likes to be treated, with scenes, fireworks, and his own writings. A good new play I never expect to see more; nor have seen since the *Provoked Husband*, which came out when I was at school."

Goldsmith adds to the outcry. "Our poet's performance," says he, "must undergo a process truly chemical before it is presented to the public. It must be tried in the manager's fire, strained through a licenser, suffer from repeated corrections, till it may be a mere *caput mortuum* when it arrives before the public. . . . Getting a play on even in three or four years is a privilege reserved only for the happy few who have the arts of courting the manager as well as the muse; who have adulation to please his vanity, powerful patrons to support their merit, or money to indemnify disappointment. Our Saxon ancestors had but one name for a wit and a witch. I will not dispute the propriety of uniting those characters then; but the man who under present discouragements ventures to write for the stage, whatever claim he may have to the appellation of a wit, at least has no right to be called a conjurer."

But there is a passage which touches Garrick to the quick. "I have no particular spleen against the fellow who sweeps the stage with the besom, or the hero who brushes it with his train. It were a matter of indifference to me whether our heroines are in keeping, or our candle snuffers burn their fingers, did not such make a great part of public care and polite conversation. Our actors assume all that

[105]

state off the stage which they do on it; and to use an
expression borrowed from the green room, every one is up
in his part. I am sorry to say it, they seem to forget their
real characters."

These strictures rankle in Garrick's mind when Goldsmith solicits his vote for the vacant secretaryship of the
Society of Arts of which the manager is a member.

A little doll of a figure in dark blue with dark eyes
and laced ruffles to his shirt front and sleeves, receives
Goldsmith in his office at Drury Lane.

"Sir," remarks Garrick, "you have taken pains to deprive yourself of my assistance by an unprovoked attack
upon the management of this theatre in your *Present State
of Learning*. How is it possible for you to lay claim to my
recommendation?"

Goldsmith, instead of apologizing for his conduct,
bluntly replies, "In truth, sir, I spoke my mind, and I believe
what I said is very right." The manager dismisses him with
civility.

Goldsmith makes no further application, fails to get the
appointment, and considers Garrick his enemy. In the second edition of his treatise, he expunges or modifies the
passages which have given the manager offense, but Garrick for a time remains cool. . .

Little mercurial Davy Garrick, young and light and
alive in every muscle and in every feature comes bound-
ing on the stage. The very flaps and skirts of his coat seem
animated. He is brisk, brisk, and knowing—his smart hat
cocked airily a little on one side and not in the least over-
shadowing his brilliant face, full of confidence in his
calves, with firmness and decision in every movement. His
voice is distinct, melodious, commanding. . . .

Garrick, as all of us know, was born under a lucky

star—the son of a recruiting captain whose family was originally French (the name was Garrique) and from whom he inherits his little figure, his expressive eye, his happy buoyancy of spirit, and his restless vivacity. He begins the world with a great hunger for money. The son of a half-pay officer, he is bred in a family whose study it is to make four pence do as much as others make four half penny do. But when he has got money, he is very liberal. He is not mean, but naturally careful.

Now Garrick is always on a fidget for attention and adulation. When he thinks himself free and adored, he prattles such stuff as would disgrace an eight year old child in conversation with its doting and admiring grandmother. He is a glutton in praise, stealing sidelong glances at a duke's table to ascertain whether he has made a hit upon the butler and footmen. . . . Envy is his torment.

His hesitation and never giving a direct answer arise from two causes—affectation and a fear of being led into promises which he never means to perform. And therefore—— "By—nay—why—now, if you will not—why, I cannot say, but I may settle that matter, and as I shall see you on Tuesday, why, then—hey—you know that—Mrs. Garrick's coach is waiting—and you now—I say now—hey—now Tuesday. You will remember Tuesday? . . ." A salad, Goldsmith calls him, oil, vinegar, sugar, and saltness.

To paint Garrick is to come into direct competition with all the notable portrait painters of the time. Everybody paints Garrick—Reynolds, Gainsborough, Hayman, Dance, Cotes, Hone, Zoffany, Angelica Kauffman.

Noblemen have him to their houses. The great Murray, leader of the King's bench, forgets his briefs and his politics to entertain him at supper in Lincoln's Inn Fields. Ladies fall in love with him. "All the run is now after Garrick," says Walpole. "The Duke of Argyll says he is superior to Betterton. . . ." Yet he is capable of mutilating *Hamlet* and degrading the *Midsummer Night's Dream* into a ballet opera. . . .

GOLDY

Here lies David Garrick, describe me who can
An abridgment of all that was pleasant in man.
As an actor, confessed without rival to shine:
As a wit, if not first, in the very first line.
Yet with talents like these, and an excellent heart,
The man had his failings, a dupe to his art.
Like an ill judging beauty, his colors he spread,
And beplastered with rouge his own natural red.
On the stage he was natural, simple, affecting;
'Twas only that, when he was off, he was acting.
With no reason on earth to go out of his way,
He turned and he varied full ten times a day.
Though secure of our hearts, yet confoundedly sick
If they were not his own by finessing and trick.
He cast off his friends, as a huntsman his pack,
For he knew when he pleased, he could whistle them back.
Of praise a mere glutton, he swallowed what came;
And the puff of a dunce, he mistook it for fame;
Till his relish grown callous, almost to disease,
Who peppered the highest was surest to please.
But let us be candid, and speak out our mind,
If dunces applauded, he paid them in kind.
Ye Kenricks, ye Kellys, and Woodfalls so grave,
What a commerce was yours, while you got and you gave!
How did Grub Street re-echo the shouts that you raised,
While he was be-Rosciused, and you were bepraised.
But peace to his spirit wherever it flies,
To act as an angel and mix with the skies;
Those poets who owe their best fame to his skill
Shall still be his flatterers, go where he will;
Old Shakespeare receive him with praise and with love,
And Beaumonts and Bens be his Kellys above.

CHAPTER 12

GRUB STREET

1.

THE HALCYON DAYS of literature are come. Booksellers are never more active than at the close of 1759. Every week has its spawn of periodical publications, feeble but of desperate fecundity—the Babblers and Schemers, Friends and Advisers, Auditors, Comptrollers, and Grumblers, Spendthrifts and Bachelors (they go hand in hand), Free Inquirers, Scrutators, and Investigators, Englishmen, Freeholders, and Moderators, Sylphs and Triflers, Rangers and Cottagers, Templars, Gentlemen, and Skeptics. Many of these choke each other at the outset; few of them escape oblivion. Enrolled is a host from the ranks of Grub Street— the favorite Purdons, Hills, Wilkingtons, Kenricks, Shiels, Bakers, Guthries, Wotys, Ryders, Collyers, Joneses, Pilkingtons, Huddlestone Wynnes, and Hiffernans.

In their midst is the author of the English Dictionary. For in Grub Street, as occasion calls, he is still to be seen— poor, persevering, proud, "tugging at the oar."

Goldsmith has mounted the wagon of industry and is writing for *The Lady's Magazine* and for *The Busy Body*. Then bookseller Wilkie of the Bible in St. Paul's Churchyard makes an offer to him to edit and write another magazine—a freshly born one. True, magazines and periodicals are issued by the score, but Wilkie has read the *Inquiry* and come to the conclusion that its writer is the man to nurse his child into manhood—possibly. At any rate, if it dies, it can be dressed up in other clothes and baptized by another name—and no one will be any the wiser.

"A man of your genius, sir, could, if you were the sole contributor and editor, produce something which might catch the town." (Mild interest. Goldsmith crosses his legs.)

"The magazine is to make its appearance every Saturday—once a week, instead of the usual twice." (Goldsmith uncrosses his legs.)

"You will be left free, sir, to give a spice of variety to its contents." (Extreme interest, but hesitation.)

"And you will receive two guineas a week—of which this is an advance payment." (Oh! the thrifty canny Scot!)

Goldsmith agrees *con amore*—and goes away dreaming of future greatness, when tailor bills will be mere bagatelles, and he will be president of the Charity Society. (Oliver Goldsmith is devoid of ambition. He has no desire to become a great writer. He only becomes a great writer to save himself from starvation.)

The Bee consists of a variety of essays on amusements, follies, and vices in fashion, topics of conversation, remarks on theatrical exhibitions, and memoirs of modern literature, etc., etc.—all for three pence. To maintain a steady output he depends on his past experience, his reading, and on outright pilfering from the Dutch essayist Justus van Effen and Diderot's and D'Alembert's *Encylopédie*. The first number issues from St. Paul's Churchyard on Saturday, the sixth of October.

2.

With nightcap on his head and pen in hand, Goldsmith is nodding drowsily over his work in his room near the Old Bailey. He fancies himself placed in the yard of a large inn, in which there are an infinite number of wagons and stage coaches, attended by fellows who either invite the company to take their places, or are busied in packing their baggage. Each vehicle has its inscription, showing the place of its destination. On one he can read, The Pleasure Stage Coach; on another, The Wagon of Industry; on a third, The Vanity Whim; and on a fourth, The Landau of Riches. He has some inclination to step into each of these, one after another, but he knows not by what means, he passes them by, and at last fixes his eye upon a small carriage, Berlin fashion, which seems the most convenient vehicle at a distance in the world, and upon his nearer approach finds it to be The Fame Machine.

He instantly goes up to the coachman, whom he finds to be an affable and seemingly good-natured fellow. The coachman informs him that he has but a few days ago returned from the Temple of Fame, to which he was carrying Addison, Swift, Pope, Steele, Congreve, and Colley Cibber, that they made but indifferent company by the way, and that he once or twice was going to empty his Berlin of the whole cargo.

"However," says he, "I got them all safe home, with no other damage than a black eye, which Colley gave Mr. Pope, and am now returned for another coachful."

"If that be all," says Goldsmith, "and if you are in want of company, I'll make one with all my heart. Open the door. I hope the machine rides easy."

"Oh, for that, sir, extremely easy." But still keeping the door shut, and measuring Goldsmith with his eye, "Pray, sir, have you no luggage? You seems to be a good-natured sort of gentleman, but I don't find you have got any luggage, and I never permit any to travel with me but such as have something valuable to pay for coach hire."

Examining his pockets, our poet is not a little disconcerted at this unexpected rebuff, but considering that he carries a number of the *Bee* under his arm, he is resolved

GOLDY

to open it in his eyes and dazzle him with the splendor of
the page. The coachman reads the title and contents, however, without any emotion, and assures him he has never
heard of it before. "In short, friend," says he, now losing
all his former respect, "you must not come in. I expect
better passengers, but as you seem a harmless creature,
perhaps, if there be room left, I may let you ride a while
for charity."

Goldsmith now takes his stand by the coachman at the
door, and since he cannot command a seat, is resolved
to be as useful as possible, and earn by his assiduity what
he cannot by his merit.

The next that presents himself for a place is a most
whimsical figure indeed. He is hung round with papers of
his own composing, not unlike those who sing ballads in
the streets, and comes dancing up to the door with all the
confidence of instant admittance. The volubility of his
motion and address prevents Goldsmith from being able to
read more of his cargo than the word *Inspector,* which is
written in great letters at the top of some of the papers.
He opens the coach door himself without any ceremony,
and is just slipping in, when the coachman, with as little
ceremony pulls him back. The figure seems perfectly angry
at this repulse and demands a gentleman's satisfaction.

"Lord, sir!" replies the coachman, "instead of proper
luggage, by your bulk you seem loaded for a West India
voyage. You are big enough, with all your papers, to crack
twenty stage coaches. Excuse me, indeed, sir, for you must
not enter."

The figure now begins to expostulate. He assures the
coachman that though his baggage seems so bulky, it is
perfectly light, and that he will be contented with the
smallest corner of room. But Jehu is inflexible, and the
carrier of the *Inspectors* is sent to dance back again, with
all his papers fluttering in the wind. They expect to have
no more trouble from this quarter, when, in a few minutes,
the same figure changes his appearance, like Harlequin

[112]

upon the stage, and with the same confidence, again makes his approaches, dressed in lace, and carrying nothing but a nosegay. Upon coming nearer, he thrusts the nosegay to the coachman's nose, grasps the brass, and seems now resolved to enter by violence. Goldsmith finds the struggle soon begin to grow hot, and the coachman, who is a little old, unable to continue to contest; so, in order to ingratiate himself, he steps in to his assistance, and their united efforts send this literary Proteus (who is none other than John Hill), clear off, dancing a rigadoon, and smelling to his own nosegay.

Another figure comes forward but is likewise turned away. Then comes a very grave personage, whom at some distance, they take for one of the most reserved, and even disagreeable figures they have ever seen; but as he approaches, his appearance improves, and when they can distinguish him thoroughly, they perceive that, in spite of the severity of his brow, he has one of the most good-natured countenances that can be imagined. Upon coming to open the stage door, he lifts a parcel of folios into the seat before him, but our inquisitorial coachman at once shoves them out again.

"What! not take in my *Dictionary?*" exclaims the other in a rage.

"Be patient, sir," replies the coachman. "I have drove a coach, man and boy, these two thousand years, but I do not remember to have carried above one dictionary during the whole time. That little book which I perceive peeping from one of your pockets, may I presume to ask what it contains?"

"A mere trifle," replies the author. "It is called *The Rambler.*"

"*The Rambler!*" says the coachman, "I beg, sir, you'll take your place. I have heard our ladies in the court of Apollo frequently mention it with rapture, and Clio, who happens to be a little grave, has been heard to prefer it to the *Spectator;* though others have observed, that the reflections, by being refined, sometimes become minute."

This grave gentleman is scarcely seated, when another, whose appearance is something more modern, seems willing to enter, yet afraid to ask. He carries in his hand a bundle of essays, of which the coachman is curious enough to inquire the contents.

"These," replies the gentleman (whom Goldsmith now recognizes as Mr. Hume) "are rhapsodies against the religion of my country."

"And how can you expect to come into my coach, after thus choosing the wrong side of the question?"

"Ay, but I am right," replies the other, "and if you give me leave, I shall, in a few minutes, state the argument."

"Right or wrong," says the coachman, "he who disturbs religion is a blockhead, and he shall never travel in a coach of mine."

"If, then," says the gentleman mustering up all his courage, "if I am not to have admittance as an essayist, I hope I shall not be repulsed as an historian. The last volume of my history met with applause."

"Yes," replies the coachman, "but I have only heard the first approved at the temple of Fame, and as I see you have it about you, enter, without further ceremony."

Their attention is now diverted to a crowd which is pushing forward a person that seems more inclined to the Stagecoach of Riches; but by their means he is driven forward to the same machine, which he, however, seems heartily to despise. Impelled, however, by their solicitations, he steps up, flourishing a voluminous history and demanding admittance.

"Sir, I have formerly heard your name mentioned," says the coachman, "but never as an historian. Is there no other work upon which you may claim a place?"

"None," replies the other (who is Dr. Smollett) "except a romance, but this is a work of too trifling a nature to claim future attention."

"You mistake," says the inquisitor, "a well-written romance is no such easy task as is generally imagined. I remember formerly to have carried Cervantes and Segrais, and if you think fit, you may enter."

Upon our three literary travellers coming into the same coach, Goldsmith listens attentively to hear what may be the conversation that passes upon this extraordinary occasion, when, instead of agreeable or entertaining dialogue, he finds them grumbling at each other, and each seems discontented with his companions. Strange! thinks Goldsmith to himself, that they who are thus born to enlighten the world, should still preserve the narrow prejudices of childhood, and, by disagreeing, make even the highest merit ridiculous. Were the learned and the wise to unite against the dunces of society, instead of sometimes dividing into opposite parties within themselves, they might throw a luster upon each other's reputation, and teach every rank of subordinate merit, if not to admire, at least not to avow dislike.

In the midst of these reflections, Goldsmith perceives that the coachman, unmindful of him, has now mounted the box. Several are approaching to be taken in, whose pretensions are very just. He therefore desires the coachman to stop and take in more passengers, but he replies that as he has now mounted the box, it would be improper to come down, but that he shall take them all, one after the other, when he returns. So he drives away, and as for Goldsmith, as he cannot get in, he mounts behind, in order to hear the conversation on the way. . . .

A loud knocking below. The landlady opens the door— a gentleman asks to see her lodger and goes unannounced upstairs. She then hears Goldsmith's door banged open, closed again sharply from within, and the key turned in the lock. After this the sound of a noisy argument reaches her, but it soon subsides, and to her surprise, the perfect silence that follows, continues for more than three hours. Then the door is again opened, and the gentleman, descending more cheerfully than he has entered, sends her out to a neighboring tavern for some supper . . . Mr. Wilkie has obtained his arrears of copy . . .

Sad to say, on November 20, the *Bee's* brief life closes, and obsequies are said with its eighth number. Goldsmith turns to another short-lived venture—*The Weekly Magazine*, but in a few days, he is sought out by that distinguished author, Dr. Tobias Smollett. Smollett has read the *Bee* and has decided to enlist Goldsmith's services in launching his new venture, *The British Magazine*.

The sea has hardly tended to soften Dr. Smollett's manners. Essentially a fighter, his theory of life is the eternal traditions of the navy—whatever the force of the enemy, always attack. And so he fights endless literary battles and braves for years the cudgels of controversy. He is oppressed by illness, age, narrow fortune, but his spirit is resolute and independent, and his courage sturdy. He has a marked dislike of modish society and hates ceremony of every kind. He has tried to establish a practise in Downing Street and then in Mayfair, but has failed. He cannot be a fashionable physician—among his many gifts the bedside manner is hardly included.

Religion does not appeal to him. His Christ would always find it difficult to love an enemy unless he has drubbed him soundly first. He is far ahead of his times— he believes in fresh air and cold water . . .

"Many a time do I stop my task and betake me to a game of romps with Betty while my wife looks on smiling and longing in her heart to join in the sport"—poor Betty whose early death he never quite gets over.

Among his multifarious labors, he runs a literary factory, where he turns out every kind of production from a Universal History to a translation of Voltaire. To get through his work, he employs an army of hacks in constant labor, and every Sunday he entertains them with dinner at his house in Chelsea. Here the unfortunate brothers of the quill are treated to beef, pudding, and potatoes, port punch and Calvert's entire butt beer . . .

On January 1, 1760, the first venture appears. It is published for six pence, embellished with curious copper plates, and entitled, *The British Magazine, or Monthly Repository for Gentlemen and Ladies. By T. Smollett, M.D. and others.* It is dedicated with much fervor to Mr. Pitt.

The first number has the tale of Sir Launcelot Greaves. Though Sir Launcelot is mad, wise thoughts have made him so, and in the hope to "remedy evils which the law cannot reach, to detect fraud and treason, to abase insolence, to mortify pride, to discourage slander, to disgrace immodesty, and to stigmatize ingratitude," he stumbles through his odd career. . . . But the magazine is suddenly snuffed out after twenty odd numbers. Smollett, pining for the loss of his only daughter, sails for the Continent never to return to a fixed or settled residence in London.

3.

Good-natured Mr. Newbery with his red pimpled face is at the door of Oliver Goldsmith. He is no sooner alighted than he is in haste to be gone, for he is ever on business of the utmost importance, and is at this time actually compiling materials for the history of Mr. Thomas Trip. When he enters the house, his first declaration is that he cannot sit down, and so short is his visit that he appears to have come for no other reason but to say he must go. He has published for one Dr. Primrose against the Deuterogamists of the age, but now his object is to secure the alliance and services of Oliver Goldsmith. . . .

He is a bustling, multifaceted man, essentially commercial, essentially enterprising, rigorously exacting his money's worth of work, keeping a prudent record of all casual cash advances, but on the whole not unkindly, in his business fashion, to the needy brethren of the pen by whom he is surrounded. His wig is often awry and his spectacles often mislaid in that perpetual journey from pillar to post which ultimately lands him at the comparatively early age of fifty-four in his grave at Waltham St. Lawrence.

John Newbery is engaged in two distinct branches of business—the sale of books and the sale of patent medicines. He is part owner of Dr. Hooper's Female Pills and sole manager of Dr. James's Fever Powders. The latter have an extraordinary vogue. The King doses the Princess Elizabeth with them; Gray and Cowper both believe in their efficacy. Fielding praises them in his *Amelia,* and Horace Walpole declares he should take them if the house were on fire. In any other country but England, they would bring public honors and rewards. . . .

Besides, John Newbery is the first bookseller who has made the issue of books, specially intended for children, a business of any importance. He has small presses constructed and imports from Holland or Germany gay flowered and gilt paper for bindings. His little books, radiant with gold and rich with bad pictures, have an enormous sale—many thousands being exhausted during the Christmas holidays. As publisher of the renowned history of Giles Gingerbread—a little boy who lives upon learning—of Mrs. Margery Two-shoes, and of the redoubtable Tommy Trip and his dog Jowler, an artless appeal is made to all little Masters and Misses who are good—or intend to be good. Naughty boys are thrust into the jaws of dragons, and good boys are elevated to ride in King Pepin's coach. And in *Goody Two Shoes* we are told, for instance, that the heroine's father died miserably, because he was "seized with a violent fever in a Place where Dr. James's Powder was not to be had. . . ."

Smollett has little of the Pickle in him, and John Newbery much of the Mr. Trip. . .

The newspaper venture of good Mr. Newbery starts twelve days after Smollett's, the first number of *The Public Ledger* appearing January 12, 1760—a daily short sheet of gossip, commercial information, records of political events, editorial comment, and literary essays on books, town topics, and social life. Goldsmith undertakes to write two articles per week at one guinea per article.

Into the *Ledger* go the Chinese Letters. At the close of 1760 ninety-eight have been published; within a few months they are brought to completion; and in the following year they are republished by Mr. Newbery in two volumes, but without the author's name, as *The Citizen of the World*. (Most of Goldsmith's borrowings are from French or English writers—Montesquieu, Marana, Lord Lyttelton, Voltaire and numerous others.

If to London of 1760 the *true* East is an undiscovered bourne, a craze for pseudo-Orient, especially China, is almost at fever pitch—in works of history, travel, fiction, "Oriental" letters and tales in newspapers and magazines, and dozens of books on Chinese gardening, music, furniture, cookery, architecture. Ladies cover their mantelpieces with idols, pagodas, mandarins. "Every chair in an apartment," says John Shebbeare, "the frames of glasses and tables, must be Chinese, the walls covered with Chinese paper filled with figures which resemble nothing of God's creation and which a prudent nation would prohibit for the sake of pregnant women. . . . Nay, so excessive is the love of Chinese architecture become that at present the fox hunters would be sorry to break a leg in pursuing their sport in leaping any gate that was not made in the Eastern taste of little bits of wood standing in all directions." Dr. Johnson publishes several Oriental tales in the *Rambler* and in 1759 writes *Rasselas*.

The Monthly Review is now decently resolved to swallow its leek, and its obedient Mr. Kenrick is put under orders not to bite or even to bark at Dr. Goldsmith, but to profess admiration and supplicate forgiveness.

As we read the Chinese Letters, those actual days come

back vividly to us. Earl Ferrers glides through them with his horrible passion and yet more ghastly composure. The theaters again contend with Pollys and Macheaths, and the town with perpetual Beggars' Operas. Merry and fashionable crowds repeople White Conduit Gardens and Vauxhall. Old George II dies and young George III ascends the throne. Churchill makes his hit with the *Rosciad,* and Sterne, having startled the town with the humor and extravagance of *Tristram Shandy,* comes up from the country quiet to enjoy his popularity.

This tall, thin, hectic looking Yorkshire parson is everywhere the honored guest of the rich and noble. His book is become the fashion and east and west are moved alike. Mr. Dodsley offers him £650 for a second edition of two more volumes; Lord Falconberg gives him a curacy of £150 a year; Mr. Reynolds paints his portrait; Warburton, not having yet pronounced him an "irrecoverable scoundrel," goes round to the bishops and tells them he is the English Rabelais. And Sterne is boasting to his friends of dinner engagements fourteen deep.

The way to fame is like that to heaven, through much tribulation, and Sterne describes himself in the midst of his triumph as "attacked and pelted from cellar and garret."

4.

About this time there is a city campaign of peculiar cruelty. On the groundless cry of hydrophobia, dogs are slaughtered wholesale, and their bodies block up the streets. "The dear, good-natured, honest, sensible creatures," exclaims Horace Walpole, "Christ! How can anybody hurt them?"

But the epidemic terror rages, and the whole nation is actually groaning under the malignity of its influence. The people sally from their houses with that circumspection which is prudent in such as expect a mad dog at every turning. The physician publishes his prescription; the beadle prepares his halter, and a few of unusual bravery arm themselves with boots and buff gloves, in order to face the enemy if he should offer to attack them. In short, the whole people stand gravely upon their defense, and seem by their present spirit, to show a resolution of not being tamely bit by mad dogs any longer.

Their manner of knowing whether a dog be mad or not somewhat resembles the ancient European custom of trying witches. The old woman suspected was tied hand and foot and thrown into the water. If she swam, then she was instantly carried off to be burnt for a witch; if she sank, then indeed she was acquitted of the charge, but drowned in the experiment. In the same manner a crowd gathers around a dog suspected of madness, and they begin by teasing the devoted animal on every side. If he attempts to stand upon the defensive and bite, then he is unanimously found guilty, for "a mad dog always snaps at everything." If, on the contrary, he strives to escape by running away, then he can expect no compassion, for "mad dogs always run straight forward before them."

It is pleasant enough for a neutral being (like me), who has no share in these ideal calamities, to mark the stages of this national disease. The terror at first feebly enters with a disregarded story of a little dog that went through a neighboring village, and was thought to be mad by several that had seen him. The next account comes that a mastiff ran through a certain town and bit five geese, which immediately ran mad, foamed at the bill, and died in great agonies soon after. Then comes an affecting history of a little boy bit in the leg and gone down to be dipped in the salt water. When the people have sufficiently shuddered at that, they are next congealed with a frightful account of a man who was said lately to have died from a bite he had received some years before. This relation only prepares the way for another still more hideous, as how the master of a family, with seven small children, were all bit by a mad lapdog; and how the poor father first perceived the infection by calling for a draught of water where he saw the lapdog swimming in the cup.

When epidemic terror is thus once excited, every morning comes loaded with some new disaster. As in stories of ghosts each loves to hear the account, though it only serves to make him uneasy, so here each listens with eagerness and adds to the tidings new circumstances of peculiar horror. A lady, for instance, in the country, of very weak nerves, has been frighted by the barking of a dog, and this, alas! too frequently happens. The story soon is improved and spreads that a mad dog had frighted a lady of distinction. These circumstances begin to grow terrible before they have reached the neighboring village, and there the report is that a lady of quality was bit by a mad mastiff. This account every moment gathers new strength and grows more dismal as it approaches the capital; and by the time it has arrived in town the lady is described, with wild eyes, foaming mouth, running mad upon all fours, barking like a dog, biting her servants, and at last smothered between two beds by the advice of her doctors—while the mad mastiff is in the meantime ranging the whole country over, slavering at the mouth, and seeking whom he may devour. . . .

Goldsmith's landlady, a good-natured woman, but a little credulous, wakes him one morning, with horror and astonishment in her looks. She desires him, if he has any regard for his safety to keep within, for a few days ago so dismal an accident happened, as to put all the world upon their guard. A mad dog down in the country, she assures him, bit a farmer, who soon becoming mad ran into his own yard and bit a fine brindled cow. The cow quickly became as mad as the man, began to foam at the mouth, and raising herself up, walked about on her hind legs, sometimes barking like a dog, and sometimes attempting to talk like the farmer. Upon examining the grounds of this story, Goldsmith finds his landlady had it from one neigh-

bor, who had it from another neighbor, who heard it from
very good authority. . . .

Good people all, of every sort,
  Give ear unto my song,
And if you find it wondrous short,
  It cannot hold you long.

In Islington there was a man,
  Of whom the world might say,
That still a godly race he ran,
  Whene'er he went to pray.

A kind and gentle heart he had,
  To comfort friends and foes;
The naked every day he clad,
  When he put on his clothes.

And in that town a dog was found,
  As many dogs there be,
Both mongrel, puppy, whelp, and hound,
  And curs of low degree.

This dog and man at first were friends;
  But when a pique began,
The dog to gain some private ends,
  Went mad, and bit the man.

Around from all the neighboring streets
  The wond'ring neighbors ran,
And swore the dog had lost his wits
  To bite so good a man.

The wound it seem'd both sore and sad
  To every Christian eye;
And while they swore the dog was mad,
  They swore the man would die.

But soon a wonder came to light,
  That show'd the rogues they lied!
The man recover'd of the bite—
  The dog it was that died.

CHAPTER 13

THE ROBIN HOOD

"A HIGH BORLACE will be held this evening at the Robin Hood in the Butcher Row, Temple Bar, to which all *Choice Spirits* in general are invited. The Stars will shine early."

This Robin Hood Society is chiefly composed of lawyers, clerks, petty tradesmen, and the lowest mechanics—between forty to sixty good citizens of London who meet every Monday evening to debate any questions which the members choose to submit. No restriction is put on membership except the payment of sixpence. There is Bob Booty, a strict Hobbian, John Dismal, a merchant, Thomas Broadcloth, citizen and mercer, Richard Goosequill, attorney-at-law, Jeremy Crispin, cordwainer, Mat Prig, a merchant's clerk, Will Positive, a strong fatalist, and others.

Every sect that was known among the Grecians and Romans has its votaries here also. There is a tailor, a stoic; a shoemaker, a Platonist; and a cook, an Epicurean. They affect to entertain a profound veneration for Socrates, often preferring him to the Apostles, though instead of declaring with this wise philosopher that they know nothing, the members of the Robin Hood Society profess to know everything. They pun with grave faces, and make quibbles and conundrums with the air of philosophers.

So great a universitie,
    I think there ne'er was any,
In which you may a scholar be
    For spending of a penny.

Demosthenes, on being asked what was the first quality in an orator, replied action; what the second—action; what the third—action. Upon this principle one of the members is the greatest orator that has ever lived. He never troubles himself about the order or substance of what he delivers but waves his hands, tosses his head, abounds in several new and beautiful gestures, and from the beginning of his speech to the end of it, takes no care but to set it off with action.

On first being ushered into the society, one is surprised to find such amazing erudition among them. Toland, Collins, Chubb, and Mandeville seem to have been learned by heart. A shoemaker takes pains to show his disbelief of the Gospel by unsainting the Apostles, and calling them by no other title than plain Peter or plain Paul. Many wise tradesmen settle the most important articles of faith over a pint of beer. A midshipman swears that the Bible is all a lie for he has sailed around with Lord Anson, and if there were any Red Sea, he would have met it. A barber surgeon sets forth the opinion that it is impossible for the Saviour to have fasted forty days in the wilderness. And a bricklayer, who during the day works by line and rule and carefully lays one brick upon another, argues with a fellow laborer that the world was made by chance. . . .

This affectation of freethinking is happily confined to the men. On Sundays while their husbands are toping at the alehouse, the good women, their wives, think it their duty to go to church, say their prayers, bring home the text, and hear the children recite their catechism. . . .

Goldy becomes a member of the society and speaks there occasionally. He is a politician, logician, geometrician, physician, metaphysician, casuist, moralist, theologist, mythologist, or anything but an atheist. The members look upon him as "a candid disputant, with a clear head and an honest heart, though coming but seldom."

On first being introduced to the club by his Irish friend Samuel Derrick, he is struck with the self important appearance of the chairman ensconced in a large gilt chair.

"This," says Goldy, "must be the Lord Chancellor at least."

"No, no," replies Derrick, who recognizes Caleb Jeacocke, the baker, "he is only master of the rolls. . . ."

Samuel Derrick's story is interesting. Diminutive Samuel Derrick lives in a second floor attic in Shoe Lane, Holborn, with Mrs. Lessingham, the actress, whom he has trained for the stage. But the lady hankers after diamonds and fine dresses and soon abandons her lover and his attic near the heavens. Years later when affairs are in a more prosperous condition, Derrick calls upon her, wishing to renew his acquaintance, but the little man receives such a snub that he departs in all haste.

There is a charming *savoir faire* about Derrick. One evening having quitted his attic indefinitely—for the very good reason that he has no money to pay for it—he finds himself near the docks, and for want of a more luxurious couch, falls asleep upon a hulk. An equally impecunious author spies out his old acquaintance and wakes him. Upon which Derrick exclaims, "My dear Floyd, I am sorry to see you in this destitute state. Will you go home with me to my lodgings?"

Through the interest of his friends, who make most of his talents, Derrick becomes, on the death of Beau Nash, Master of the Ceremonies at Bath and Tunbridge Wells. He now thinks himself no end of a fine fellow and for five years hops about the rooms and streets in a white hat—for in that respect he imitates his predecessor Beau Nash. In spite of his insignificant appearance Derrick is so absurdly vain that when he blossoms forth as a man of fashion, he always makes the footman walk behind him and will constantly cross the street with the man at his heels so that there can be no mistake about it. . . .

CHAPTER 14

WHITE MICE

BEING NOW in easier circumstances and in
receipt of frequent sums from the booksellers, Goldsmith
in the middle of 1760 emerges from his dismal abode in
Green Arbour Court and takes respectable apartments in
Wine Office Court, Fleet Street. But still he looks back
with kindness to his old hostess and often supplies her
with food from his own table and visits her frequently
"with the sole purpose to be kind to her."

In his new lodgings he begins to receive visitors and
to entertain his literary friends—among them Guthrie,
Murphy, Christopher Smart, and Bickerstaffe. There is also
a numerous class of Irish hangers-on—honey seeking bees
who scent the perfume of the guinea and make direct
for it.

Jack Pilkington, a shifting adventurer, calls on him one
day with a smiling face. Good luck has dawned on him at
last, and his troubles are over. A very small sum—and he
runs about the room for joy of the announcement—is all he
wants to make his fortune. A great duchess has a most
surprising passion for white mice. Two have been procured already, and for years he has been looking for two
more, which she is ready to offer a most extravagant price
for. Aware of her grace's weakness, he has long ago im-

plored his friend going out to India to procure him—if possible—two white mice; and here they are actually arrived—in the river at that moment—and a small sum is all that stands between Jack Pilkington and independence for life. Yes, all he wants is a cage for the creatures sufficiently handsome to be received by the duchess.

"How much will a cage cost?" asks Goldsmith.

"About two guineas," replies Pilkington.

"In truth, Jack, then you're out of luck, for I have got but half a guinea in the world."

"Ay, but my dear Doctor," continues Pilkington, "you have got a watch, and though I would rather die than propose such an indelicacy upon any other occasion than the present, if you could let me have that, I could pawn it across the way for two guineas, and be able to repay you with heartfelt gratitude in a few days."

This last bait takes poor Goldsmith, and Pilkington carries off the watch.

A paragraph later informs him of certain equivocal modes "whereby Mr. P-lk—g-on is endeavoring to raise money"—yet a messenger not long afterwards carries to the starving creature's death bed "a guinea from Mr. Goldsmith."

He takes solitary rambles sometimes extending to the walls of White Conduit House. One day while strolling about the gardens, he meets the wife and two daughters of a respectable tradesman whom he knows. With a desire to please, he conducts them about the garden, treats them to tea and runs up a bill in the most open-handed manner imaginable. When he comes to pay, he finds himself in one of his old predicaments—he has no money. The waiter sneers; the people at the next table look at each other and smile; then some acquaintances in whose eyes he wishes to stand well come up and amuse themselves at his expense.

"A shilling, Bob . . . Will, a few pence—you know I . . . John? . . ."

"Sorry, old man. . . . Haven't a half penny. . . . Why, my tailor. . . . Wish I—but. . . . So you can't pay, Goldy?"

When they have sufficiently enjoyed themselves, a few pence are scraped together, the waiter is paid, and poor Goldy is enabled to convoy off the ladies with flying colors.

So passes the thoughtless life of Oliver Goldsmith in the first year of his success. He is at the theater enjoying Garrick's Abel Drugger and laughing at all who call it "low," a little tired of Polly and the *Beggar's Opera,* not at all interested in the fortunate tumbler who between the acts of tragedies as well as farces balances a straw upon his nose—and after all is over zigzagging his way home through coach wheels and palanquin poles, "like a bird in its flight through the branches of a forest."

"What!" he says to his friend Derrick, "Polly and the Pickpocket tonight, Polly and the Pickpocket tomorrow night, and Polly and the Pickpocket again! I want patience. I'll hear no more. My soul is out of tune—all jarring discord and confusion. Rest, rest, ye dear three clinking shillings in my pocket's bottom—the music you make is more harmonious to my spirit, than catgut, rosin, or all the nightingales that ever chirruped in petticoats!"

But if he escapes the wiles of Macheath, he is more beset by fretting, disdainful Queens (who come in curtsying to the audience) and violent Kings. Kings are men of spirit. Unlike your phlegmatic sons of clay, they feel at every pore. They are for immediate tenderness or instant death. Death and tenderness are leading passions with every buskined hero. This moment they embrace, and the next stab, mixing daggers and kisses in every period.

He goes away impressed with the fact that there is nothing easier than to write properly for the theater, and is amazed that none are apprenticed to the trade—for an author, when well acquainted with the value of thunder and lightning, when versed in all the mystery of scene shifting and trapdoors, when skilled in the proper periods to introduce a wire walker or a waterfall, when instructed

[129]

in every actor's peculiar talent, and capable of adapting his speeches to the supposed excellency—when thus instructed, knows all that can give an audience pleasure. One player shines in an exclamation, another in a groan, a third in a horror, a fourth in a start, a fifth in a smile, a sixth faints, and a seventh fidgets around the stage with peculiar vivacity. That piece, therefore, succeeds best, where each has a proper opportunity of shining. The actors' business is not so much to adapt himself to the poet, as the poet's to adapt himself to the actor. . . .

CHAPTER 15

CLUBS

LET A MAN'S CHARACTER, sentiments, or complexion be what they will, he can find company in London to match them. If he be splenetic, he may every day meet companions on the seats in St. James's Park, with whose groans he may mix his own, and pathetically talk of the weather. If he be passionate, he may vent his rage among the old orators at Slaughter's Coffee House, and damn the nation, because it keeps him from starving. If he be phlegmatic, he may sit in silence at the Humdrum Club in Ivy Lane; and if actually mad, he may find very good company in Moorfields, either at Bedlam or the Foundery, ready to cultivate a nearer acquaintance.

For societies, meetings, clubs swarm in London—the No Nose Club, the Surly Club, the Scatterwit Club, the Club of Ugly Faces, consisting of those to whom nature has been unkind, the Split Farthing Club, the Atheistical Club—whimsical physicians, half-learned gentlemen, crack-brained philosophers, and conceited libertines—the Bird Fancier's Club, the Beau's Club, a finikin society or Lady's lap dog club kept at a tavern near Covent Garden where the members assemble themselves to compare dresses and invent new fashions, the Quacks' Club, the Beggars' Club, the Yorkshire Club—held at a house in the Rounds in

Smithfield, upon every market day, "where Northerners, by consulting one another, may be better able to exercise their cunning in this southern air, and maintain that character they have justly deserved"—the Club of Broken Shopkeepers, the Florist's Club or Odoriferous Society—consisting of pink and tulip worshipers who will walk ten miles to see a new stripe in a clove gilliflower or gaze away whole hours upon an odd-colored daisy—the Thieves' Club, a society of audacious desperadoes who keep a daily rendezvous at the sign of the Half Moon in the Old Bailey—and the Wrangling Club, Lying Club, Smoking Club, Mock Heroes Club, Oddfellows' Club, Humbugs' Club, the Society of Bucks, the Thespian Club, the Great Bottle Club, the small coalmen's Music Club, held at a tavern in Clerkenwell—and a thousand and one others.

But, although such as have a knowledge of the town may easily class themselves with tempers congenial to their own, a countryman who comes to live in London finds nothing more difficult. With regard to Goldsmith, none ever tries with more assiduity or comes off with such indifferent success. He spends a whole season in the search during which time his name is enrolled in societies, lodges, convocations, and meetings, without number. To some he is introduced by a friend, to others invited by an advertisement. To these he introduces himself, and to those he changes his name to gain admittance. In short, no coquette is ever more solicitous to match her ribbons to her complexion, than he to suit his club to his temper, for he is too obstinate to bring his temper to conform to it.

An odd acquaintance of Goldsmith's proposes to bring him to the club that he frequents which he fancies will suit the poet's temper exactly. "We have at the Muzzy Club," says he, "no riotous mirth nor awkward ribaldry, no confusion or bawling. All is conducted with wisdom and decency; besides, some of our members are worth forty thousand pounds—men of prudence and foresight every one of them. These are the proper acquaintances, and to such I will tonight introduce you." Goldsmith is charmed at the proposal. To be acquainted with men worth forty thousand pounds and to talk wisdom the whole night are offers that throw him into a rapture.

At seven o'clock he is accordingly introduced by his friend, not indeed to the company—for though he makes his best bow, they seem insensible of his approach—but to the table at which they are sitting. Upon his entering the room, he cannot avoid feeling a secret veneration from the solemnity of the scene before him. The members keep a profound silence, each with a pipe in his mouth, and a pewter pot in his hand, and with faces that may easily be construed into absolute wisdom. Happy society, thinks Goldsmith to himself, where the members think before they speak, deliver nothing rashly, but convey their thoughts to each other pregnant with meaning and matured by reflection.

In this pleasing speculation he continues a full half hour, expecting each moment that somebody will begin to open his mouth. Every time the pipe is laid down, he believes it is to speak, but it is only to spit. At length, resolving to break the charm himself, and overcome their extreme diffidence—for to this he imputes their silence—he rubs his hands, and looking as wise as possible, observes that the nights begin to grow a little coolish at this time of the year. This, as it is directed to none of the company in particular, none thinks himself obliged to answer, wherefore Goldsmith continues still to rub his hands and look wise. His next effort is addressed to a gentleman who sits next to him, to whom he observes that the beer is extremely good. His neighbor makes no reply but by a large puff of tobacco smoke.

He now begins to be uneasy in this dumb society, till one of them a little relieves him by observing that bread has not risen these three weeks.

"Ay," says another, still keeping the pipe in his mouth, "that puts me in mind of a pleasant story about that—

hem—very well. You must know—but before I begin—sir, my service to you—where was I? . . ."

His next club goes by the name of the Harmonical Society, probably from that love of order and friendship which every person commends in institutions of this nature. The landlord is himself the founder. The money spent is fourpence each, and they sometimes whip for a double reckoning. To this club few recommendations are requisite, except the introductory fourpence, and my landlord's good word, which, as he gains by it, he never refuses.

They all here talk and behave as everybody else usually does on his club night. They discuss the topics of the day, drink each other's health, snuff the candles with their fingers, and fill their pipes from the same plate of tobacco. The company salute each other in the common manner. Mr. Bellowsmender hopes Mr. Currycombmaker has not caught cold going home the last club night, and he returns the compliment by hoping that young Master Bellowsmender has got well again of the chin-cough. Dr. Twist tells them a story of a parliament man with whom he is intimately acquainted, while the bagman, at the same time, is telling a better story of a noble lord with whom he can do anything. A gentleman in a black wig and leather breeches, at t'other end of the table, is engaged in a long narrative of the Ghost in Cock Lane. He has read it in the papers of the day and is telling it to some that sit next to him, who cannot read. Near him, Mr. Dibbins is disputing on the old subject of religion with a pedlar, over the table, while the president vainly knocks down Mr. Leathersides for a song. Besides the combination of these voices which form an upper part to the concert, there are several others playing under parts by themselves, each endeavoring to fasten the attention of some luckless neighbor, who is himself bent upon the same design against another.

"So, sir, d'ye perceive me, the ghost giving three loud raps at the bedpost—Says my lord to me, my dear

Smokeum, you know there is no man upon the face of the yearth for whom I have so high—A damnable false heretical opinion of all sound doctrine and good learning, for I'll tell it aloud and spare not, that—Silence for a song. Mr. Leathersides for a song—'As I was a-walking upon the highway, I met a young damsel'—Then what brings you here? says the parson to the ghost—As for Abel Drugger, sir, he's damned low in it. My 'prentice boy has more of the gentleman than he—For murder will out one time or another, and none but a ghost, you know, gentlemen, can—Sour grapes, as the fox said once when he could not reach them; and I'll, I'll tell you a story about that that will make you burst your sides with laughing. A fox once— Will nobody listen to the song—'As I was a-walking upon the highway, I met a young damsel both buxom and gay,'—No ghost, gentlemen, can be murdered, nor did I ever hear but of one ghost killed in all my life, and that was stabbed in the belly with a—My blood and soul if I don't—Mr. Bellowsmender, I have the honor of drinking your very good health—Blast me if I do—dam—blood— bugs—fire—whiz—blid—tit—rat—trip—" The rest all riot, nonsense, and rapid confusion.

(Were I to be angry at men for being fools, I could here find ample room for declamation, but alas! I have been a fool myself, and why should I be angry with them for being something so natural to every child of humanity?)

Fatigued with this society, Goldsmith is introduced the following night to a club of moral philosophers. He finds the members very warmly disputing when he arrives, not indeed about religion or ethics, but about who neglected to lay down his preliminary sixpence upon entering the room. The president swears that he has laid his own down, and so swear all the company.

During this contest Goldsmith has an opportunity of observing the laws, and also the members of the society. The president, who has been, as our poet is told, lately a bankrupt, is a tall, pale figure, with a long black wig;

the next to him is dressed in a large white wig and a black cravat. A third, by the brownness of complexion, seems a native of Jamaica, and a fourth by his hue, appears to be a blacksmith. But their rules will give the most just idea of their learning and principles.

I. We, being a laudable society of moral philosophers, intend to dispute twice a week about religion and priest-craft, leaving behind us old wives' tales, and following good learning and sound sense; and if so be, that any other persons have a mind to be of the society, they shall be entitled so to do, upon paying the sum of three shillings, to be spent by the company in punch.

II. That no member get drunk before nine of the clock, upon pain of forfeiting three pence, to be spent by the company in punch.

III. That, as members are sometimes apt to go away without paying, every person shall pay sixpence upon his entering the room; and all disputes shall be settled by a majority; and all fines shall be paid in punch.

IV. That sixpence shall be every night given to the president, in order to buy books of learning for the good of the society. The president has already put himself to a good deal of expense in buying books for the club, particularly the works of Tully, Socrates, and Cicero, which he will soon read to the society.

V. All them who brings a new argument against religion, and who being a philosopher and a man of learning, as the rest of us is, shall be admitted to the freedom of the society, upon paying sixpence only, to be spent in punch.

VI. Whenever we are to have an extraordinary meeting, it shall be advertised by some outlandish name in the newspapers.

> SAUNDERS MAC WILD, *President.*
> ANTHONY BLEWIT, *Vice President.*
> his + mark
> WILLIAM TURPIN, *Secretary.*

CHAPTER 16

DR. JOHNSON AND
MR. BOSWELL

1.

"I CAME TO LONDON," says Dr. Johnson, "with two pence half penny in my pocket."

"Eh, what's that you say?" cries Garrick, his fellow wayfarer and adventurer, "with two pence half penny in your pocket?"

"Why, yes, I came with two pence half penny in *my* pocket, and thou, Davy, with but three half pence in thine."

So poor were they that after their arrival they had with difficulty raised five pounds by giving their joint note to a bookseller in the Strand.

Many, many years has Johnson gone on obscurely in London, enduring all the hardships of Grub Street. He is so destitute at one time that he and Savage, the poet, walk all night about St. James's Square, both too poor to pay for a night's lodging, yet both full of poetry and patriotism and determined to stand by their country. He is so shabby in dress another time that when he dines at Cave's, his bookseller, while there is prosperous company, he cannot make his appearance at table but has his dinner handed to him behind a screen.

Yet through all the long and dreary struggle, often diseased in mind as well as in body, he has been resolutely proud and independent. He has fufilled his college vow of "fighting his way by his literature and his wit." His *Rambler* and *Idler* have made him the great moralist of the age. His *Dictionary and History of the English Language* has excited the admiration of the learned world. He is now at the head of intellectual society. He has built up his fame with his writings, and he now puts a tower on his fame with his conversation. He becomes as much an autocrat in his sphere as David Garrick becomes of the stage. He is, as Smollett humorously dubs him, "The Great Cham of Literature."

The 31st of May, 1761. Goldsmith meets Dr. Johnson. Thomas Percy has arranged the meeting, and Goldsmith is giving a supper in honor of his visitor.

Percy calls to take up Johnson at Inner Temple Lane and finds him in a marked condition of studied neatness—without his rusty brown suit, soiled shirt, loose knee breeches, unbuckled shoes, or old little shrivelled, unpowdered wig—and not at all to be taken for a beggarman. Percy has not seen him in so respectable a garb since he appeared behind Garrick's scenes on the first of the nine nights of *Irene*—in a scarlet gold—laced waistcoat, and rich gold-laced hat. For now he is arrayed in a new suit, a new hat, and a well-powdered wig—uncommonly spruce.

Percy asks the cause of this singular transformation. "Why, sir," replies Johnson, "I hear that Goldsmith, who is a very great sloven, justifies his disregard of cleanliness and decency by quoting my practise, and I am desirous this night to show him a better example."

The acquaintanceship thus started ripens into friendship in the course of frequent meetings at the shop of Davies, the bookseller, in Russell Street, Covent Garden.

Thomas Davies, ex-performer of Drury Lane, has now with his "mighty pretty wife" left the stage and taken wholly to bookselling. The *Rosciad* has put an end to his theatrical existence. He never afterwards mouths a sentence but that he thinks of Churchill's image:

> Statesman all over, in plots famous grown,
> He mouths a sentence as a cur mouths a bone.

—and is confused in the line that follows. His eye never falls upon any prominent figure in the front row of the pit that he does not tremble to fancy it the brawny person of Churchill. What Davies loses in self possession, Garrick meanwhile loses in temper, and matters come to a head. . . .

At the *Rosciad* the players run about like stricken deer and strive to extract the arrow from their wound by communicating the knowledge of it to their friends. But their friends, so far from being aggrieved, enjoy their distress. . . .

"Pretty Mrs. Davies" is the loadstar of her husband's fortune. Her tea table is as much a literary lounge as his shop. She finds favor by her sweet eyes and her winning ways, pouring out to Johnson cups of his favorite beverage. Indeed, it is suggested that she is the leading cause of his coming to this literary haunt.

And so it is as natural for people interested in Johnson to repair to Davies', as for those who want to hear of George Selwyn, Lord March, or Lord Carlisle, to call at Betty's the fruiterer in St. James's Street.

A frequent visitor is Goldsmith—his thick, short, clumsy figure oddly contrasting with the precise, stately Percy. High bred and courtly Beauclerc saunters in, and here often may be seen the broad, fat face of Foote, beaming with fun and waggery, and sometimes the mild, long face of Bennet Langton. Bland and gracious Reynolds is a rarer visitor, but to Tom Davies even swashbuckling Warburton will drive on some proud business of his own, in his equipage "besprinkled with mitres" after calling on Garrick in Southhampton Street. For Garrick this is the only place of meeting he cares to avoid, as he thinks most of the authors go there to abuse him.

Davies is as much a king in his own shop as ever he was on the stage. Encouraged by authors, he grows in amusing importance, sets up for quite a patron of the players, affects the insides as well as the outsides of books, becomes critic, pronounces upon plays and actors, and discusses themes of scholarship. When George Steevens calls one day to buy the Oxford Homer, which he has seen tossing about upon his shelves, he is told by the modest bookseller that he has but one copy, and keeps it for his own reading.

Struck with the odd habits and appearance of Johnson and Goldsmith, now so often brought together in Davies' shop, Foote talks of putting on the stage a farce called *The Orators*. The play in intended as a hit at the Robin Hood Debating Club and is to show up the two doctors in it for the entertainment of the town.

"What is the common price of an oak stick, sir?" says Johnson to Davies. "Sixpence," is the reply. "Why, then, sir, give me leave to send your servant to purchase a shilling one. I'll have a double quantity, for I am told Foote means to take me off, as he calls it, and I am determined the fellow shall not do it with impunity."

Foote has no desire to undergo the criticism of the cudgel wielded by Johnson, and so the farce of *The Orators* appears without the caricatures of the lexicographer and the essayist.

2.

"This is not a poetical age," says Goldsmith, dining at Davies'. "There is no poetry produced in it."

"Nay," returns Dodsley, "have you seen my collection? You may not be able to find palaces in it like Dryden's 'Ode,' but you have villages composed of very pretty houses."

Johnson is not present, but there is another guest at the table—a youth of two and twenty, son of a Scottish judge, urged to enter law, but eager to bestow himself on the army. The study of law has not extinguished his love of London for which he has as violent an affection as the most romantic lover ever has for his mistress. He has come up from Edinburgh to see Johnson and the wits and is not a little anxious that Johnson and the wits should see him. He expects to meet the great lexicographer. He meets only Oliver Goldsmith—and is much disappointed. The feeling is mutual.

While Goldsmith and Dodsley speak on poetry, little Davies endeavors to console Boswell for his disappointment by giving him imitations of Johnson—mouthing his words, rolling his head, and assuming as ponderous a manner as his petty person will permit. The bottle flows round, and Bozzy's tongue is loosed. The youthful Scot tells them what he has seen in London, and all that have seen him. Wilkes has said, "how d'ye do" to him; Churchill has shaken hands with him, Scotsman though he is; and he has been to Bedford to see that comical fellow Foote and has heard him dashing away at everybody and everything. In imitation:

"Have you had good success in Dublin, Mr. Foote?"

"Poh, damn 'em! There was not a shilling in the country except what the Duke of Bedford and I and Mr. Rigby have brought away."

And he goes on to tell them how he has seen Garrick in the new farce of the *Farmer's Return,* and gone and peeped over Hogarth's shoulder as he sketched little David in the *Farmer* and how—above all—he has the other night given prodigious entertainment in the Drury Lane Pit, by *extempore* imitations of the lowing of a cow— Moo!—Moo!—

"The universal cry of the galleries was, encore the cow! encore the cow! In the pride of my heart I attempted imitations of some other animals, but with very inferior effect."

Dr. Blair interrupts—"Stick to the cow, mon."

GOLDY

3.

At the Mitre Tavern, Fleet Street. The doors are guarded by a life-sized figure of a Scotchman in kilts eternally engaged in the act of taking snuff. Boswell, having been made happy by an introduction to the Great Master, spends his first evening in company with him and Goldsmith. The trio sup together and pass some time in literary conversation. On quitting the tavern Johnson goes as usual to drink tea with his pensioner, blind and peevish Miss Williams. Goldsmith, being a privileged man, goes with him, strutting away and calling to Boswell with an air of superiority, "like that of an esoteric over an exoteric disciple of a sage of antiquity, 'I go to Miss Williams.'"

Boswell envies Goldsmith this mighty privilege, of which he seems to be so proud, but it is not long before he obtains the same mark of distinction.

"Who is this Scotch cur at Johnson's heels?" asks someone noting the sudden intimacy.

"He is not a cur," replies Goldsmith, "you are too severe; he is only a bur. Tom Davies flung him at Johnson in sport, and he has the faculty of sticking."

CHAPTER 17

MERRY ISLINGTON

NOTWITHSTANDING his growing success, Goldsmith continues to consider literature a mere makeshift. His vagrant mind teems with plans of a grand nature. One is for visiting the east and exploring the interior of Asia. He has a vague notion that valuable discoveries are to be made there and many useful inventions in the arts brought back to the stock of European knowledge.

"Thus in Siberian Tartary," he observes, "the natives extract a strong spirit from milk, which is a secret probably unknown to the chemists of Europe. In the most savage parts of India they are possessed of the secret of dyeing vegetable substances scarlet, and that of refining lead into a metal which, for hardness and color, is little inferior to silver."

In 1761, when Lord Bute becomes prime minister, Goldsmith draws up a memorandum on the subject and the better to insure success, precedes his application by an ingenious essay to the same effect in the *Public Ledger.*

His memorial and essay are fruitless, his project deemed visionary. Still it continues to haunt his mind, and he often talks of making an expedition to Aleppo.

Johnson treats the project scoffingly. "Of all men," says

he, "Goldsmith is the most unfit to go out upon such an inquiry, for he is utterly ignorant of such arts as we already possess, and, consequently, could not know what would be accessions to our present stock of mechanical knowledge. Sir, he would bring home a grinding barrow, which you see in every street in London, and think that he had furnished a wonderful improvement."

Goldsmith's connection with Newbery, the bookseller, now leads him into a variety of literary hack jobs. He compiles anthologies, edits manuscripts, corrects proof sheets, digests biographies, writes histories and abridgments of them for schools, and rewrites children's tales. For fourteen guineas, he writes a life of Richard Nash.

He likes Nash—he has a fellow feeling for Beau who like himself is a good-natured, easy going fellow, careless with money, with a nice taste in dress, and a naive vanity in adorning his person with fine clothes. Added to which, he has more than a passing pleasure in riffling the cards and is very generous. So he touches his vices with a gentle hand and never fails to bring out his virtues.

It is a delightful book and important in the development of English biography. In his insistence on candor and accuracy in reporting the facts, his realization that any man may be worthy of biographical notice, his portrayal of character by means not only of lofty deeds but of humble trifles, his belief that the author should interpret his subject sympathetically, and that biography is worthy of artistic effort, Goldsmith does much to raise biography to its status as literature.

At the close of 1762 Goldsmith removes to a country lodging in Merry Islington, kept by a stout and elderly lady named Mrs. Elizabeth Fleming. He goes there to be near Newbery who resides in the Canonbury House (used at one time by Queen Elizabeth as a hunting lodge), but a stronger inducement is the quiet and the country air. There are still green fields and lanes in Islington—and woodlands where houses are not.

Newbery is to pay for his board and lodging fifty pounds a year, to be paid quarterly. In return the author is in honor bound to furnish "copy."

Among the various productions thrown off by him is a small work in two volumes, *The History of England, in a Series of Letters from a Nobleman to his Son*—a digest of Hume, Rapin, Carte, Burke and White Kennet. These authors he reads in the morning, noting down passages with remarks. Then he rambles with a companion about the skirts of Merry Islington and returns to a temperate dinner and a cheerful evening. Finally, before going to bed, he writes off what has arranged itself in his head from the studies of the morning.

The work, like the others he has written, is anonymous. Some attribute it to Lord Chesterfield, others to Lord Orrery, and others to Lord Lyttelton. The last is pleased, and never disowns the bantling thus laid at his door. The book goes through twenty-five editions in the first sixty years after its publication.

Mrs. Fleming does not charge for extras but notes down her magnanimity:

	£	s.	d.	
Tea			18	
Wines and cakes			18	
Bottle of port		2		
10 sheets of paper	0	0	5	
Penns	0	0	2¾	
Gave the boy for carrying parcel to Pall Mall	0	0	8	
Laundry, Extra		18	½	
Sasafras	0	0	6	
Paid the Newes man	0	16	10½	
A pint of ale	0	0	2	
Mr. Baggott and Doctor Reman dinner and tea	0	0	0	etc. etc.

Among the anonymous entries are some relating to more distinguished visitors.

CHAPTER 18

HOGARTH AND REYNOLDS

THE CORNER OF Castle Street, London. A stout, active, bustling little man in a sky blue coat is watching two boys quarrelling. Patting the weaker one on the back, while looking intently at the expression in his face, he spirits him up to a fresh encounter. "At him again! Damn him, if I would take it of him! At him again!"

The little man, William Hogarth by name, is a sturdy, outspoken, honest, obstinate, pugnacious man with a somewhat combative head and a scar over his right eye. He once pummels a fellow soundly for maltreating the beautiful drummeress whom he drew in Southwark Fair.

He likes good clothes, good living, good order in his household, and is proud of the rewards of industry and respectability. In his impatience with the parrot raptures of pretentious persons, he utters blasphemous expressions against the divinity of Corregio—Raphael Urbino—Michelangelo! He hates all foreigners—and especially the French. His pictures are dramas with the moral written in large letters after the fable . . .

Wilkes he rails against; Churchill he condemns, and Johnson he loves. "I'll tell you what," he says to Goldsmith, "Samuel Johnson's conversation is to the talk of

other men like Titian's painting compared to Hudson's—
but don't you tell people, now, that I say so, for the connoisseurs and I are at war, you know, and because I hate
them, they think I hate Titian—and let them." Goldsmith
and the connoisseurs are at war too.

To mitigate Mrs. Fleming's impatience, to moderate
her wrath, and—when money is not at hand—to minister
to her vanities, Hogarth brings an easel in a coach one
day and paints her. . . .

She is different from the sort of sitters whose coroneted
coaches crowd the west side of Leicester Square.

"My prices—for a head, 35 guineas; as far as the knees,
70 guineas; and for a whole length, 150 guineas; the time
required being in general three sittings, about an hour
and a half each time."

Everybody goes to Reynolds—the members of the
Royal Family, the archbishops of York and Canterbury,
the actress Mrs. Abington, William Pitt, General Oglethorpe, and Walpole, Sterne, Foote, Goldsmith, Johnson,
and the two famous courtesans, Kitty Fisher and Nelly
O'Brien. Sir Joshua is very impartial.

His success is so great that the number of sitters increases from one hundred and twenty in 1755 to one hundred fifty-six in 1759. He receives five or six or seven
sitters a day, and some of these as early as six or seven in
the morning. To keep pace with the demand, he employs
several assistants. "No man," he says, "ever made a fortune
with his own hands." And so now he begins to make a
good deal of money, and in a few years' time, his income
reaches six thousand pounds a year.

He has moved from St. Martin's Lane into Newport
Street and from Newport Street into Leicester Square. He
opens his house with a ball and sets up a magnificent
chariot richly carved and gilded and adorned with panels
painted by Chas. Catton, the elder, representing the four
seasons. The liveries of his servants are laced with silver.

This showy equipage he seldom uses himself but bids his sister Frances go out with it as often as possible, much to her annoyance, and let it be seen. It acts as a valuable advertisement. People inquire whose grand chariot this is—it gives a strong indication of his great success and by that means tends to increase it. . . .

Yet no one grudges Reynolds his good fortune, which is worn with generosity and grace and justified by his noble qualities.

The keynote of his whole life is his art—and he acts up to the ideal of a perfect portrait painter. His business is not to criticize but to observe, not to direct but to reflect the currents of society. "I go," he says, "with the great stream of life."

Reynolds has two permanent physical defects—a scar on his lip, from an accident at Minorca, and deafness contracted from a cold at the Vatican while copying Raphael.

"Study the great works of the great masters, forever," says Reynolds.

"There is only one school," cries Hogarth, "and that is kept by Nature." "Talk of sense and study and all that," he says to Walpole, "why it is owing to the good sense of the English that they have not painted better. The people who have studied painting least are the best judges of it. There's Reynolds—why, but t'other day, he offered a hundred pounds for a picture that I would not hang in my cellar."

The great men live separate to the last. The only feeling they share in common is that kindness to Oliver Goldsmith.

While Hogarth is propitiating and painting Mrs. Fleming, Reynolds is founding the Club, later called the Literary Club.

CHAPTER 19

LANKY AND BEAU

1.

FLEET STREET. The wooden balconies of the timber-framed and gabled houses project over the rugged pavement. Grotesque signs and quaint carvings swing from projecting iron rods.

From one of the courts a man emerges and walks westward. A tall, burly man, large, fat, and ungainly, and with a great stoop. He is dressed in a brown coat like Scotch snuff, black worsted stockings, and large easy shoes with silver buckles. On his head is a flowing greyish bobwig on which is perched a large looped up hat. He rolls in his gait, going zigzag to and fro like a ship rolling and tacking in a heavy sea, and swinging his arms backwards and forwards as he shambles along. Up Wyck Street and Drury Lane, laying his hand on every post he passes. One indeed he misses while lost in thought, but he quickly discovers the omission and turns back to the post to touch it. And so he goes on till he reaches Gerrard Street, Soho Square, and stands at the threshold of the Turk's Head Tavern.

He bangs the door open and enters. A snug room warmed with brash and faggot—and a large table set with refreshments. Eight or ten men are there already. They are apparently awaiting his advent and now they all sit down to their meal.

That face, long and rather thin, with its finely curved outline and delicately chiselled nose, betokening taste and acuteness, with its broad brow and full eyes, is William Jones, orientalist. Next to him sits small and graceful Garrick dressed as a man of fashion, with embroidered neckcloth, laced ruffles and trim wig.

Across the table is Reynolds in sober brown—middle aged—with a round and florid face—full lips, nose somewhat lumpish—wearing eyeglasses and carrying an ear trumpet. His forehead, though low, is broad.

Burke sits erect and firm—cherub cheeks, little bob wig with curls and spectacles, comfortable underchin, and a delicate flutter of lace ruffles to light up his tight plain brown coat. Above all a forehead visibly bulging with genius. Every Irishman has a potato in his brain. Mr. Burke has two.

One near burly Johnson has a cocked nose, bag cheeks, protruding shelf mouth, and fat developed chin—and is dressed foppishly with very conspicuous ruffles over his hands. He is now watching the Doctor—how he eats, how he drinks, how he mutters, how he rolls his head about, what he says, how he says it, to whom he says it—so that when he goes home in the night he may put it all down in notes for his journal. And he lives in and for his journal. When the great man gives a roll or two in his chair and purses out his lips in the act of speaking, this admiring gentleman turns an eager face towards him so that he may not lose a word that falls from his oracle. Inseparable as Castor and Pollux—each lacking the other would lack half himself.

At the head of the table sits Johnson—in his old shrivelled and unpowdered wig, his brown coat with the metal buttons, and his rumpled neckcloth, which ought to be at the wash—blinking, puffing, half whistling, clucking like a hen, rolling his head, drumming with his fingers, tearing his meat like a tiger and swallowing his tea in oceans.

He loves not to talk much while eating. "For my part," he says, "I mind my belly very studiously and very carefully, for I look upon it that he who does not mind his belly will hardly mind anything else."

And so he pays little attention to what is said around him. Now his eyes are riveted on the plate, into which he peers, for he is short sighted, and he is eating with such fierce intensity that the veins of his forehead are swollen and perspiration stands in beads on his brow. He is devouring a veal pie, with plums and sugar, which exhales an odor too strong for the nostrils of those who sit near him. Beau asks him with sly humor how he likes it. His reply is a grunt and a demand for a second portion. . . .

Well, the eating is over. *"Esto perpetua"* (may she endure forever), the charter toast of the Club, is duly drunk and the bottles go their rounds.

Burke fills his glass with claret whereupon the Doctor shakes his head and says, "Poor stuff, sir. Claret is the liquor for boys, port for men, but he who aspires to be a hero must drink brandy." (His sayings would not appear so extraordinary were it not for his bow-wow way.)

Burke lifts the glass to his lips and replies, "Then, sir, give me claret, for I like to be a boy and partake of the honest hilarity of youth."

Sir Joshua puts his trumpet to his ear to catch the conversation. He loves a glass of something stronger than claret, and more than one of them, and so he says, "Sir, I think wine is very useful. The pleasure of drinking wine is so connected with pleasing your company that altogether there is something of social goodness in it."

"Why, no, sir," replies Johnson, waving his flag of defiance. . . . Beauclerc smiles. Thickset, pockmarked Goldy in butterfly brilliancy of colors fidgets and shifts on his chair as if ready to explode with some remark. Jones and Garrick stir bishop in their glasses. And tall, stooping Bennet Langton, sitting with one leg twisted round the other, takes an oblong gold mounted snuff box from his waist-coat, helps himself to a pinch, taps the lid with his long, thin, carefully kept fingers, and places the snuff box on the table. . . .

In 1763 the Club is founded. Reynolds is its Romulus, but Johnson catches eagerly at the notion and suggests as its model a club he formed fourteen years before in Ivy Lane.

The members are limited to nine. They are to meet and sup together once a week on Monday night, 7 o'clock, at the Turk's Head Tavern in Gerrard Street, Soho, where Johnson is in the habit of dining to encourage the hostess who is a good civil woman and has not too much business. Two members are to constitute a meeting and each one present is to bear his share of the reckoning.

Mr. Hawkins, as an original member of the Ivy Lane, is invited to join. Topham Beauclerc and Bennet Langton are also asked and welcomed earnestly—and of course, Mr. Edmund Burke. The notion delights Burke and he asks admission for his father-in-law Doctor Nugent, a Roman Catholic physician, who lives with him. Beauclerc in a like manner suggests his friend Chamier, secretary in the war office. Oliver Goldsmith completes the number. But another member of the original Ivy Lane society, Samuel Dyer, makes an unexpected appearance from abroad in the following year and is joyfully admitted.

Mr. Hawkins is out of place. Neither in habits nor opinions does he harmonize with the rest. Bishop Percy calls him "a most detestable fellow." But other adjectives are applied to him—obstinate, contentious, quarrelsome, haughty, ignorant, mean, grovelling, absolutely dishonorable and sanctimonious.

He has been an attorney for many years, dabbling in literature and music, but so large a fortune has fallen to him in right of his wife that he withdraws from law and lives and judges with severity as a Middlesex magistrate.

He is absurdly proud of his coach, rough to inferiors,

and humble to men like Walpole. The honor of knight-hood means a stiffening of his mental and physical gait into a strut so that he strides the earth a ridiculous sawdust-stuffed Colossus.

He charges *Tom Jones* with having "corrupted the rising generation," and sapped "the foundation of that morality which it is the duty of parents and all public instructors to inculcate in the minds of young people." This is his common style of talk. He speaks contemptuously of Hogarth as a man who knows nothing out of Covent Garden. And Richardson, Fielding, Smollett, Sterne are— "stuff."

He laments that in no less than fourteen cases it is still possible to cheat the gallows. He wants every prisoner convicted and every convict hanged—and he does his best to counteract the perverse spirit of humanity coming into fashion. . . . He is a regular Churchman. . . .

Mr. Hawkins, after the first four meetings, begs to be excused his share of the reckoning on the ground that he does not partake of the supper. "And was he excused?" asks Dr. Burney.

"Oh yes, sir," replies Johnson, "and very readily. No man is angry at another for being inferior to himself. We all admitted his plea publicly, for the gratification of scorning him privately. Sir John, sir, is a very unclubbable man. Yet I really believe him to be an honest man at bottom, though, to be sure, he is penurious, and he is mean, and it must be owned he has a tendency to savageness."

He does not remain a member for more than two or three years. He withdraws, so he says, because its late hours are inconsistent with his domestic arrangements, but the fact is that one evening he attacks Mr. Burke in so rude a manner that all the company testify their displeasure—and at the next meeting he is *persona non grata*.

Altogether his existence is a kind of pompous, parsimonious, drawl:

GOLDY

Here lies Sir John Hawkins
Without his shoes and stauckins. . . .

2.

"What I most envy Burke for," says Johnson, "is, his
being constantly the same. He is never what we call humdrum, never unwilling to begin to talk, nor in haste to
leave off. Take up whatever topic you please, he is ready
to meet you. His stream of mind is perpetual. I cannot
say he is good at listening . . . So desirous is he to talk,
that if one is speaking at this end of the table, he'll speak
to somebody at the other end. Burke, sir, is such a man
that if you met him for the first time in the street, where
there was a shower of cannon bullets, and you and he ran
up a stair to take shelter but for five minutes, he'd talk to
you in such a manner that, when you parted, you would
say, 'This is an extraordinary man.'"

For Mr. Burke, when all is said, is a "style." He puts
forth a superb plumage glittering all over with a hundred
eyes of fancy. His gait is awkward and heavy, and his
voice seems rather to scare than attract. But his blemishes
are all Irish—his luxuriance of expression, his vehemence,
his impetuosity, his tendency to excessive gesture, his
strong Irish brogue and animal spirits.

He talks like the striking illustrations in a book. On
Boswell's mention of Croft's *Life of Young* as a pretty
successful imitation of Johnson's style, he replies, "No, no,
it is not a good imitation of Johnson. It has all his pomp
without his force. It has all the nodosities of the oak without
its strength." Then after a pause, "It has all the contortions
of the Sibyl without the inspiration."

He is a vast storehouse of knowledge, an exhaustless
mind. It is contrary to his nature to be pent up within a
narrow compass. He must have room. He is not to be
hampered by commonplace trammels. Merchants are astonished by his knowledge of commerce, philologists by

his knowledge of language, antiquarians by his knowledge
of antiquities. He is a prodigy of nature and of acquisition—he reads everything—he knows everything—he sees
everything—he foresees everything . . . The only subjects
he does not understand are music and gaming.

He is in the habit of drinking quantities of hot water,
as hot as he can bear it. Hot water, he says, is the finest
stimulant in the world . . .

Johnson rushes at him striking blows as heavy as a
battle axe of Coeur de Lion. Burke evades the stroke, and
like Saladin wheels around his foe with arguments as keen
as the Paynim's scimitar—assailing, evading, thrusting,
parrying . . . While good Dr. Nugent, half in pride, half
in terror, watches each effort of his son-in-law. . . .

3.

A youth of eighteen is so delighted with reading
Johnson's *Rambler* that he comes up to London to obtain
an introduction to the author. He expects to find a decent,
well-dressed, remarkably decorous philosopher. Instead of
which, down from his bed chamber at noon comes a large
uncouth figure, with a little shrivelled wig sticking on top
of his head, a pair of old shoes by way of slippers and
his clothes hanging loose about him. But his conversation
is so rich, so animated, so forcible—and his opinions so
congenial with his own—that an instant and lasting friendship is started.

Bennet Langton is of an ancient family with an ancestral estate in Lincolnshire. "Langton, sir," says Johnson
with awe, "has a grant of free warren from Henry the Second; and Cardinal Stephen Langton, in King John's reign,
was of this family."

Langton is six feet tall, slenderly built, and slightly
stooping. In drawing rooms, the ladies gather about him
like maids about the Maypole. His friend Beauclerc compares him to the stork standing upon one leg in Raphael's

cartoon of the miraculous draught of fishes. He has a habit of sitting with one leg twisted round the other, and of locking his hands on his knee, as if fearing to occupy more space than is equitable.

His queer constitution seems to leave him at his lowest ebb every afternoon about two. He is forgetful, weary, confused, and without an idea in his head, but after a little food, he is himself again. At dinner parties he usually rises fasting—such is the perpetual flow of his conversation, and such the incessant demand made upon him.

A morning call from Mr. Langton is a thing to suggest the eternal years. The family may drive out two or three hours, return, and dress, and mother may turn in her mind the postponement of dinner before he makes his appearance.

His courteous smile and mild beauty endear him to all. He never oppresses any man's parts or puts any man out of countenance. His Greek serenity fulfills beautifully the pious injunction of Sir Thomas Browne "to sit quietly in the soft showers of Providence."

He teaches modesty and Greek. In the midst of a talk he will fall into the vowelled undertones of the tongue he loves, correcting himself with a little wave of the hands and the apologetic phrase—"And so it goes on."

Speaking to a company one chilly forenoon in his own house, he pauses to remark that if the fire lacks attention, it may go out—a brief, casual, murmurous interruption. He resumes his discourse, breaking off presently and pleading abstractedly with his eyes in the air, "Pray ring for coals." All sit looking at the fire, and so little solicitous about the impending catastrophe that presently Langton is off again on the stream of his softened eloquence. In a few minutes comes another lull. "Did anybody answer that bell?" A general negative. "Did anybody ring that bell?" A sly shaking of heads. And once more the inspired monody soars among the clouds, at last dropping meditatively to the hearthstone—"Dear, dear, the fire is out. . . ."

Johnson values Langton for his piety, his ancient descent, his amiable behavior, and his mastery of Greek. "Who in this town knows anything of Clenardius, sir, but you and I," he says. . . .

4.

Alternating, as in his Oxford career, pleasure and literature, the tavern and court, books and the gaming table, Topham Beauclerc has in London but widened the scene of his wit and folly, his reasoning and merriment, his polished manners and well-bred contempt, his acuteness and maliciousness. He is familiar with Fox, Selwyn, Walpole, and with the glittering loungers in St. James's Street who do not ache to consort with Johnson—and he is quite their match in acuteness and ease. He walks through the modish world where Langton cannot and will not follow. He combines the Ship Tavern with the court levées, Davies' shop with the golden insipidities of the drawing room, *la comédie, la danse, l'amour même* with the intellectual tie wigs of Soho. He is fastidious in everything he does. He makes one hour of conversation at Elmsley's his standard of enjoyment and his imagined extreme of annoyance is to be clapped on the back by Tom Davies.

Everything comes from him easily. No man is ever so free when he is going to say a good thing from a look which expresses that it is coming or when he has said it from a look that expresses it has come. During one of the disputes when the Whigs, "the cursed Whigs," "the bottomless Whigs," as Johnson calls them, have become predominant in the Club, and when, in the course of repelling a bitter attack on Fox and Burke, Beauclerc has fallen foul of George Steevens, Boswell interposes, "The gentleman, Mr. Beauclerc, against whom you are so violent, is, I know, a man of good principles." Beauclerc: "Then he does not wear them out in practice."

He is, moreover, the only son of Lord Sidney Beauclerc, grandson of the Duke of St. Albans, and is thought in

some ways to resemble Charles the Second. These are high
recommendations with Johnson. But when the youth testi-
fies a profound respect for the man, and an ardent admiration of his writings, the conquest is complete. The moral,
pious Johnson and the laughing young rake become
companions.

The uncouth, unwieldy Johnson is flattered at finding
himself an object of idolatry to two high born, high bred,
aristocratic young men, and throwing gravity aside, is
ready to play the part of "a young man upon town."

One night when Beauclerc and Langton have supped
at a tavern and sat until three in the morning, it comes
into their heads to go and wake up Johnson. They accordingly rap violently at the door of his chambers in the
Temple till at last he appears in his shirt with a little
black wig on top of his head, instead of a nightcap, and
a poker in his hand—imagining that some ruffians are come
to attack him. When he discovers Lanky and Beau sum-
moning him forth to a morning ramble, his whole manner
changes, "What, is it you, you dogs! I'll have a frisk with
you."

They sally forth together in Covent Garden, figure
among the green grocers and fruit women just come in
from the country with their hampers, repair to a neighboring tavern where Johnson brews a bowl of bishop,
grows merry over his cups, and anathematizes sleep in
Lord Lansdowne's lines:

> "Short, very short, be then thy reign
> For I'm in haste to laugh and drink again."

They then take a boat, row to Billingsgate, and Johnson
and Beauclerc like mad wags determine to "persevere in
dissipation for the rest of the day." Langton, however,
pleads an engagement to breakfast with some young ladies,
and is scolded by the great moralist for leaving his social
friends to go and sit with "a set of wretched un-idea'd girls."

"I heard of your frolic t'other night," says Garrick to

Johnson. "You'll be in the *Chronicle*." He utters worse forebodings to others. "I shall have my old friend to bail out of the roundhouse."

Johnson crows over Garrick on this occasion. "He durst not do such a thing!" he chuckles. "His wife would not *let* him."

Soon after, Beauclerc's mother angrily rebukes him. An old man should not put such thoughts into young people's heads. But the frisking philosopher has as little respect for Lady Sidney's anger as for Garrick's alarm. "She has no notion of a joke, sir," says he, "has come late into life, and has a mighty unpliable understanding. . . ."

Beauclerc's "air of the world" fascinates Johnson. It gives the youth an influence, a superiority, a secret charm which Johnson very frankly confesses to. No one can take more liberty with him. When his friends are studying stately congratulations on his pension, Beau scans his person and simply hopes that like Falstaff "he'd in future purge and live cleanly like a gentleman." Johnson laughs at the advice and profits by it.

Yet fond of him as he is, he sometimes loses patience. "Sir," he says to Beauclerc, after one of his malicious sallies, "you never open your mouth but with intention to give pain, and you have often given me pain, not from the power of what you have said, but from seeing your intention."

The habit is doubtless an evil one, and few suffer from it so much as Goldsmith.

When it is first proposed to enroll Goldsmith in the Club, there is some demur. As he writes for the booksellers, they look on him as a mere literary drudge, equal to the task of compiling and translating, but little capable of original production. Even after his admission, some of the members regard him in a dubious light. Johnson and Reynolds, of course, know his merits. Burke is not a stranger to them. But to the others, he is a sealed book. And his outside is not prepossessing.

GOLDY

His ungainly figure and awkward manners are against him. He is not sufficiently at home to give play to his humor. He is strange and out of place. He feels at times the cool satirical eye of courtly Beauclerc scanning him, and the more he attempts to appear at his ease, the more awkward he becomes. . . .

CHAPTER 20

A DEDICATION

ONE MORNING Johnson receives a message from poor Goldsmith that he is in great distress, and begging him to come as soon as possible. Johnson sends him a guinea and promises to come to him directly. He accordingly goes as soon as he is dressed and finds that Goldsmith's landlady has arrested him for his rent, at which he is in a violent passion. He sees that Goldsmith has already changed his guinea and has a bottle of Madeira and a glass before him. Johnson puts the cork into the bottle, desires him to be calm, and begins to talk to him of the means by which he may be extricated. Goldsmith then tells him that he has a manuscript of a novel ready for the press, which he has sold to Francis Newbery for £60 but on which he has received only twenty. Johnson looks into it and sees its merit, tells the landlady he will soon return, and having gone to the bookseller, obtains the balance of forty pounds. He brings the money to Goldsmith who discharges his rent, not without berating his landlady in a high tone for having used him so ill.

All this takes place at 6 Wine Office Court. Goldsmith is about to leave his lodgings altogether for a final sojourn at Islington, and his landlady thinks that she will never see him again. Then Newbery, a relation of hers, tells her of the author's broken financial condition, and she, there-fore, takes quick and drastic action to compel him to pay his rent.

The novel is *The Vicar of Wakefield*. It is so little appreciated by the bookseller that he keeps it by him for nearly two years unpublished and sells a third share of it to a printer Benjamin Collins of Salisbury.

Not having seen him for some time, Reynolds calls upon Goldsmith, and as no one answers the door, he opens it unannounced and walks in. His friend is at his desk but looking at another part of the room where a little pet dog is sitting on his haunches. At one time he glances down at his paper, at another shakes his finger at the dog in re-buke for toppling over. Reynolds advances and looks past Goldsmith's shoulder at the writing on his desk. It seems to be some portion of a poem, and looking more closely, he is able to read a couplet which has been that instant written. The ink of the second line is still wet:

"By sports like these are all their care beguiled,
The sports of children satisfy the child. . . ."

"This day is published," says the *Public Advertiser* of the nineteenth of December, 1764, "price one shilling and six pence, *The Traveller or a Prospect of Society, a Poem*, By Oliver Goldsmith. M.B. Printed for J. Newbery in St. Paul's Churchyard."

It is the first time that Goldsmith's name has been an-nounced in connection with anything he has written, and with it he resolves to associate his brother Henry. "DEAR SIR,—I am sensible that the friendship between us can acquire no new force from the ceremonies of a Dedication, and perhaps it demands an excuse thus to prefix your name to my attempts, which you decline giving with your own. But as a part of this poem was formerly written to you from Switzerland, the whole can now, with propriety, be only inscribed to you. It will also throw a light upon many parts of it when the reader understands that it is addressed to a man who, despising fame and fortune, has retired early to happiness and obscurity, with an income of forty pounds a year.

"I now perceive, my dear brother, the wisdom of your humble choice. You have entered upon a sacred office where the harvest is great and the laborers are but few; while you have left the field of ambition, where the laborers are many, and the harvest not worth carrying away. But of all kinds of ambition, what from the refinement of the times, from different systems of criticism, and from the divisions of party, that which pursues poetical fame is the wildest . . ."

Mr. Johnson aids the launching of the poem by a favorable notice in the *Critical Review*. Other periodicals come out in its favor. In three months there is a second edition issued; shortly afterwards a third, then a fourth, and before the year is out, the author is pronounced the best poet of the time—and obtains a bonus of twenty guineas.

The appearance of *The Traveller* alters Goldsmith's intellectual standing at the Club. They are astonished that a newspaper essayist—a bookseller's drudge—should have written such a poem. They cannot reconcile his heedless garrulity with the sound good sense of his poetry. "Well," exclaims Chamier, "I do believe he wrote this poem himself and, let me tell you, that is believing a great deal."

At the next meeting of the Club, Chamier sounds the author a little about his poem. "Mr. Goldsmith," says he, "what do you mean by the last word in the first line of your *Traveller*, 'remote, unfriended, solitary, slow?' Do you mean tardiness of locomotion?"

"Yes," replies Goldsmith flurried at the moment.

"No, sir," interposes Johnson, "you did not mean tardiness of locomotion; you meant that sluggishness of mind which comes upon a man in solitude."

"Ah," exclaims Goldsmith, "*that* was what I meant." (Perhaps Goldy had two meanings in mind—steps literally slow but also the forlornness of mind they can betray.)

Chamier believes that Johnson is the author of the line and a rumor goes around that he wrote many of the finest passages. But it is ultimately laid to rest by Johnson himself who marks with a pencil all the verses he contributed—nine in number, and by no means the best. He pronounces it the finest poem that has appeared since the days of Pope.

"There is not a bad line in the poem," Langton declares, "not one of Dryden's careless verses."

"I was glad," observes Reynolds, "to hear Charles Fox say it was one of the finest poems in the English language."

"Why was you glad?" rejoins Langton. "You surely had no doubt of this before."

"No," remarks Johnson decisively, "the merit of *The Traveller* is so well established that Mr. Fox's praise cannot augment it, nor his censure diminish it."

Crusty Samuel Johnson is certainly stirred by its power. Boswell mentions that once during their tour of the Hebrides, after a good night's rest and a leisurely breakfast, while he is helping the lexicographer on with his greatcoat, Johnson repeats from *The Traveller* the character of the British nation, which he does with such energy that the tear starts into his eye—

> Stern o'er each bosom Reason holds her state,
> With daring aims irregularly great;
> Pride in their port, defiance in their eye,
> I see the lords of humankind pass by. . . .

"Well, I never more shall think Doctor Goldsmith ugly," is the frank tribute of Miss Frances Reynolds, after hearing Johnson read the poem aloud from the beginning to the end of it a few days after it is published.

"Renny dear" is now a mature and very fidgety lady of seven and thirty. She nourishes a singularity which is her bane, as if it were her greatest blessing. It is that of living in an habitual perplexity and irresolution—which to herself is restlessly tormenting and to all around her teasingly tiresome. Whatever she suggests or plans one day, she reverses the next—and so on, endlessly. This lady paints miniatures and copies her brother's pictures. Of these copies, he says, "They make other people laugh and me cry."

Miss Reynolds founds her admiring promise about *The Traveller* on what she has herself said at a party in her brother's house some days before. It is suddenly proposed, as a social game after supper, to toast ugly women and have them matched by ugly men. Whereupon one of the gentlemen giving Miss Williams, Johnson's blind old pensioner, Miss Reynolds instantly matches her with Goldsmith. This whimsical union so enchants Mrs. Cholmondeley (Peg Woffington's sister, who has married an honorable and reverend gentleman well known to the set) that, though she has some pique with Renny dear, she runs around the table, kisses her, and says she forgives her everything for her last toast.

"Thus," exclaims Johnson, who is present and whose wit is rewarded with a roar, "thus the ancients, on the making up of their quarrels, used to sacrifice a beast betwixt them."

Since recognition comes so suddenly, Goldsmith cannot take it gracefully. When Hugh Kelly congratulates him on his success and invites him to dinner, he earnestly replies, "I would with pleasure accept your kind invitation . . . but to tell you the truth, my dear boy, my *Traveller* has found me a *home* in so many places that I am engaged, I believe, three days—let me see—today I dine with Edmund Burke, tomorrow with Dr. Nugent, and the next day with Topham Beauclerc—but I'll tell you what *I'll do* for *you*, I'll dine with you on Saturday." (Kelly accepts the offer.)

Absent from England at the time of the publication of *The Traveller*, Boswell returns to find Goldsmith suddenly elevated almost to a par with his idol. "He imitates you, sir," says he to Johnson.

"Why, no, sir," replies Johnson, "Jack Hawksworth is one of my imitators, but not Goldsmith. Goldy, sir, has great merit."

"But, sir, he is much indebted to you for his getting so high in the public estimation."

"Why, sir, he has, perhaps, got *sooner* to it by his intimacy with me."

~~~~~~~~~~~~~~~~~~~~~~~~~~~~~~~~~~~~~

CHAPTER 21

A NEW PARNASSUS

Now THAT HE IS RISING in the world, Goldsmith feels himself called upon to improve his style of
living. He accordingly emerges from Wine Office Court
and takes chambers on the library staircase in the Temple.
They are humble quarters and he is an inmate with Jeffs,
the butler of the society. Still he is in the Temple, a place
associated with the illustrious names of English literature—
the Dorsets, Raleighs, Seldens, Clarendons, Beaumonts,
Fords, Marstons, Wycherleys, and Congreves. . . . He has
a key resembling a battle axe.

Johnson soon after pays him a visit. On his prying and
peering about in the rooms after his short sighted fashion,
flattening his face against every object he looks at, Goldsmith uneasily blurts out, "I shall soon be in better chambers, sir, than these."

"Nay, sir," answers Johnson, "never mind that. *Nil te
quaesiveris extra.*" (You need not look for anything more.)

Among the persons of rank who have been struck with
the merits of *The Traveller* is the Earl of Northumberland,
Lord Lieutenant of Ireland. Understanding that Goldsmith
is an Irishman, he is disposed to extend to him the patronage which his high post affords. He intimates the same to
his relative Dr. Percy and expresses a wish that Goldsmith

wait upon him. Unluckily the poet blunders at the outset. He dresses himself in the best manner he can, and, after studying some compliments he thinks necessary on such an occasion, proceeds to Northumberland House, and acquaints the servants that he has particular business with the duke. They show him into an antechamber, where he meets Mr. John Hawkins, also calling on the duke, and where, after waiting some time, a gentleman, very elegantly dressed, makes his appearance. Taking him for the duke, he delivers all the fine things he has composed in order to compliment him on the honor he has done him— when to Goldsmith's great astonishment, the gentleman tells him that he has mistaken him for his master, who will see him immediately. At that instant the duke comes into the apartment, and Goldsmith is so confounded that he wants words to express the sense he entertains of the duke's politeness and goes away exceedingly chagrined at the blunder he has committed.

Upon his coming out, Mr. John Hawkins, who has stayed to take him home, asks him the result of his conversation, "His lordship," says Goldy, "told me he had read my poem, meaning *The Traveller*, and was much delighted with it; that he was going to be Lord Lieutenant of Ireland, and that, hearing I was a native of that country, he should be glad to do me any kindness."

"And what did you answer," says Hawkins, "to this gracious offer?"

"Why," says Goldy, "I could say nothing but that I had a brother there, a clergyman, that stood in need of help. As for myself, I have no great dependence on the promises of great men. I look to the booksellers for support. They are my best friends, and I am not inclined to forsake them for others. . . ."

After all, the introduction to Northumberland House does not prove so complete a failure. Dr. Percy acquaints the poet with his kinswoman, the duchess—a lady of literary taste and talent: one of her poems has been given to the world. The French fashion of Bouts Rimés has become quite tonish among the quality at Bath, although laughed at in London, and a new Parnassus has been erected—composed of three laurels, a myrtle tree, a weeping willow, and a view of the Avon which has been christened Helicon. Lady Miller, who invites the water drinkers, is returned a beauty, a genius, a Sappho, a tenth Muse, as romantic as Mme. Scudery, and as sophisticated as Mrs. Vesey. She holds a Parnassus fair every Thursday, gives out rhymes and themes, and all the flux of quality at Bath contend for the prizes. A Roman vase, dressed with pink ribbons, receives the poetry which is drawn out every festival. Six judges of these Olympic Games retire and select the brightest compositions—and the successful kneel to Calliope Miller, kiss her fat hand, and are crowned with myrtle by her.

The duchess gets very jollily through her task and is finished. Her Grace must not be held responsible for attempting to make "puffing" rime with "muffin" to which certain captious critics may object. When Dr. Johnson is told that an acquaintance has written for Lady Miller's vase, without a moment's hesitation, he pronounces him to be "a blockhead for his pains." But when it is added that the duchess has also contributed, he replies, "Sir, the Duchess of Northumberland may do what she pleases. Nobody will say anything to a lady of her high rank. . . ." Therefore, for the following lines the duchess is crowned:

> The pen which I now take and   brandish
> Has long lain useless in my   standish,
> Know every maid from her in   patten
> To her who shines in glossy   satin,
> That could they now prepare an   olio
> From best receipt of book in   folio
> Ever so fine for all their   puffing
> I should prefer a buttered   muffin
> A muffin Jove himself might   feast on
> If ate with Miller at   Batheaston.

The Countess is patroness as well as poet, and so under her auspices, a poem of Goldsmith's, based on Percy's version of the old ballad, "Gentle Herdsman," is given an aristocratic introduction to the world. "Edwin and Angelina: A Ballad. By Mr. Goldsmith. Printed for the Amusement of the Countess of Northumberland."

As in this fashionable age, there are many of Lord Foppington's opinion "that a book should be recommended by its outside to a man of quality and breeding," it is encumbent on all authors to let their works appear as well dressed as possible if they expect them to be admitted into polite company. And the name of a duchess on the title page is the highest stamp of fashion. . . . Yet we should not lay too much stress on the decorations but rather remember Tully's precept to all who build that "the owner should be an ornament to the house and not the house to the owner."

The circle at Northumberland House is too stately and aristocratical for Goldy, and we find he does not become familiar in it.

He is more at home at Gosfield, the seat of his countryman, Robert Nugent, afterwards Viscount Clare—a jovial voluptuary who has left the Roman Catholic for the Protestant Church to benefit his fortunes. Squire Gawky, as he is called, has an Irishman's propensity for rich widows, and an Irishman's luck—having been thrice married and gained a fortune with each wife. He is now near sixty, tall, stout, with a remarkably loud voice, and a broad Irish brogue.

With the Nugents Goldsmith can relax, say whatever pops into his head, and be sure it will not be greeted with scorn. He can, as always, enjoy a joke on himself too. One day, Mary, Lord Clare's daughter, ties his wig to a chair while he is napping, and when he awakes and stands up, the wig is pulled off his head. But he takes the joke in good part, makes use of it in one of his comedies, and settles his debt to Mary Nugent by writing a riddle for her:

"The clothes we love best, and the half of an agent,
Is the name of a Lady, to whom I'm obadient."

Children do not share Queeney Thrale's opinion of
Goldsmith. George Colman the Younger says that Goldsmith is his favorite. The first time they meet, when the
boy is only five years old and Goldsmith is having tea with
Colman's father, Goldsmith picks up the youngster and
dandles him on his knee—only to be greeted with a smart
slap in the face. Young George is punished by being
locked up in an adjoining room to undergo solitary con-
finement in the dark, and there he begins to howl and
scream. At length Goldsmith appears with a lighted candle
in his hand and a smile on his countenance. Colman sulks
and sobs, and Goldsmith fondles and soothes till the
youngster begins to brighten. Finally Goldsmith puts down
the candle and begins to conjure. He places upon the
carpet three hats which happen to be in the room, a
shilling under each, and the shillings he tells Colman are
England, France, and Spain. "Hey, presto, cockolorum!"
cried the Doctor, and lo! on uncovering the shillings, they
are all found congregated under one hat. As young Colman is no politician at five, he does not wonder at the
sudden revolution which brings England, France, and
Spain all under one crown. But as he is also no conjuror,
it amazes him beyond measure. Colman and Goldsmith become cordial friends and merry playfellows. When he
reaches manhood, Colman declares that Garrick lacks the
bonhomie of Goldsmith, for while Garrick plays with a
child to please himself, Goldsmith plays to please the
child.

The fame Goldsmith has gained by the publication of
his *Traveller* occasions a resuscitation of many of his
anonymous pieces from the various magazines and newspapers in which they lie dormant. These are published in
1765 under the title, *Essays by Mr. Goldsmith.* His only

motive for collecting such fragments is self-preservation—
that is, twenty guineas.

"The following Essays have already appeared at different times and in different publications. The Pamphlets in
which they were inserted being generally unsuccessful,
these shared the common fate, without assisting the bookseller's aims, or extending the writer's reputation. The public were too strenuously employed with their own follies
to be assiduous in estimating mine, so that many of my
best attempts in this way have fallen victims to the tran-
sient topic of the times—the Ghost in Cock Lane, or the
siege of Ticonderoga.

"But though they have passed pretty silently into the
world, I can by no means complain of their circulation.
The magazines and papers of the day have indeed been
liberal enough in this respect. Most of these essays have
been regularly reprinted twice or thrice a year, and conveyed to the public through the kennel of some engaging
compilation. If there be a pride in multiplied editions, I
have seen some of my labours sixteen times reprinted, and
claimed by different parents as their own. . . . These gentlemen have kindly stood sponsors to my productions, and
to flatter me more, have always taken my errors on themselves.

"It is time, however, at last, to vindicate my claims;
and as these entertainers of the public, as they call themselves, have partly lived upon me for some years, let me
now try if I cannot live a little upon myself. I would desire, in this case, to imitate that fat man whom I have
somewhere heard of in a shipwreck, who when the sailors,
pressed by famine, were taking slices from his posteriors to
satisfy their hunger, insisted, with great justice, on having
the first cut for himself. . . ."

The volume sells reasonably well. It goes into a second
edition and is reissued eight times before the end of the
century.

Without its dignified doctoral prefix, Goldsmith's name

is now seldom mentioned. Even Newbery is careful to preserve it. Indeed Goldsmith, at the suggestion of Reynolds, tries to make professional use of it. It is much to have a regular calling, says the successful painter—it gives a man social rank and consideration in the world. Then again, advantage should be taken of the growing popularity of *The Traveller*. To be at once a physician and man of letters is the most natural thing possible. There were the Arbuthnots and Garths, to say nothing of Cowley, among the dead; there are the Akensides, Graingers, Armstrongs, and Smolletts among the living.

Who, his friends ask him, leads in this honorable profession? There is Doctor Richard Rock, F.U.N., for instance, the first upon the list of glory. This great man, short of stature, is fat, and waddles as he walks. He always wears a white three-tailed wig nicely combed and frizzed upon each cheek. Sometimes he carries a cane, but a hat never. It is indeed very remarkable that this extraordinary personage should never wear a hat, but so it is, he never wears a hat. He is usually drawn at the top of his own bills, sitting in his arm chair, holding a little bottle between his finger and thumb, and surrounded with rotten teeth, nippers, pills, packets, and gallipots. No man can promise fairer nor better than he, for as he observes, "Be your disorder never so far gone, be under no uneasiness, make yourself quite easy—I can cure you. . . ." If such a man is in the public eye, why, friends ask, is not Dr. Goldsmith?

And so out comes Dr. Goldsmith in June of 1765, according to the account books of Mr. William Filby, the tailor, in purple silk small clothes, a handsome scarlet roquelaure buttoned close under the chin, a full dress professional wig, deep ruffles, a sword, and a gold-headed cane shaped like the staff of a parish beadle. He amazes his friends with no less than three similar suits not less expensive in the next six months. Thus arrayed he struts into the sick rooms of his patients, his scarlet roquelaure flaunting from his shoulders, and his queer little figure stuck through with a huge pin by his wandering sword.

He soon, however, gets tired of the duties and restraints of his profession. He finds it hard to give up his old humble haunts—his tea at the White Conduit Gardens, his ale house club at Islington, his nights at the Wrekin or St. Giles. "In truth," he says—"in truth" is a favorite phrase of his—"one has to make vast sacrifices for good company's sake, for here am I shut out of several places where I used to play the fool very agreeably."

At length, on prescribing to a lady of his acquaintance, a Mrs. Sidebotham, a warm dispute arises between him and the apothecary as to the amount of medicine to be administered. The doctor stands on the rights and dignity of his profession and resents the interference of a compounder of drugs. But the lady thinks her apothecary the safer counsellor, and the doctor flings out of the house in a passion. "I am determined henceforth," says he to Topham Beauclerc, "to leave off prescribing for friends."

"Do so, my dear Doctor," is the reply, "whenever you undertake to kill, let it be only your enemies."

This is the end of Goldsmith's medical career.

CHAPTER 22

NOTTINGHAM ALE

"No, sir," says Dr. Johnson, "there is nothing which has yet been contrived by man by which so much happiness is produced as by a good tavern. . . ."

A big open fireplace "brought well out" throws a glow of warmth over all in winter. A large room low and wainscotted, with heavy timbers on the ceiling—and the floor strewn with clean sawdust. . . . Against the windows on Wine Office Court are straight, high-backed benches, unrelenting in their stiffness, forming cubicles, each enclosing a small table with a neat white cloth, to dine six at a time. Dr. Johnson's table is laid each day. And here Goldsmith often comes to dine with him. They sup on the historic dish of the tavern—a beefsteak pudding with larks and oysters. . . .

> The Modern world so stiff and stale,
> You leave behind you when you please,
> For long clay pipes and great old ale,
> And beefsteaks in the Cheshire Cheese. . . .
> If doubts or debts thy soul assail,
> If Fashion's forms its current freeze,
> Try a long pipe, a glass of ale,
> And supper at the Cheshire Cheese. . . .

But the social dignities here and at Gerrard Street do not suffice for the clubbable propensities of Goldsmith. Wholly at ease he cannot always be, and so he joins a Shilling Whist Club at the Devil Tavern.

The Devil Tavern is the resort of lawyers, wits, and literary men. It is the habit of young barristers from the Temple, when going out to lunch, of placing on their doors a notice—"Gone to the Devil." Roistering days the house has known when three bottles were still the measure of a gentleman. But wine still warms the veins and loosens the throat, and clumsy Goldy with his companions troll lustily the old drinking song:

> I cannot eate but little meat,
>   My stomach is not good,
> But sure I think that I can drink
>   With him that wears a hood.
> Though I go bare, take ye no care,
>   I nothing am acold,
> I stuff my skin so full within
>   With jolly good ale and old.

> CHORUS

> Back and sides, go bare, go bare,
>   Both foote and hand go cold,
> But belly! God send thee good ale enough
>   Whether it be new or old. . . .

Goldsmith is the butt of his card club at the tavern, and they occupy the intervals of their favorite game with practical jokes upon him. Once, coming to the club in a hackney coach, he gives the coachman by mistake a guinea, instead of a shilling—which he sets down as a dead loss as there is no likelihood that a fellow of this class will return the money. On the next night, he is told that a person at the street door wishes to speak to him. He goes forth but soon returns with a radiant countenance. To his surprise and delight, the coachman has actually brought back the guinea. Such honesty, he declares, ought not to go unrewarded. Collecting together a small sum from the club and increasing it largely from his own purse, he dismisses Jehu with many encomiums. He is still chanting his praises when a member of the club asks to see the guinea. To Goldsmith's confusion, it proves a counterfeit. A burst of laughter—the joke is discovered—the pretended coachman is as much a counterfeit as the guinea. . . .

Another of his clubs, in the style of The Three Jolly Pigeons, meets every Wednesday evening at the Globe Tavern in Fleet Street. Here is Tom King, the comedian, with an old hard rough withered face like a john apple, puckered up into a thousand wrinkles, with shrewd hints and tart replies. King is a performer who throws novelty into old characters, consequence into new, and nature into all. He is the best speaker of prologues and epilogues, rendering them little dramas in themselves. His acting leaves a taste on the palate sharp and sweet like a quince. Integrity is the guiding principle of his acting and of his life. He loses all his money through gambling. . . .

Here, too, is Hugh Kelly, a young Irishman of twenty-eight, originally apprenticed to a staymaker in Dublin, then writer to a London attorney, then a Grub Street hack, scribbling for magazines and newspapers. Of late he has set up as theatrical censor and satirist, in a paper called *Thespis*, in emulation of Churchill's *Rosciad*. He has harassed the poor actors without mercy but has lavished his incense on Garrick, who, in consequence, takes him into favor.

He is an author with a sufficient vogue to inflate his vanity. This, however, is severely mortified on his first introduction to Johnson. After sitting a short while, he gets up to take leave, expressing a fear that a longer visit may be troublesome. "Not in the least, sir," says the surly moralist, "I had forgotten you were in the room."

When Kelly requests permission to converse with him, Johnson remarks, "Sir, I never desire to converse with a man who has written more than he has read."

GOLDY

A prime wag of the club is one of Goldsmith's Irish hangers-on, Glover. Originally educated for medicine, he has taken in early life to the stage, though without success. While performing at Cork, he attempts in jest to restore the life of a criminal who has just been executed. To the astonishment of every one, himself included, he succeeds. The miracle takes wind. He abandons the stage, resumes the wig and cane, and considers his fortune made. Unluckily there are not many dead people to be restored in Ireland. His practice does not equal his expectations, and so he comes to London where he continues to dabble indifferently in medicine and literature.

He is a great frequenter of the Globe and Devil taverns—and amuses the company by mimicking Garrick, Foote, Colman, Sterne, and others. He has seldom money to pay for his reckoning, but he is always sure to find some ready purse—especially Goldsmith's.

Another attendant at the club is a certain Mr. B———, a pig butcher. Mr. B. piques himself very much on his good fellowship with the author of *The Traveller* and his constant manner of drinking to him is, "Come, Noll, here's my service to you, old boy." Glover, shocked by this free and easy tone, whispers to Goldsmith that he should not allow such liberties. "Let him alone," is the reply, "you'll see how civilly I'll let him down." After a time, he calls out, with marked ceremony and politeness, "Mr. B. I have the honor of drinking your good health."

"Thank'ee, thank'ee, Noll," nods the pig butcher, scarce pulling the pipe out of his mouth.

"I don't see the effect of your reproof," whispers Glover.

"I give it up," replies Goldsmith, with a good-humored shrug, "I ought to have known before now there is no putting a pig in the right way."

At every meeting of the club, a huge "tun" of a man delights Goldsmith by singing that jovial song with its rousing chorus, Nottingham Ale:

Fair Venus, the goddess of beauty and love
Arose from the froth that swam on the sea,
Minerva leap'd out of the cranium of Jove!
A coy, sullen slut, as most authors agree;
Bold Bacchus, they tell us, the prince of good fellows,
Was his natural son, but attend to my tale,
For they that thus chatter mistake quite the matter,
He sprung from a barrel of Nottingham Ale,
      Nottingham Ale!
      Nottingham Ale!
No liquor on earth like Nottingham Ale! . . .

The Man in Black (by that name is he known) first introduces Goldsmith to a club of authors that meets every Saturday at seven, at the sign of the Broom near Islington. Upon their entrance, they find the members all assembled and engaged in a loud debate. The poet in shabby finery, holding a manuscript in his hand, is earnestly endeavoring to persuade the company to hear him read the first book of a heroic poem, which he has composed the day before. But against this, all the members very warmly object. They know no reason why any member of the club should be indulged with a particular hearing, when many of them have published whole volumes which were never looked in. They insist that the law shall be observed, where reading in company is expressly noticed. It is in vain that the poet pleads the peculiar merit of his piece. He speaks to an assembly insensible to all his remonstrances. The book of laws is opened and read by the secretary, where it is expressly enacted. "That whatsoever poet, speechmaker, critic, or historian, should presume to engage the company by reading his own works, he is to lay down sixpence previous to opening the manuscript, and shall be charged one shilling an hour while he continues reading—the said shilling to be equally distributed among the company, as a recompense for their trouble."

Our poet seems at first to shrink at the penalty, hesitating for some time whether he shall deposit the fine or shut up the poem, but looking round, and perceiving two strangers in the room, his love of fame outweighs his prudence, and laying down the sum by law established, he insists on his prerogative.

A profound silence ensuing, he begins by explaining his design. "Gentlemen," says he, "the present piece is not one of your common epic poems, which come from the press like paper kites in summer. There are none of your Turnuses or Didos in it—it is a heroical description of nature. I only beg you'll endeavor to make your souls unison with mine, and hear with the same enthusiasm with which I have written. The poem begins with the description of an author's bedchamber. The picture was sketched in my own apartment, for you must know, gentlemen, that I am myself the hero." Then putting himself into the attitude of an orator, with all the emphasis of voice and action he proceeds:

> Where the Red Lion, flaring o'er the way,
> Invites each passing stranger that can pay,
> Where Calvert's butt and Parson's black champagne
> Regale the drabs and bloods of Drury Lane;
> There, in a lonely room from bailiffs snug,
> The Muse found Scroggen stretched beneath a rug.
> A window, patched with paper, lent a ray,
> That dimly showed the state in which he lay;
> The sanded floor, that grits beneath the tread;
> The humid wall, with paltry pictures spread;
> The royal game of goose was there in view,
> And the twelve rules the Royal Martyr drew;
> The Seasons, framed with listing, found a place
> And brave Prince William showed his lamp black face.
> The morn was cold; he views with keen desire
> The rusty grate, unconscious of a fire;
> With beer and milk arrears the frieze was scored,
> And five cracked teacups dressed the chimney board.
> A nightcap decked his brows instead of bay;
> A cap by night—a stocking all the day!!

With this last line he seems so much elated that he is unable to proceed. "There, gentlemen," cries he, "there is a description for you. Rabelais' bedchamber is but a fool to it.

A cap by night—a stocking all the day!

There is sound, and sense, and truth, and nature in the trifling compass of ten little syllables."

He is too much employed in self admiration to observe the company, who by nods, winks, shrugs, and stifled laughter, testify every mark of contempt. He turns severally to each for his opinion and finds all, however, ready to applaud. One swears it is inimitable, another says it is damned fine, and a third cries out in a rapture, *Carissimo!* At last, addressing himself to the president, "And pray, Mr. Squint," says he, "let us have your opinion."

"Mine," answers the president, taking the manuscript out of the author's hand, "may this glass suffocate me, but I think it equal to anything I have seen, and I fancy," continues he, doubling up the poem and forcing it into the author's pocket, "that you will get great honor when it comes out, so that I shall beg leave to put it in. We will not intrude upon your good nature, in desiring to hear more of it at present; from the claw we may infer the lion —*ex ungue Herculem*, we are satisfied, perfectly satisfied."

The author makes two or three attempts to pull it out a second time, and the president makes as many to prevent him. Thus, though with reluctance, he is at last obliged to sit down, contented with the commendations for which he has paid.

When this tempest of poetry and praise is blown over, one of the company changes the subject by wondering how any man can be so dull as to write poetry at present, since prose itself will hardly pay. "Would you think it, gentlemen," continues he, "I have actually written last week sixteen prayers, twelve bawdy jests, and three sermons, all at the rate of sixpence a piece, and what is still more extraordinary, the bookseller has lost by the bargain.

Such sermons would once have gained me a prebend's stall,
but now! alas! we have neither piety, taste, nor humor
among us. Positively, if this season does not turn out better
than it has begun, unless the ministry commit some blunders to furnish us with a new topic of abuse, I shall resume
my old business of working at the press, instead of finding
it employment."

The whole club seems to join in condemning the season, as one of the worst that has come for some time. A
gentleman particularly observes that the nobility is never
known to subscribe worse than at present. "I know not
how it happens," says he, "though I follow them up as
close as possible, yet I can hardly get a single subscription
in a week. The houses of the great are as inaccessible as a
frontier garrison at midnight. I never see a nobleman's
door half opened, that some surly porter or footman does
not stand full in the breach. I was yesterday to wait with
a subscription proposal upon my Lord Squash, the Creo-
lian. I had posted myself at his door the whole morning,
and just as he was getting into his coach, thrust my proposal snug into his hand, folded up in the form of a letter
from myself. He just glanced at the superscription, and,
not knowing the hand, consigned it to his valet de chambre. This respectable personage treated it as his master,
and put it into the hands of the porter. The porter grasped
my proposal frowning, and measuring my figure from top
to toe, put it back into my own hands unopened."

"To the devil I pitch all the nobility," cries a little man,
in a peculiar accent. "I am sure they have of late used me
most scurvily. You must know gentlemen, some time ago,
upon the arrival of a certain noble duke from his travels,
I sat myself down, and vamped up a fine flaunting pane-
gyric, which I had written in such a strain, that I fancied
it would have even wheedled milk from a mouse. In this
I represented the whole kingdom welcoming his grace to
his native soil, not forgetting the loss France and Italy
would sustain in their arts by his departure. I expected to

touch for a bankbill at least, so folding up my verses in gilt paper, I gave my last half crown to a genteel servant to be the bearer. My letter was safely conveyed to his grace, and the servant, after four hours' absence, during which time I led the life of a fiend, returned with a letter four times as big as mine. Guess my ecstasy at the prospect of so fine a return. I eagerly took the packet into my hands, that trembled to receive it. I kept it sometime unopened before me, brooding over the expected treasure it contained; when opening it, as I hope to be saved, gentlemen, his grace had sent me, in payment for my poem, no bankbills, but six copies of verses, each longer than mine, addressed to him upon the same occasion. . . ."

CHAPTER 23

FAMILY PORTRAITS

STRASBOURG. Johann Gottfried Herder is reading aloud *Der Landpriester von Wakefield* to a young man of twenty-one, Goethe, and his companion Peglow. Herder, dressed in a black suit, with powdered hair in round curls, oval face, big clerical nose, and coal black eyes—one of which is inflamed—is a striking contrast to the elegantly clad, sparrowish Goethe. He reads in an easy quiet way, unmoved and monotonous, as if the characters do not affect him in a lifelike manner, but only glide gently by. But the two young men take the story as present, real, and living; show much emotion, and rejoice like children when the poor wretched vagrant turns out to be a rich powerful Herr.

Wolfgang is especially captured, as the Vicar and his family remind him of Fredericka and his Sessenheim friends. . . .

Roused by the success of *The Traveller,* Newbery (through his nephew Francis) has finally published the novel on March 27, 1766—almost two years after it has slumbered on his hands. There is no noise made about it, no trumpets blown for it. *St. James' Chronicle* does not condescend to notice its appearance; the *Monthly Review* confesses frankly that nothing is to be made of it; none of the Club, excepting Burke, cares for it. But its popularity slowly widens—other editions appear—and it is translated into seven languages. However, it is no very great financial success.

ADVERTISEMENT. "There are an hundred faults in this thing, and an hundred things might be said to prove them beauties. But it is needless. A book may be amusing with numerous errors, or it may be very dull without a single absurdity. The hero of this piece unites in himself the three greatest characters upon earth; he is a priest, an husbandman, and the father of a family. He is drawn as ready to teach, and ready to obey, as simple in affluence and majestic in adversity. In this age of opulence and refinement, whom can such a character please? Such as are found of high life will turn with disdain from the simplicity of his country fireside; such as mistake ribaldry for humour will find no wit in his harmless conversation; and such as have been taught to deride religion will laugh at one whose chief stores of comfort are drawn from futurity. . . ."

The Vicar's wife and daughters, happening to return a visit at their neighbor Flamborough's, find that the family has lately got its pictures drawn by a limner, who travels the country, and takes likenesses for fifteen shillings a head. As this family and his have long a sort of rivalry in point of taste, his wife's spirit takes alarm at this stolen march upon her, and notwithstanding all the Vicar can say—and he says much—it is resolved that the family have its picture done too.

Having, therefore, engaged the limner—for what can the Vicar do—their next deliberation is to show the superiority of their tastes in the attitudes. As for the rosy Flamboroughs—there are seven of them and they do nothing but flaunt in red top knots, hunt the slipper, burn nuts, play tricks, dance country dances, and scream with laughter—they are drawn with seven oranges, a thing quite out of taste, no variety in life, no composition in the world.

The Vicar's family desires to have something in a brighter style, and, after many debates, at length comes to a unanimous resolution of being drawn together, in one large historical family piece. This will be cheaper, since one frame will serve for all, and it will be infinitely more genteel, for all families of any taste are now drawn in the same manner.

Accordingly Olivia Primrose, who to her mother's knowledge has a great deal to say upon every subject and is well skilled in controversy, who has read Thwackum and Square's disputes in *Tom Jones* as well as the argument of man Friday and his master in *Robinson Crusoe* and is not without hopes of converting her rake of a lover by means of the dialogues in *Religious Courtship*—it is as natural for ambitious little Livy that she should wish to be drawn as an Amazon sitting upon a bank of flowers, dressed in a green joseph richly laced with gold, a whip in her hand, and the young squire as Alexander the Great lying captive at her feet—as it certainly suits the more sober simplicity of her sister Sophy to figure in the same composition as a shepherdess with as many sheep as the painter can put in for nothing. Honest old Dick and Chubby little Bill are Cupids. Mrs. Deborah Primrose, triumphing in her lamb's wool and gooseberry wine, is represented as the Mother of Love with plenty of diamonds in her hair and stomacher. While the Vicar in gown and band presents her with his books on the Whistonian controversy—and Moses is dressed out with a hat and white feather. . . .

The piece is large, and it must be owned, the painter did not spare his colors, for which Mrs. Primrose gives him great encomiums. They are all perfectly satisfied with his performance, but an unfortunate circumstance now occurs which strikes them with dismay. The picture is so very large that they have no place in the house to fix it. How they all came to disregard so material a point, is inconceivable, but certain it is, they were all greatly amiss. The picture, therefore, instead of gratifying their vanity, as they hope, leans, in a most mortifying manner, against the kitchen wall, where the canvas is stretched and painted much too large to be got through any of the doors, and the jest of all their neighbors. One compares it to Robinson Crusoe's long boat, too large to be removed; another thinks it more resembles a reel in a bottle; some wonder how it can be got out, but still more are amazed how it ever got in. . . .

"Anyone who would truly appreciate it [*The Vicar of Wakefield*] should not try to criticize it or analyze it."

"On Saturday will be published in two vols. the second edition of *The Vicar of Wakefield. A Tale*. Supposed to be written by himself." And on that very Saturday, a bill which Oliver Goldsmith has drawn upon Mr. John Newbery for fifteen guineas is returned dishonored. . . . He continues, therefore, his usual job work for the press, writing introductions and prefaces, revising, touching up, and modifying travels and voyages, making compilations of prose and poetry—"building books," as he sportively terms it. His terms begin to be proportioned to his celebrity. . . .

CHAPTER 24

MEETING HIS MAJESTY

An Irishman's ideas, says a countryman in palliation, rush out of his mind like the inhabitants of a house on fire—undressed, half dressed, or grotesquely dressed in the first garments to hand, tumbling too one over another in their wild scurry; whereas the ideas of an ordinary Englishman issue forth from his mind like a Presbyterian household on a Sabbath morn, marching in due order and decorous dress to the kirk. Thus the Irishman in England talks often too much, too fast, too light, too figuratively, too discursively. . . .

Oliver Goldsmith has more than a common share of that hurry of ideas which is found in his countrymen.

He has become one of the lions of the day. Literary society is open to him, but he is not prepared to move in it with confidence and success. Ballymahon has been a poor school of manners. He has brought from Ireland, as he says, nothing but his brogue and his blunders, and they have never left him.

"No man," says Johnson, "is more foolish than Goldsmith when he has not a pen in his hand, or more wise when he has." Yet with all this deficiency, he feels that as he has become a notoriety, he has entered the lists and is expected to fight, and so with Hibernian heedlessness, he dashes on at a venture, trusting to chance to make a lucky hit.

"The misfortune of Goldsmith in conversation is this, he goes on without knowing how he is to get off. His genius is great, but his knowledge is small. As they say of a generous man it is a pity he is not rich, we may say of Goldsmith it is a pity he is not knowing. He will not keep his knowledge to himself. . . . Rather than not talk, he will talk of what he knows himself to be ignorant, which can only end in exposing him. If in company with two founders, he would fall atalking on the method of making cannon, though both of them would soon see that he did not know what metal a cannon is made of. . . . Sir, he is so much afraid of being unnoticed that he often talks merely lest you should forget that he is in the company."

Boswell. "Yes, he stands forward."

Johnson. "True, sir, but if a man is to stand forward, he should wish to do it not in an awkward posture, not in rags, not so as that he shall only be exposed to ridicule."

Boswell. "For my part, I like very well to hear honest Goldsmith talk away carelessly."

Johnson. "Why, yes, sir—but he should not like to hear himself."

And again—"Goldsmith should not be forever attempting to shine in conversation. He has no temper for it; he is so much mortified when he fails. Sir, a game of jokes is composed partly of skill, partly of chance. A man may be beat at times by one who has not the tenth part of his wit. Now Goldsmith, putting himself against another, is like a man laying a hundred to one who can not spare the hundred. It is not worth a man's while. A man should not lay a hundred to one unless he can easily spare it, though he has a hundred chances for him. He can get but a guinea, and he may lose a hundred. Goldsmith is in this state. When he contends, if he gets the better, it is a very little addition to a man of his literary reputation; if he does not get the better, he is miserably vexed. . . ."

GOLDY

(The original version of Johnson's words as set forth in Boswell's *Journal* reads—"He should not attempt as he does, for he has not temper for it, he's so much hurt if he fails.")

Johnson is not aware how much he is himself to blame for producing this vexation. The great lexicographer spoiled by the homage of society, is prone to lose his temper when the argument goes against him. He cannot brook being worsted, but will attempt to bear down his adversary by the rolling thunder of his periods. When that fails, he becomes downright insulting. Boswell calls it "having recourse to some sudden mode of robust sophistry," and gives an instance of it. Once when he is pressing the Master with visible advantage, he stops him thus, "My dear Boswell, let's have no more of this; you'll make nothing of it. I'd rather hear you whistle a Scotch tune."

"There is no arguing with Johnson," remarks Goldsmith, "for when his pistol misses fire, he knocks you down with the butt end of it."

At times, however, he is very fortunate. Sir Joshua Reynolds is in company with them one day when Goldsmith says that he thinks he can write a good fable and observes that in most fables the animals introduced seldom talk in character. "For instance, the fable of the little fishes, who saw birds fly over their heads, and, envying them, petitioned Jupiter to be changed into birds. The skill consists in making them talk like little fishes." While indulging himself in this reverie, he observes Johnson shaking his sides and laughing. "Why, Dr. Johnson, this is not so easy as you seem to think, for if you were to make little fishes talk, they would talk like WHALES."

"Sir," says Goldsmith to Boswell, who has been talking of Johnson as entitled to the honor of unquestioned superiority, "you are for making a monarchy of what should be a republic. . . ."

Sir Joshua is generally tolerant of his friend's follies in conversation. He believes Goldy deliberately plays the clown because of his innate honesty and hatred of all that is pompous. Besides the Doctor has come late into the great world. He has lived a great part of his life with mean people. All his old habits are against him. It is too late to learn new ones or at least for the new to sit easy on him. With his fighting opinions, absurdity, and ridiculous kind of envy, he makes always a sort of bustle: the conversation never stagnates or languishes. The same company that, at the moment he has turned his back, are in open cry on his absurdity are still desirous of meeting him again the next day. Wherever Goldy is, insists Sir Joshua, there is no yawning.

But he never makes common observations with an air as if he has spoken oracles.

2.

In February, 1767, there happens an incident in Johnson's life which gratifies the lexicographer's Tory enthusiasm. He is in the habit of visiting the royal library at the Queen's House, a noble collection of books which he has helped form. Mr. Barnard, the librarian, takes care that everything shall contribute to his ease and enjoyment, while indulging his literary tastes, so that he has here a very agreeable retreat at leisure hours.

His Majesty George III, being informed of his occasional visits, signifies a desire to be told when Dr. Johnson comes next to the library. Accordingly the next time that Johnson does come, as soon as he is fairly engaged with a book, on which, while he sits by the fire, he seems quite intent, Mr. Barnard steals round to the King's apartment and mentions that Dr. Johnson is then in the library. His Majesty says he is at leisure, and will go to him. Upon which Mr. Barnard takes one of the candles that stand on the King's table and lights His Majesty through a suite of rooms, till they come to a private door in the library, of which His Majesty has the key. Being entered, Mr. Barnard steps forward hastily to Dr. Johnson, who is still intently studying, and whispers to him, "Sir, here is the King." Johnson starts up and stands still. His Majesty approaches him and is at once courteously easy.

The conversation is varied and discursive, the King shifting from subject to subject according to his wont. During the whole interview Johnson talks to His Majesty with profound respect, but still in his open, manly manner, with a sonorous voice, and never in that subdued tone which is commonly used at the levée and in the drawing room.

"I found His Majesty wished I should talk," says Johnson, "and I made it my business to talk. I find it does a man good to be talked to by his sovereign. In the first place, a man cannot be in a passion."

After the King withdraws, Johnson shows himself highly pleased with His Majesty's conversation. "Sir," he says to Mr. Barnard, "they may talk of the King as they will, but he is the finest gentleman I have ever seen." And he subsequently observes to Bennet Langton, "Sir, his manners are those of as fine a gentleman as we may suppose Louis the Fourteenth or Charles the Second."

Still radiant with the reflex of royalty, he holds forth one day to a listening group at Sir Joshua Reynolds', who are anxious to hear every word of this memorable conversation.

Among other things, His Majesty inquired whether he was writing anything, and he replied that he thought he had already done his part as a writer. "I should have thought so too," said the King, "if you had not written so well." "No man," observes Johnson, commenting on this speech, "could have made a handsomer compliment, and it was fit for a King to pay. It was decisive."

"But did you make no reply to this high compliment?" asks one of the company.

"No, sir," replies Johnson, "when the King had said it, it was to be so. It was not for me to bandy civilities with my sovereign."

[192]

During all the time in which Johnson is thus relating the incidents of the conversation, Goldsmith remains unmoved upon a sofa at a distance, appearing not to take the slightest interest in the royal theme. At length recollecting himself, he springs up from the sofa, advances to Johnson, and in a kind of flutter, exclaims, "Well, you acquitted yourself in this conversation better than I should have done, for I should have bowed and stammered through the whole of it. . . ."

CHAPTER 25

SENTIMENTAL COMEDY

WHEN ALL THE WORLD goes to see Rous-
seau, including the King and Queen, when their majesties
look more at the philosopher than at the players, and when
poor Mrs. Garrick, who has exalted him on a seat in her
box and is rewarded for her pains by his laughing at
Lusignan and crying at Lord Chalkstone, not understanding a word of either, holds him back by the skirts of his
coat all night in continual terror that "the recluse philosopher" will tumble over the front of the box into the pit
from his eager anxiety to show himself, Goldsmith can
hardly have stayed away. Nor is he likely to be absent
when the Drury Lane Players make a grand rally for a rival
fund, and in defiance of outlawry, Wilkes unexpectedly
shows himself in the theater more bent on seeing Garrick's
Kitely than keeping faith with the ministry whom he has
promised the day before to go back to Paris more secretly
and quickly than he has come to London. Least of all can
the poet absent himself when the last new comedy is
played, the *Clandestine Marriage*, by Colman and Garrick,
suggested by Hogarth's pictures of Marriage à la Mode. It
takes the town by storm, crowds the house with fashionable audiences, and forms one of the leading literary topics
of the day. It turns Goldsmith's thoughts to the theater.

[194]

He is in debt and what wonder then that he should look for hope there. Besides the tempting profits of an author's night, which, with any reasonable success, can hardly average less than from three hundred to four hundred pounds, nothing makes the town half so fond of a man as a successful play.

He takes for a model the older English comedy. He thinks Congreve's astonishing wit too exuberant for the stage, and for truth to nature, vivacity, life and spirit, places Farquhar first. With what is called the genteel or sentimental school that is all the mode and of which Cibber and Steele were the originators, he feels no sympathy. What Farquhar has done, he will do.

The English nation is just falling into lethargy. Their comedies which should enliven them like sparkling champagne are become mere syrup of poppies, gentle soporific draughts. Pleasantry which moves anyone to more than a grave smile is reprobated as low. If there is no interruption to this, their audiences will go to the theaters with their night caps, and settees will be furnished in Covent Garden and Drury Lane and commodiously adjusted for repose. . . .

"A new species of dramatic composition," says Goldsmith, in one of his essays, "has been introduced under the name of *sentimental comedy,* in which the virtues of private life are exhibited, rather than the vices exposed; and the distresses rather than the faults of mankind make our interest in the piece. In these plays almost all the characters are good and exceedingly generous. They are lavish enough of their tin money on the stage, and though they want humor, have abundance of sentiment and feeling. If they happen to have faults or foibles, the spectator is taught not only to pardon, but to applaud them in consideration of the goodness of their hearts, so that folly, instead of being ridiculed, is commended, and the comedy aims at touching our passions, without the power of being truly pathetic. In this manner we are likely to lose one great source of entertainment on the stage, for while the comic poet is invading the province of the tragic muse, he leaves her lively sister quite neglected. Of this, however, he is no ways solicitous, as he measures his fame by his profits. . . ."

The manuscript of *The Good Natured Man* is placed in Garrick's hands at the painter's house in Leicester Square. Garrick, unable to put off the mock majesty of the stage, means to be civil but is rather too gracious and condescending. He expects the author to esteem his patronage a favor. He is willing to accept the play but wishes to be courted to it. But Goldsmith rejects all ideas of kindness in a bargain intended to be of mutual advantage to both parties.

They separate, however, with an understanding on Goldsmith's part that the play is to be acted. The conduct of Garrick proves evasive. He does not think the piece likely to succeed and avows his opinion to Johnson and Reynolds—but he hesitates to say as much to Goldsmith through fear of wounding his feelings. Repeated interviews take place, some correspondence follows—without bringing matters to a head. In the meantime the theatrical season passes away.

Goldsmith's pocket suffers grievously by the delay, and he calls upon the manager, who still talks of acting the play, to advance him forty pounds upon a note of the younger Newbery. Garrick readily complies but again suggests certain alterations. These are indignantly rejected by the author. The manager insists and proposes to leave the matter to the arbitration of Whitehead, the laureate, who officiates as his reader and elbow critic. Goldsmith is more indignant than ever, and a violent dispute follows—which is only calmed by the interference of Burke and Reynolds.

Just at this time, Colman, having parted from Garrick, becomes manager and part proprietor of Covent Garden, and is preparing to open a powerful competition with his former colleague. On hearing this, Goldsmith makes overtures to Colman, who, without waiting to consult his fellow proprietors, who are absent, gives instantly a favorable reply. And the play is abandoned to his discretion. "Dear Sir," says Goldsmith, in a letter dated July 9, "I am very much obliged to you for your kind partiality in my favor, and your tenderness in shortening the interval of my expectation. That the play is liable to many objections I well know, but I am happy that it is in hands of the most capable in the world of removing them. If then, dear sir, you will complete your favor by putting the piece into such a state as it may be acted, or of directing me how to do it, I shall ever retain a sense of your goodness to me. And indeed, though most probably this be the last I shall ever write, yet I cannot help feeling a secret satisfaction that poets for the future are likely to have a protector who declines taking advantage of their dreadful situation and scorns that importance which may be required by trifling with their anxieties."

The next day Goldsmith writes to Garrick at Lichfield, informing him of the transfer. "As I found you had very great difficulties about that piece, I complied with his desire. . . . I am extremely sorry that you should think me warm at our last meeting. Your judgment certainly ought to be free, especially in a matter which must in some measure concern your own credit and interest. I assure you, sir, I have no disposition to differ with you on this or any other account, but am, with a high opinion of your abilities, and a very real esteem, Sir, your most obedient humble servant. OLIVER GOLDSMITH."

In reply. "I was, indeed, much hurt that your warmth at our last meeting mistook my sincere and friendly attention to your play for the remains of a former misunderstanding, which I had as much forgot as if it had never existed. What I said to you at my own house I now repeat, that I felt more pain in giving my sentiments than you possibly would in receiving them. It has been the business, and ever will be, of my life to live on the best terms with men of genius, and I know that Dr. Goldsmith will have no reason to change his previous friendly disposition toward me, as I shall be glad of every future opportunity to convince him how much I am his obedient servant and well wisher. D. GARRICK."

CHAPTER 26

"FALSE DELICACY"

THE COMEDY is not to be performed before Christmas, and Goldsmith again has to resort to literary jobs for his daily support. These secure him petty occasional sums, the largest of which is ten pounds from the elder Newbery for a historical compilation. But this scanty rill soon ceases as Newbery becomes too ill to attend to business and has to transfer the whole management to his nephew.

Then no less a person than Tom Davies comes to his rescue. Davies' business has thriven since he left the stage, and he is determined to speculate in a history. He therefore proposes an easy popular history of Rome in two volumes, which Goldsmith is to complete in two years, if possible, for a sum of two hundred and fifty guineas. An arrangement is soon made, and as usual Goldsmith seeks a retreat in Merry Islington during the summer months, where he may alternate his literary labors with strolls about the green fields. He has an old oak room in the turret of Canonbury House, a genuine relic of Elizabeth's hunting set and now a favorite nestling place of authors and publishers. A number of these fellow occupants of the castle form a temporary club which holds its meetings at the Crown Tavern on the Islington lower road, and here he presides in genial style and is the life of the company.

Here too he gets those plain and perfect English dinners which are the delight of all travellers stopping at roadside inns—mutton broth, rich in meat and herbs, fresh water fish in every form, eels—stewed, fried, boiled, baked, spitchcocked and water souchie—salmon, the purest butter, green gooseberries, the earliest cucumbers, saddle of Southdown mutton, kept to a moment and done to a turn, mutton chops, hot and hot, Irish stews, rumpsteaks, tender and juicy, chicken and ham, plum pudding (ah!), fruit tarts and trifle and gooseberry fool. . . .

At the close of the year Goldsmith is back at the Temple, in communication with Burke about his comedy, and again in attendance at Gerrard Street.

While he is living from hand to mouth, his independence is subjected to a severe trial. The opening of Lord North's administration is a time of great political excitement. The public mind is agitated by the question of American taxation. Junius and Wilkes and other powerful writers are attacking the administration with all their force. Grub Street is stirred to its lowest depths. Inflammatory talent of all kinds is in full activity, and the kingdom is deluged with pamphlets, lampoons, and libels of the grossest sort. The ministry, looking anxiously around for support, thinks the pen of Goldsmith may be readily enlisted. His hospitable friend and countryman, Robert Nugent, has come out strenuously for colonial taxation, been selected for a lordship on the board of trade, and raised to the rank of Baron Nugent and Viscount Clare. His example, it is thought, will be enough of itself to bring Goldsmith into the ministerial ranks. . . . Then what writer of the day is proof against a full purse or a pension?

Parson Scott, Lord Sandwich's chaplain, one of the servants of religion who like the Reverend Mr. Thwackum believes in grace—the grace of the empowered rich—calls upon Goldsmith to induce him to write in favor of the

administration. He tells him his authority, assures him that
he will pay most liberally for his exertions—but Goldsmith
remarks, "I can earn as much as will supply my wants
without writing for any party. The assistance you offer is
therefore unnecessary to me."

And so Parson Scott leaves him in his garret. . . .

The comedy of *The Good Natured Man* is doomed to
experience delays and difficulties to the very last. Garrick
still has a lurking grudge against the author and tries to
boost Hugh Kelly, Goldsmith's boon companion of the
Wednesday Club, as a kind of rival. Kelly has written a
comedy called *False Delicacy* in the style of the sentimental school. Garrick, though he has decried the school
and produced *The Clandestine Marriage* in opposition to it,
lauds Kelly's play to the skies—writes a prologue and epilogue to it, and on January 23, 1768, brings it out with the
greatest possible dramatic effect. The town is taken by
storm. Packed houses applaud it to the echo, newspapers
outdo each other in their praises, and night after night
seems to give it a fresh triumph.

Kelly, when he goes to the playhouse treasury to receive the profits of his first third night, which amount to
£150, not having ever seen so much money of his own
before, is all astonishment. He puts the money into his
pocket as fast as he can and runs home to his wife in a
rapture to communicate the pleasure he has enjoyed.

The booksellers vie with the manager in enhancing the
play's success. They announce that the first impression of
three thousand copies has been exhausted before two
o'clock on the day of publication. Four editions amounting
to ten thousand copies are sold in the course of the
season. It is translated into German, into French, into
Portuguese. . . .

A public breakfast is given to Kelly at the Chapter
Coffee House and a piece of plate presented to him. . . .
Kelly is so fond of displaying the plate on his sideboard
that he adds to it his silver spurs, and he exhibits his fat

little person in a flaming broad silver laced waistcoat, bag-wig and sword.

It is reported that he has done Goldsmith, who admires Mrs. Kelly's amiability, the service of dissuading him from marrying Mrs. Kelly's bad-tempered sister.

While *False Delicacy* is born on the wings of fictitious prosperity, *The Good Natured Man* is creeping through the last rehearsals at Covent Garden. The success of the rival piece has thrown a damper on the author, manager, and actors. Goldsmith goes about with a face of anxiety; Colman loses what little faith he had in it; and all the actors are discontented with their parts, excepting Ned Shuter, an excellent low comedian, and pretty Miss Walford. Johnson stands by Goldsmith in unwavering kindness, attends rehearsals, furnishes a prologue according to an early promise, and pishes and pshaws at the doubts and fears on part of the author.

CHAPTER 27

THE GOOD NATURED MAN

WHU-DUB—DUB—DUB—"Throw him over"—
"Won't ye ha some orange chips?"—"Ay, what an over-
flowing house!"—"Keep down your elbows or you'll break
my ribs"—"The gallery gods so well pressed"—"Zounds,
how you squeeze! What do you think one is made of"—
"From left ot right"—"Is this your wig?"—"No, it's that
there Lady's" "There's Alderman Cramp with his young
wife"—"Ho-hum"—"Madam, you're a charming spouse, so
neat in limb, er, tomorrow at the fruit shop, at twelve
o'clock, will you come at twelve o'clock"—"Sir, I don't understand you, I'd only dropped my glove"—"Here, Miss, are
these my places? No? Then I'll go back"—"You can't"—
"You can," she fibs. . . .

Much beglassed carriages rumble up to the theater and
arrogantly servile footmen in livery leap down, open the
doors, and place the steps in position for the descent of
my Lady. She is gallantly handed down by her sigisbée,
magnificent in mauve shot with silver, and peering with
fashionable affected myopia at the loungers through his
gold lorgnette. . . .

The fine ladies and gentlemen now stroll in to show
themselves. The former spread their fans upon the ledges,
make curtsy to their acquaintances, and then talk and

[203]

laugh as loud as they are able. They do not come to the
theater out of any regard to Colman or Garrick, but, like
the fine lady in Lethe, because everybody is there. The
silent courtship of the eyes, ogles, nods, glances, and
curtsies from one to another may be allowed them the
same as at church. In her stage box my Lady D—— interrupts with peals of silvery laughter the exquisite who is
relating a scandalous anecdote about the detested Mr.
B——. At every word a reputation dies.

The gods crowded in the upper gallery deem it incum-
bent upon themselves to create as much noise as possible
and to manifest their resentment by an occasional shower
of oranges and half-eaten pippins. Young bloods, reeling
from the taverns about Covent Garden, tumble drunk into
the boxes and roll their eyes at the pretty little orange
wenches, carrying baskets laden with oranges, cakes,
peaches, snuff, and Hesperian fruit, who run about crying, "Would you have some oranges? Have some orange
chips, ladies and gentlemen! Would you have some non-
pareils? Programmes? Would you have a programme? Pardon, sir, what did you say?" . . . Mr. Town purchases his
orange, his programme, and his "pipe of to"; and awaits
the commencement of the play. . . .

> Press'd by the load of life, the weary mind
> Surveys the general toil of human kind;
> With cool submission joins the lab'ring train,
> And social sorrow loses half its pain . . .

Mr. Bensley, a stage lover of portentous utterance,
throws into the heavy opening of Johnson's prologue such
a ponderous gloom that at the outset he dashes the spirits
of the audience. Nor does Mr. Powell's Honeywood mend
matters much with the more cheerful opening of the play.
He has complained at rehearsals that the part gives him
no opportunity of displaying his abilities, and so uniform
tameness, not to say, insipidity, is his contribution. Shuter,
after a different fashion, soon warms the audience and

shocks the sentimentalists among them with his boisterous laughter that he sends ringing through the house. But then come the bailiffs, and as they are poorly acted, the disaffected party is able to take full revenge for the indelicacy of all such farcical mirth. When good Mr. Timothy Twitch is describing his love of that jewel, humanity, and little Flanigan is damning the French for making the beer three pence half penny a pot, the people in the pit cry out, "Low—language, uncommonly low—low—oo!" Hisses, catcalls, shouts. The comedy is trembling in the balance. But Shuter comes on with the "incendiary letter" in the last scene of the fourth act and reads it with such humor that he carries the fifth act through.

Meanwhile poor Goldy is suffering in exquisite distress. He has lost all his faith in the comedy and in himself, and when the curtain falls, he can only think of his debt of gratitude to Shuter. He hurries to the Green Room and thanks the actor in his honest manner before all the performers, declaring that he has made the character appear as new to him as to any other person in the audience. Then with little heart for doubtful congratulations he turns off to meet his friends in Gerrard Street. By the time he arrives, he has entirely forgotten the catcalls and hisses, and he chats gaily as if nothing happened amiss. He even sings his favorite song about an old woman tossed in a blanket seventeen times as high as the moon, and is altogether very noisy and loud. His friends "never perceive his not eating, nor image to themselves the anguish of his heart." But when all are gone, except Johnson, he bursts out crying and swears by God that he will never write again.

A captious critic in the *London Magazine* (February, 1768) attacks Goldy for lack of originality and asserts that he is indebted to six French plays for characters and situations. But the charge is exaggerated, for only two plays contain material sufficiently similar to *The Good Natured*

GOLDY

Man: 1) in *Le Philantrope ou l'ami de tout le monde* by Le Grand, a brief scene adapted to help illustrate the character of the good natured man and 2) in *L'Important* by de Brueys, the character of Lofty, which Goldy has lifted out of the French play and adapted.

The comedy is played ten consecutive nights, but rather drags than supports itself buoyantly through the remainder of the season. Shuter gives it an eleventh night a month later by selecting it for his benefit, and Goldsmith in a fit of extravagant good nature sends him ten guineas for a box ticket. . . .

Shuter is the delight of the galleries and the fiddle of every company he enters. His humor is broad and voluptuous. But the bottle is the sun of his table, and he neither has nor seeks any higher inspiration. To ebriety he adds gaming, and so loses his money soon after his wits. The supplies frequently run low, and friends, however much wanted, are not always at home.

When he appears before a crowded house, he is perfectly easy. Yet when he appears before a small and select audience, especially ladies, he betrays the strongest marks of shyness—even bashfulness. . . .

Goldsmith's three nights net him four hundred pounds. Griffin pays him a hundred pounds more for publication. . . . Five hundred pounds and all at one miraculous draught! It appears to him wealth inexhaustible. So little is he used to receive money in a lump sum that when, at a time before, Newbery made him his first advance of twenty guineas, his embarrassment was as great as Captain Brazen's in the play whether he should build a privateer or a playhouse with the money. Now he takes means hardly less effective to disembarrass himself of the profits of his comedy. He descends from the shabby attic story of Inner Temple and purchases chambers, "up two pair of stairs," in 2 Brick Court, Middle Temple, for which he gives four hundred pounds. He then goes on to furnish them with Wilton carpets, blue morine-covered mahogany sofas, blue morine curtains, chairs corresponding, chimney glasses, Pembroke and card tables and tasteful book shelves. His awkward little person he furnishes out in a style befitting his apartment. In addition to his suit of Tyrian bloom, satin grain, garter blue silk breeches, another is charged in the books of Mr. Filby in no less gorgeous terms, being lined with silk and furnished with gold buttons. Thus lodged and thus arrayed he receives his friends. He gives dinners to Johnson, Reynolds, Percy, Bickerstaffe and others; and supper parties to the young folks of both sexes. These last are preceded by blind man's buff, forfeits, or a game of cards. After supper, he dances a mock minuet, sings a song, plays the flute and puts his best wig on wrong side foremost. Then the festivities begin. . . .

At Macklin's house, he throws up his wig to the ceiling and cries out, "Men are never so much like men as when they look like boys. . . ."

Exactly below the apartments of Goldsmith, a rising young lawyer by the name of Blackstone is bent close to his desk, finishing his fourth volume of *Commentaries* and shaking his head at the distracting social noises that go on above. . . .

CHAPTER 28

A SHOEMAKER'S HOLIDAY

MR. KELLY WITHDRAWS from the Wednesday Club. Alleged attacks by Goldsmith on his comedy have been repeated to him with exaggeration and he resents the unfriendliness. Abruptly encountering each other one night in the Covent Garden Green Room, Goldsmith stammers out some awkward congratulations to Kelly on his recent success. Kelly replies, "If I thought you sincere, Mr. Goldsmith, I should thank you."

From that hour they never speak to one another, and Kelly resigns from the club.

Goldsmith begins his *Deserted Village*. First he sketches a part of his design in prose in which he throws out such ideas as occur to him; then he sits down carefully to versify them, correct them, and add such other ideas as he thinks better fitted for the subject. If sometimes he exceeds his prose design by writing several verses impromptu, these he will take singular pains afterwards to revise, lest they be found unconnected with his main design.

Ten lines are his second morning's work, and when his friend, William Cooke, a poor Irish law student, enters his chambers, he reads them aloud:

Dear lovely bow'rs of innocence and ease
Seats of my youth, when ev'ry sport could please,

How often have I loiter'd o'er thy green,
Where humble happiness endear'd each scene!
How often have I paus'd on ev'ry charm,
The shelter'd cot, the cultivated farm,
The never-failing brook, the busy mill,
The decent church that topp'd the neighb'ring hill,
The hawthorn bush, with seats beneath the shade,
For talking age and whisp'ring lovers made! . . .

"Come," he adds, "let me tell you this is no bad morning's work, and now, my dear boy, if you are not better engaged, I should be glad to enjoy a Shoemaker's Holiday with you."

A Shoemaker's Holiday is truly a very innocent enjoyment. Three or four of his jolly pigeon friends rendezvous at his chambers to breakfast about ten o'clock in the morning. At eleven the party sets on foot in high spirits making extensive rambles by lanes and fields to Blackheath, Wandsworth, Chelsea, Hampton Court and Highgate, or some other pleasant resort within a few miles of London. At one they sit down at Highbury Barn to dinner; about six they adjourn to White Conduit House to drink tea; and conclude by supping at the Grecian or Temple Exchange or at the Globe Tavern in Fleet Street. The whole expenses of the day never exceed a crown and are oftener from three and sixpence to four shillings, for which the friends obtain good air, good exercise, and good conversation.

One of the companions on the Shoemaker's Holiday, and an occasional amanuensis of Goldsmith, is Peter Barlow. Peter is very poor, very proud in his way, and appears always in the same peculiar dress. He declares himself able to give only a specified sum for his daily dinner but stands firmly on his ability to do so, and never permits anyone to do it for him. If the dinner costs even five shillings each, Peter puts down no more than his regular sum of fifteen pence, and Goldsmith makes up the difference.

There are many other pensioners on less liberal terms than Peter. Goldsmith has two or three poor authors always on his list, besides several widows and poor house-keepers. When he has no money to give them, he sends them away with shirts or old clothes and sometimes with the contents of his breakfast table. "Now let me only suppose," he says, after they are gone, "that I have eaten a much heartier breakfast than usual, and I'm nothing out of pocket."

On one occasion, being temporarily short of money, Conversation Cooke, as he is called, asks his friend for a loan. The request is made at a time when Goldsmith has not a guinea in his pocket, so he is compelled to tell Cooke that he cannot oblige him. Cooke receives the refusal with such chagrin that Goldsmith rushes out and borrows the money. On returning with it, he finds that his friend has locked the door and gone out. When Cooke comes home in the "wee sma' hours of the mornin'," he has some difficulty in opening the door and discovers that a paper package of silver money has been pushed beneath it. He immediately goes and thanks Goldsmith, also pointing out that anyone passing the door might have made off with the money. "In truth, my dear friend," remarks our poet, "I did not think of that."

As little does he trouble himself to think when a French adventurer goes to him with proposals for a history of England in French which is not only to be completed in fifteen volumes at the cost of seven guineas and a half, and to be paid for in advance, but to have the effect of bringing into more friendly relations the literary men of both countries. Straightway he gives his name and guinea— and in the Colonel Chevalier de Champigny's advertisements, jostling the names of crowned heads and ambassadors, there figures the "Author of *The Traveller*."

NEWS

IN 1768 GOLDSMITH GOES for a summer retreat into a cottage eight miles down the Edgeware road and takes with him Mr. Edmund Bott, barrister and man of letters, his neighbor in the Temple. The cottage belongs to a rich shoemaker of Piccadilly who has embellished his little domain of half an acre with flying mercuries, *jets d'eau,* and other preposterous ornaments. To set off his Shoemaker's Holiday, Goldsmith calls this Shoemaker's Paradise.

As Mr. Bott is one of those respectable gentlemen who keep a horse and a gig, Goldsmith accompanies him sometimes to town, partakes of a social dinner, and returns with him in the evening. On one occasion they linger too long over their bottle and come near breaking their necks on the way homeward by driving into a ditch—while Mr. Bott proves with professional eloquence that at the instant they are exactly in the center of the road.

At Edgeware, the *History of Rome* is again undertaken for Davies, and here the new poem is worked out in adjoining lanes and in pleasant strolls along the shady hedges. So engaged, he is not much interested in what is going on elsewhere.

Walpole, mourning for the loss of his Lady Hervey and

his Lady Suffolk, is reading his tragedy of *The Mysterious Mother* to his lady friends that remain and rejoicing that he does not need to expose himself to "the impertinences of that jackanapes Garrick, who lets nothing appear but his own wretched stuff, or that of creatures still duller, who suffer him to alter their pieces as he pleases." Hume is receiving a considerable increase in his pension with the significant intimation of the royal wish that he should apply himself to the continuation of his English History. Great lords are fondly dandling Robertson into the good graces of the booksellers, and the Chief Justice is admiringly telling the Duke of Bedford that £4500 is to be paid him for his history of Charles the Fifth. Having made an unavailing effort to empty his head of Corsica, Boswell himself has visited Johnson in the spring, followed him to Oxford, and is now making him the hero of dinner parties at the Crown and Anchor in the Strand—where Percy is attacked, Robertson slighted, and Davies turned to ridicule. The Wilkes fever is raging in London with the virulence of a plague, and the town is topsy turvy. The *Sentimental Journey* is giving pleasure to not a few. Even Walpole declares it "infinitely preferable to the tiresome *Tristram Shandy*." While, within a few months, at a grand dinner table around which are seated two dukes, two earls, Mr. Garrick and Mr. Hume, a footman in attendance announces Sterne's lonely death in a common lodging house in Bond Street. . . .

In the course of this summer Goldsmith's career of gayety is suddenly brought to a halt by news of the death of his brother Henry. At the age of forty-five he has closed a quiet blameless life amid the scenes of his youth, fulfilling the simple duties of a village pastor:

> At church, with meek and unaffected grace,
> His looks adorn'd the venerable place;
> Truth from his lips prevail'd with double sway,
> And fools, who came to scoff, remain'd to pray.

The service past, around the pious man,
With steady zeal, each honest rustic ran;
E'en children follow'd, with endearing wile,
And pluck'd his gown, to share the good man's smile
His ready smile a parent's warmth express'd,
Their welfare pleas'd him, and their cares distress'd;
To them his heart, his love, his griefs were giv'n,
But all his serious thoughts had rest in Heav'n. . . .

CHAPTER 3 0

GRUB STREET PROTEGÉS

1.

GOLDSMITH IS ALL in a fidget to get back to London—to the sights, smells and cries of its streets. . . . They begin early and go on all day long. A ballad singer bawls in the road; a chimney sweep shouts from the house top; the scavenger rings the bells on his cart; the tumbler and dancing girl set up their pitch with pipe and drum; and the bearward comes along with his animal and his dogs. Nobody minds how much noise is made. Shouts of chair menders, knife grinders, broom-sellers, o'clo' men, lusty Turks in turbans and red breeches are mingled with those of hawkers of cherries, saloop, barley, broth, rice, milk, Shrewsbury cakes, eggs, rabbits, pippins, oysters, honey, matches, tarts, tripe, greens, shrimps, lace, ribbons, combs, buckles, pots, brooms, flint, steel, scissors, straps, and a thousand and one things.

June is marked by the bawling of mackerel, autumn by plums, pears, and walnuts; Christmas by the appearance in the barrows of rosemary, bay, holly, laurel, and mistletoe; spring by sweet smelling flowers. And so with the days of the week. On Mondays and Thursdays the bear and the bull are led out to the baiting at Hockley in the Hole; on Wednesday and Friday the fish stalls are covered with double their customary store—luscious scallops, jointed lobsters, red speckled trouts, and salmon's silver jowl; and Saturday is marked by universal washing, when dirty waters drop from the balconies and dexterous damsels twirl the sprinkling mop, cleanse the spattered sash, and scrub the stairs. . . .

And so Goldsmith packs his things, and in October is again at the Temple, at his old haunts and in the theater.

He consents to take part in the editing of a new *Gentleman Journal* in which Kenrick, Hiffernan, Kelly, and some others are engaged. It dies soon after it is born, and on someone remarking what an extraordinary thing so sudden a death was, Goldsmith replies, "Not at all, sir, a very common case. It died of too many doctors. . . ."

Isaac Bickerstaffe, a clever and facile Irishman, who ten years before suddenly withdrew his commission in the marines, took to theatrical writing for subsistence, and since obtained repute as the author of *Love in a Village,* invites his literary friends to a party. The dinner is to be followed by a reading of Bickerstaffe's new play. Among the guests are Goldsmith and Paul Hiffernan, a Grub Street protegé of the Purdon and Pilkington class.

Hiffernan is an eccentric, drunken, idle creature, educated as a physician, not without talent, but a continual victim of what he calls, *impecuniosity*. He writes newspaper paragraphs in the morning, forages for his dinner, sleeps out the early part of the night in one of the theaters, and in return for his convivial talents, which make his company attractive after play hours, is always sure of a closing entertainment at the Black Lion in Russell Street or the Cyder Cellar in Maiden Lane. Latterly he has taken to dramatic criticism which has gained him the invitation to Bickerstaffe's party.

A good dinner precedes the reading and much justice is done to this—and to the bottle which follows. At the end of the first act, the first batch of opinions is collected.

"Very well, by—, very well!" mumbles Hiffernan. About

the middle of the second act, he begins to nod, and in a little time snores outright. Bickerstaffe feels a little embarrassed, but raising his voice, continues on. The louder he reads, the louder Hifferman snores, until the author comes to a pause. Goldsmith can hold out no longer and cries out, "Never mind the brute, Bick! Go on. So he would have served Homer if he was here, and reading his own works."

Kenrick's malice twists this into a comparison of Bickerstaffe to Homer, and no laugh is heartier than Garrick's at the new proof of Goldsmith's folly:

> "What are your Bretons, Romans, Grecians,
> Compared with thoroughbred Milesians!
> Step into Griffin's shop, he'll tell ye
> Of Goldsmith, Bickerstaffe, and Kelly . . .
> And take one Irish evidence for t'other,
> Ev'n Homer's self is but their foster brother."

Johnson is a rough consoler. "Never mind, sir," says he to Goldsmith, when he sees that the poet feels the sting. "A man whose business it is to be talked of is much helped by being attacked. Fame, sir, is a shuttlecock; if it be struck only at one end of the room, it will soon fall to the ground. To keep it up, it must be struck at both ends."

Sometimes a Grub Street protegé turns up rather awkwardly when Goldsmith is entertaining his aristocratic friends. One with the worst qualities of the tribe appears suddenly at the Temple. "And how do you think he served me?" says he to a friend. "Why, sir, after staying away two years, he came one evening into my chambers, half drunk, as I was taking a glass of wine with Topham Beauclerc and General Oglethorpe; and sitting himself down, with most intolerable assurance inquired after my health and literary pursuits, as if he were upon the most friendly footing. I was at first so much ashamed at ever having known such a fellow that I stifled my resentment and drew him into a conversation on such topics as I knew he could talk upon—in which, to do him justice, he acquitted himself very reputably; when all of a sudden, as if recollecting something, he pulled two papers out of his pocket, which he presented to me with great ceremony, saying, 'Here, my dear friend, is a quarter of a pound of tea, and a half pound of sugar, I have brought you, for though it is not in my power at present to pay you the two guineas you so graciously lent me, you, nor any man else, shall ever have it to say that I want gratitude.'" "This," adds Goldsmith, "was too much. I could no longer keep in my feelings, but desired him to turn out of my chambers directly, which he very coolly did, taking up his tea and sugar—and I never saw him afterward. . . ."

2.

Though Goldsmith cares little for party questions, he has something of a half fanciful Jacobite leaning, and is as much ready for a hit at the Hanoverian rat as Johnson himself. Strolling one day with the Master through Westminster Abbey, they come to Poet's Corner, and Johnson breaks the silence with a whisper:

"Forsitan et nostrum nomen miscebitur istis." ("It may be that our name too will mingle with those.") They walk from the Abbey together and arrive at Temple Bar, where the heads of Jacobite rebels executed for treason are still sticking on the spikes above, and where not long before people made a trade of letting spy glasses at halfpenny a look. Here Goldsmith stops Johnson, and pointing up, slyly whispers—

"Forsitan et nostrum . . . miscebitur *Istis*."

3.

One of the Club's associates is in dire trouble, and the members come to his aid. His misfortune is the talk of the town.

Hot-headed Italian Giuseppe Baretti is accosted in the

Haymarket by a streetwalker who asks him to give her a glass of wine and strikes him a stinging blow. Owing to the darkness and his bad sight he does not see that his assailant is with another woman sitting on a doorstep, and he strikes the latter with his open hand or fist. She gets up immediately and begins to scream like one possessed, calling him every kind of name, among others, "Woman hater" and "d—— Frenchman," for she recognizes he is a foreigner.

Three ruffians now appear upon the scene and attack him. He loses his head completely, draws a little fruit knife and stabs one of them, then runs away in terror along the kennel. Shortly afterwards he is arrested for murder. The magistrate, blind Sir John Fielding, refuses to release him on bail and sends him to Tothill Fields prison.

Goldsmith and Baretti have never been friends. Goldsmith disapproves of Baretti's conversation and considers him "an insolent, overbearing foreigner." Baretti in his turn thinks Goldsmith an unpolished man and absurd companion. But Goldsmith's animosity vanishes the moment he finds that Baretti is in trouble. He and Sir Joshua insist on accompanying Baretti to prison; he opens his purse and is willing to give the accused every shilling it contains.

Johnson and Burke have but small comfort to give him. "Why, what can he fear," says the prisoner, placing himself between them, "that holds two such hands as I do?"

At the trial a notable array of witnesses—Reynolds, Johnson, Burke, Garrick, and Goldsmith testify to the uprightness of Baretti's character. Goldsmith says, "I have had the honor of Mr. Baretti's company at my chambers in the Temple. He is a most humane, benevolent, peaceful man. I have heard him speak with regard to these poor creatures in the street, and he has got some in the hospital who have had distempers. I have known him five years. He is a man of as great humanity as any in the world."

The testimony of Baretti's distinguished friends help to secure his acquittal.

CHAPTER 31

LITTLE COMEDY AND
THE JESSAMY BRIDE

On the sixteenth of October, 1769, Boswell gives a dinner, and on that very day Mr. William Filby takes Goldsmith home "a half dress suit of ratteen lined with satin, a pair of silk stocking breeches, and a pair of bloom coloured ditto" (for which the entire charge is about sixteen pounds)—and to old Bond Street the poet goes in silk attire. Though he is last at every dinner party, arriving always in a violent bustle just as the rest are sitting down, on this occasion he is unusually early. Garrick and Johnson are there, and Garrick is playing round the Master with fond vivacity, taking hold of the breasts of his coat, archly looking up to his face, and complimenting him on the good health which he seems to enjoy, while the sage, shaking his head, beholds him with a gentle complacency. Dinner is kept waiting, however, as Reynolds has not yet arrived, and Goldsmith, to divert the tedious moments, struts about bragging of his dress.

"Come, come," says Garrick, "talk no more of that. You are perhaps the worst—eh, eh?" Goldsmith eagerly attempts to interrupt him. "Nay," continues Garrick, laughing ironically, "Nay you will always *look* like a gentleman, but I am talking of your being well or ill dressed."

[219]

"Well, let me tell you," says Goldsmith, "when the tailor brought home my bloom colored coat, he said, 'Sir, I have a favor to beg of you. When anybody asks you who made your clothes, be pleased to mention John Filby, at the Harrow in Water Lane.'"

"Why, sir," cries Johnson, "that was because he knew the strange color would attract crowds to gaze at it, and thus they might hear of him, and see how well he could make a coat of so absurd a color."

Circumstances, too, render Goldsmith more than usually attentive to his personal appearance. At the house of Sir Joshua Reynolds, he meets a most agreeable family from Devonshire—consisting of Mrs. Horneck, widow of Captain Kane Horneck, two daughters, seventeen and nineteen years of age, and an only son Charles of the Guards, the *Captain in Lace.* The daughters are uncommonly beautiful, sprightly and agreeable. Catherine, the eldest, called *Little Comedy,* is already engaged to Henry William Bunbury, second son of a Suffolk baronet, and a clever caricaturist of the day. But the younger, Mary, the *Jessamy Bride* (i.e., the fashionable Bride), has no declared suitor, and exerts a strange fascination over Goldsmith. For once he meets with polite society, where he is perfectly at home and fully appreciated, and with lovely women to whom his ugly features are not repulsive.

When not chained to his literary tasks, he pays a visit in company with the ladies of the family (and their lapdog and monkey) either to some of the many toy shops, or to the auction rooms where articles of vertu, cockle shells, looking glasses, snuff boxes, rings, masks, spectacles, and fancy china (for which beaux and belles have a perfect mania), and oriental knicknacks of all sorts are bought and sold. Or he drives with them to Tavistock Street near the Piazza, Covent Garden, the fashionable shopping quarter, where a long line of equipages is waiting for my ladies. As they glance within, the sweetest, fairest, nicest, dished out creatures salute them with—"Garden silks, ladies,

Italian silks, very fine Mantua silks, any right Genoa velvet, velvet embossed?" And as they enter, Goldy trooping behind in his green half-trimmed frock and breeches, the same little fellows press on them lutestring, buckram, tissues, brocades, Italian silks, cloths of gold and silver, peels, pantofles, buskins, garters, shoulder knots, head dresses, modesties, corkins, minnikins, slammakins, fans, patches, tuckers, and round robins, puffs, ruffs, cuffs, muffs, shoes of all kinds, and other things. These dandy shop assistants are positively the greatest fops in the kingdom. They have their toilets and their fine nightgowns, their chocolate in the morning and their green tea two hours afterwards, their turkey polts for dinner and their perfume washes and clean linen for the Parade.

The purchases made, the ladies are directed by Goldy and the gentleman usher to their coach. Mrs. Horneck, who wears a head in the extreme of fashion, finding it impossible to get in, has to place herself on the floor. . . .

At times our poet frets impatiently on a sofa in the hall while the ladies dress. For five hours there is such doing with their looking glasses, such pinning, unpinning, setting, unsetting, forming, conforming, such a stir with combs, purls, castanets, falls, squares, busks, bodices, necklaces, scarfs, carkonets, rabatoes, borders, tires, fans, palisadoes, fusles, pustles, pantlets, frislets, bandlets, fillets, corselets, bracelets, pendulets, amulets, annulets, and so many "lets" that the poor ladies of the toilet are scarce dressed to the girdle. And now there is such calling for fardingales, kirtles, busk points, shoe ties and the like, that seven pedlar shops, nay all Stourbridge Fair, can scarcely furnish. A ship is sooner rigged than a nice gentlewoman made ready.

The ladies' heads are never more exaggerated than now. As the hoop declines in size, the coiffure grows in height. The Hornecks, to be in fashion, take to wearing towers or pompons of hair, stuffed with wool, horsehair, powder, pomatum, and padding of all sorts. On these won-

derful erections are stuck ornaments of various kinds, such
as a coach and six, or a frigate in full sail, or a bunch
of flowers, vegetables, butterflies, caterpillars, etc.—all of
blown glass or some brittle substance—according to my
lady's taste.

Later the celebrated Duchess of Devonshire supports
in her hair two ostrich feathers (each more than an ell in
length) and as her pace wields an absolute sway over
fashion, the craze for towering feathers becomes well nigh
universal.

It is a trying period for the face. The complexion under-
goes as much treatment as the hair and is put on with the
gown, with infinite pains. Every kind of rouge and white,
lip salve and wash, is brought into requisition, and a lady's
toilet table, heaped with its Dutch Pink, Bavarian Red
Liquor to produce a blush, and innumerable Chinese
paints, resembles the colors of a rainbow.

If a North American Indian were to see a well-dressed
lady's stiff stays, round hoop, high-heeled shoes, her hair
stuffed with bushels of powder and paste, and her neck
overlaid with ruff, puff, frill, and tippet, he could never
suspect that an animal like his own squaw lurked within. . . .

As the French hairdresser (most sought after of his
tribe) departs with his servant and his number of boxes,
Goldy marches triumphantly into the Jessamy Bride's room,
humming the tune:

> The ladies of St. James'
> They're painted to the eyes,
>   Their white it stays forever,
> Their red it never dies;
>   The ladies of St. James'
> They are so fine and fair,
>   You'd think a box of essences
> Was broken in the air . . .

Woman's costumes are so grotesque that in 1776 a wag,
less delicate than Goldy, feels constrained to sing:

"Give Chloë a bushel of horse hair and wool,
  Of paste and pomatum a pound,
Ten yards of gay ribbon to deck her sweet skull,
  And gauze to encompass it round.

Let her gown be tucked up to the hip on each side,
  Shoes too high for to walk or to jump.
And to deck the sweet creature complete for a bride,
  Let the cork-cutter make her a rump.

Thus finished in taste while on Chloë you gaze,
  You may take the dear charmer for life:
But never undress her—for, out of her stays,
  You'll find you have lost half your wife."

CHAPTER 32

A PERSIAN TALE

IN THE WINTER of 1768-69 Goldsmith occupies himself at his quarters in the Temple slowly building up his *Roman History*. Occasionally he spends his time at the Grecian Coffee House, the favorite resort of Irish and Lancashire Templars, or gathers his friends around him at evening parties, where he amuses them with his flute or with whist. In a run of bad luck and worse play, he flings his cards upon the floor and exclaims, "Byefore George, I ought forever to renounce thee, fickle and faithless fortune."

The *Roman History* is published in the middle of May, in two volumes of five hundred pages each. Though frankly a compilation it is a readable, swift-moving survey of the subject. It is brought out without parade or pretension, and is announced for the use of schools and colleges, Goldsmith giving as his reason for writing it that other histories of the "period were either too voluminous for common use, or too meanly written to please."

The book goes through fourteen editions before 1800. It is translated into French, German, Italian, and Greek and continues to be in demand until the middle of the nineteenth century. One of the critics who receives it well has the grace to regret that "the author of one of the best

[224]

Photo: T. H. Mason, Dublin

STATUE OF GOLDSMITH

by Foley at the gate of Trinity College, Dublin

Painted by James Doyle

Engraved by J. Sartain

A LITERARY PARTY AT SIR JOSHUA REYNOLDS'S

BOSWELL

JOHNSON

REYNOLDS

GARRICK

BURKE

PAOLI

BURNEY

WARTIN

GOLDSMITH

poems that has appeared since those of Mr. Pope, should not apply himself wholly to works of imagination."

"Whether we take Goldsmith," says Johnson in a dinner conversation at Topham Beauclerc's, "as a poet, as a comic writer, or as a historian, he stands in the first class."

Boswell. "A historian! My dear sir, you surely will not rank his compilation of the *Roman History* with the works of other historians of this age."

Johnson. "Why, who are before him?"

Boswell. "Hume—Robertson—Lord Lyttelton."

Johnson. (His antipathy against the Scotch beginning to rise.) "I have not read Hume, but doubtless Goldsmith's *History* is better than the verbiage of Robertson, or the foppery of Dalrymple."

Boswell. "Will you not admit the superiority of Robertson in whose history we find such penetration, such painting?"

Johnson. "Sir, you must consider how that penetration and that painting are employed. It is not history; it is imagination. He who describes what he never saw, draws from fancy. Robertson paints minds as Sir Joshua paints faces in a history piece—he imagines an heroic countenance. You must look upon Robertson's work as romance and try it by that standard. History it is not. Besides, sir, it is the great excellence of a writer to put into his book as much as his book will hold. Goldsmith has done this in his history. Now Robertson might have put twice as much in his book. Robertson is like a man who has packed gold in wool; the wool takes up more room than the gold. No, sir, I always thought Robertson would be crushed with his own weight—would be buried under his own ornaments. Goldsmith tells you shortly all you want to know; Robertson detains you a great deal too long. No man will read Robertson's cumbrous detail a second time, but Goldsmith's plain narrative will please again and again. I would say to Robertson what an old tutor of a college said to one of his pupils, 'Read over your compositions, and whenever

you meet with a passage which you think is particularly
fine, strike it out!' Goldsmith's abridgment is better than
that of Lucius Florus or Eutropius, and I will venture to
say, that if you compare him with Vertot in the same
places of the *Roman History,* you will find that he exceeds
Vertot. Sir, he has the art of compiling, and of saying
everything he has to say in a pleasing manner. He is now
writing a *Natural History,* and will make it as entertaining
as a Persian Tale."

The Natural History to which Johnson alludes is the
History of Animated Nature which Goldsmith begins in
1769 under an agreement with Griffin, the bookseller, to
complete it as soon as possible in eight volumes, each containing upwards of four hundred pages, in pica, a hundred
guineas to be paid to the author on the delivery of each
volume in manuscript. It is Goldsmith's intention originally
to make a translation of Pliny, with a popular commentary.
But the appearance of Buffon's work induces him to change
his plan and make use of that excellent author for a guide
and model as well as lesser lights: Willughby and Pluche,
Brookes and Pennant.

"Poor fellow," observes Cumberland, on being shown
the beginning of Goldsmith's work, "he hardly knows an
ass from a mule, nor a turkey from a goose, but when he
sees it on the table."

Other friends entertain similar ideas as to his fitness for
the task, and banter him on the subject. The custom among
natives of Otaheite of eating dogs being once mentioned
in company, Goldsmith observes that a similar custom pre-
vails in China, that a dog butcher is as common there as
any other butcher, and that when he walks abroad all the
dogs fall on him.

Johnson. "That is not owing to his killing dogs. Sir, I
remember a butcher at Lichfield, whom a dog that was in
the house where I lived always attacked. It is the smell
of carnage which provokes this, let the animals he has
killed be what they may."

Goldsmith. "Yes, there is a general abhorrence in animals at the signs of massacre. If you put a tub full of blood into a stable, the horses are likely to go mad."

Johnson. "I doubt that."

Goldsmith. "Nay, sir, it is a fact well authenticated."

Thrale. "You had better prove it before you put it into your book on Natural History. You may do it in my stable if you will."

Johnson. "Nay, sir, I would not have him prove it. If he is content to take his information from others, he may get through his book with little trouble, and without much endangering his reputation. But if he makes experiments for so comprehensive a book as his, there would be no end to them. His erroneous assertions would fall then upon himself, and he might be blamed for not having made experiments as to every particular."

Johnson's original prediction, however, that Goldsmith would make his history as entertaining as a Persian tale is amply fulfilled. The facts which it contains are often facts of sentiment rather than facts of science. Marvels and conjectures are quietly accepted. He throws out the grave suggestion of improving the breed of the zebra into an animal for common use, "as large as the horse, as fleet, as strong, and much more beautiful." Speaking of the ostrich, he seriously hopes that "posterity may avail themselves of this creature's abilities; and riding upon an ostrich may one day become the favorite, as it most certainly is, the swiftest mode of conveyance." And in a like manner, when he gravely relates the story of the Arabian Caliph, who marked with an iron ring a dolphin caught in the Mediterranean, and so identified it for the selfsame dolphin caught afterwards in the Red Sea; when he transcribes from a letter in the German *Ephemendes* the details of a fight between an enormous serpent and a buffalo, wherein the bones of the latter, as the folds of the serpent entwine him, are heard to crack as loud as the report of a cannon; when he tells what he has found in Father Labat of the monkey's mode of managing an oyster in the tropics, how he will pick up a stone and clap it between the opening shells, and then return to eat the fish at leisure; when he relates the not less marvellous manner in which the same sort of intelligent monkey manages to enjoy a fine crab, by putting his tail in the water, letting it be seized, and drawing out with a violent jerk the victim of his appetite; when he repeats what he has heard of Patagonian horses not more than fourteen hands high, carrying men nine feet high; when he tells Gesner's story of the two nightingales who were heard repeating what they had overheard of a long and not remarkably decent conversation between a drunken tapster and his wife, as well as of the talk of two travellers about an impending war against the Protestants—in all these, and many others, he marshals his authorities and sees nothing that may not be believed. Perhaps the cautious reader will be ill disposed to accept for a fact that other marvel, to which "as it comes from a variety of the most credible witnesses, we cannot refuse our assent"—about the baboons who have such a love for women that they will attack a village when they know the men are engaged in their rice harvest, assail the poor deserted wives in a body, force them in the woods, keep them there against their wills, and kill them when refractory.

One of the most talked-of blunders in the book even before it is published is the following: "The under jaw in man possesses a great variety of motions, while the upper has been thought by many, to be quite immovable. However that it moves in man a very easy experiment will suffice to convince us. If we keep the head fixed, with anything between our teeth—the edge of a table, for instance—and then open our mouths, we shall find that both jaws recede from it at the same time; the upper jaw rises and the lower falls, and the table remains untouched between them. The upper jaw, therefore, has motion as well as the under."

Despite Goldsmith's credulity, however, he is country bred and has a countryman's noticing eye. He is a minute and shrewd observer of animals, especially birds, but he observes them with the eye of a poet and moralist as well as of a naturalist. Yet he is a skilful and conscientious compiler and has a varied knowledge of the eminent and scientific works available in his day. Though he plagiarizes carelessly and borrows hastily, he works hard and is not a slavish translator. He welds the material into a unity which is his own.

Its indisputable excellences outweigh by far its real and fancied shortcomings. The optimistic acceptance of a world of creatures involved in ruthless warfare, the admiration for the constant destruction which is rationally necessary in order to keep the chain of being full and intact— these find no image in Goldsmith's eyes. In the struggle for existence he neither permits, praises, nor justifies the warfare in nature on the grounds of rational and necessary evil; he escapes from the strictures of that philosophy which, as Voltaire remarked, "cried out in a lamentable voice that everything was good."

When the book appears, it is a striking success despite its cost of £2 8s per set. Eventually it goes through twenty-two editions, the last appearing in 1876.

Soon after the memorandum with Griffin is drawn up and the book begun, Davies noses in with an offer of five hundred pounds for a *History of England* in four volumes to be written and compiled in two years, but not to be paid for until complete and delivered—and this later labor supersedes that of the earlier contract.

The irons are hot in the fire. His *English History* occupies him chiefly, his *History of Animated Nature* occasionally. He has undertaken to write a life of his countryman, Parnell, for a new edition of his poems—and the speedy publication of *The Deserted Village* is twice announced. But it is not published speedily. Still it is paused over, altered, refined and polished. To save himself the trouble of transcription, he writes the lines in his first copy very wide, and then so fills up the intermediate space with corrections, that scarcely a word of his first thoughts is left unaltered.

> Keep your piece nine years.
> "Nine years," cries he, who high in Drury Lane,
> Lulled by soft zephyrs through the broken pane,
> Rhymes ere he wakes, and prints before Term ends,
> Obliged by hunger and request of friends. . . .

CHAPTER 33

VISIT TO ST. PAUL'S

LIEN CHI ALTANGI, our wandering philosopher, has since been introduced to a temple, not so ancient, but far superior in beauty and magnificence. In this, which is the most considerable of the empire, there are no pompous inscriptions, no flattery paid the dead, but all is elegant and awfully simple. There are, however, a few rags hung about the walls, which have, at a vast expense, been taken from the enemy in war.

In this temple he is permitted to remain during the whole service. As he is not yet acquainted with the religion of the English, he inclines them to be as grossly idolatrous as the disciples of Lao. The idol which they seem to address strides like a colossus over the door of the inner temple, which here, as with the Jews, is esteemed the most sacred part of the building. Its oracles are delivered in a hundred various tones, which seem to inspire the worshipers with enthusiasm and awe. An old woman, who appears to be the priestess, is employed in various attitudes as she feels the inspiration. When it begins to speak, all the people remain fixed in silent attention, nodding assent, looking approbation, appearing highly edified by those sounds which to a stranger may seem inarticulate and unmeaning.

GOLDY

When the idol has finished speaking and the priestess has locked up its lungs with a key, observing almost all the company leaving the temple, Lien concludes that the service is over, and taking his hat, is going to walk away amidst the crowd when he is stopped by Goldy and the Man in Black, who assure him that the ceremony has scarcely yet begun. "What!" he cries, "do I not see almost the whole body of the worshipers leaving the church? Would you persuade me that such numbers who profess religion and morality would, in this shameless manner, quit the temple before the service was concluded? You surely mistake; not even the Kalmucks would be guilty of such an indecency, though all the object of their worship was but a joint stool."

His friends seem to blush for their countrymen, assuring him that those whom he saw running away are only a parcel of musical blockheads, whose passion is merely for sounds, and whose heads are as empty as a fiddlecase. "Those who remain behind," says the Man in Black, "are the true religious. They make use of music to warm their hearts and to lift them to a proper pitch of rapture. Examine their behavior and you will confess there are some among us who practise true devotion."

Lien now looks around as directed, but sees nothing of that fervent devotion, which his friends have promised. One of the worshipers appears to be ogling the company through a glass; another is fervent, not in addresses to Heaven, but to his mistress; a third whispers; a fourth takes snuff; and the priest himself, in a drowsy tone, reads over the duties of the day.

"Bless my eyes," he cries, as he happens to look towards the door. "What do I see? One of the worshipers fallen fast asleep, and actually sunk down on his cushion! He is now enjoying the benefit of a trance, or does he receive the influence of some mysterious vision?"

"Alas! alas!" replies Goldy, "no such thing—he has only

had the misfortune of eating too hearty a dinner, and finds it impossible to keep his eyes open."

Turning to another part of the temple, Lien perceives a young lady just in the same circumstances and attitude. "Strange," he cries, "can she too have overeaten herself?"

"Oh, fie," replies the Man in Black, "you now grow censorious. She grow drowsy from eating too much! That would be profanation. She only sleeps now from having sat up all night from a brag party."

"Turn me where I will, then," says Lien, "I can perceive no single symptom of devotion among the worshipers, except from that old woman in the corner, who sits groaning behind the long sticks of a mourning fan. She indeed seems greatly edified with what she hears."

"Ay," replies his friend, "I knew we should find some to catch you. I know her—that is the deaf lady who lives in the cloisters. . . ."

CHAPTER 34

SIR JOSHUA'S DINNER TABLE

"THE KING," writes Goldsmith to brother
Maurice, "has lately been pleased to make me Professor of
Ancient History in the Royal Academy of Painting, which
he has just established, but there is no salary annexed, and
I took it rather as a compliment to the institution than any
benefit to myself. Honors to one in my situation are something like ruffles to one that wants a shirt."

Reynolds, who has been mainly instrumental in founding the Academy, has been unanimously elected president and has thereupon received the honor of knighthood.
Through his influence Johnson is nominated to the profes-
sorship of Ancient Literature and Goldsmith to that of
History. The sage is so jubilant on the occasion that he
breaks a rule of total abstinence in wine to drink several
bumpers.

By the by, the author of *The Traveller* figures in a
splendid mezzotinto engraving by Reynolds in company
with his illustrious friends. This is a matter of great glori-
fication to Goldsmith, and he struts down the street looking in the windows of every print shop. One day he meets
a young gentleman with a newly married wife hanging on
his arm. He recognizes Master Bishop, one of the boys he
petted and fondled with sweetmeats when a humble usher

at Milner's school. He immediately runs up to him and embraces him with delight. "Come, my boy," cries Goldsmith, as if still speaking to a schoolboy, "come, Sam, I am delighted to see you. I must treat you to something— what shall it be? Will you have some apples?"—glancing at an old woman's stall, then recollecting the print shop window. "Sam," says he, "have you seen my picture by Sir Joshua Reynolds? Have you seen it, Sam? Have you got an engraving?"

"I—no, sir, why—you see-er—I'm just furnishing my house and I've fixed upon the spot the print is to occupy."

"Ah, Sam!" rejoins Goldsmith reproachfully, "if your picture had been published, I would not have waited an hour without having it. . . ."

On another occasion he bustles into a dinner party in Leicester Square, very indignant at an insult he has received from someone in a coffee house. "Why, would you believe it," he explains, "the fellow took me for a tailor." Whereupon all the guests present either laugh aloud or show they suppress a laugh.

"Well, Sir Joshua," says lawyer Dunning, on arriving first at one of these parties, "and who have you got to dine with you today? The last time I dined in your house, the company was of such a sort, that by G—— I believe all the rest of the world enjoyed peace for that afternoon."

At his house in Leicester Square, Sir Joshua gives those famous dinners where persons of all kinds—peers, temporal and spiritual, statesmen, physicians, deans, historians, actors, men of letters, painters, musicians, and lovers of the arts—meet in accord, and where, though the wine and the dishes are excellent, there seems to be a tacit agreement among the guests that mind should predominate over body. . . . Dinner is always served precisely at five o'clock. However high the rank of the guest invited, Sir Joshua waits for no one.

It is no prim table he sets them down to. There is little order or arrangement. There is more abundance than elegance. And a happy freedom thrusts conventionalism aside. Often the dinner board set for six or seven is made to accommodate twice that number. Nor is the want of seats the only difficulty. There is an equal want of knives, forks, plates, and glasses. In something of the same style is the attendance. The two or three "occasional" domestics are undisciplined. The kitchen has to keep pace with the visitors. Everyone calls lustily for bread, wine, or beer, or there is little chance of being served. Once Sir Joshua is prevailed upon to furnish his table more amply with dinner glasses and decanters but these "accelerating utensils" are soon demolished—and he can never be persuaded to replace them.

Not the wine, dishes, cookery, not the fish and venison are talked of. Those social hours have matter of higher relish—while amid the bustle Sir Joshua sits unfussy and composed, always attentive to what is said by the help of his ear trumpet, never minding what is eaten or drunk, but leaving every one at liberty to scramble for himself.

He is a born diplomat and avoids friction by natural instinct. "He is the same all year round," exclaims Johnson with honest envy. "In illness and in pain, he is still the same. Sir, he is the most invulnerable man I know—the man with whom, if you should quarrel, you will find the most difficulty how to abuse. . . ."

A room panelled in deal; a glitter of candles on the table and wall; a cheerful fire sputtering and crackling in the iron grate. Dinner is over, but the guests linger at their wine. Beauclerc's laughter rings out, and its echoes die away in the melody of belfry clocks chiming the hour. . . .

Here at Sir Joshua's appears a dish of peas one day that is anything but their natural color, and which one of Beauclerc's waggish friends recommends should be sent to Hammersmith because "that is the way to Turnham Green (turn 'em green)." It is said in a whisper to Goldsmith, and so tickled and delighted is he that he resolves to pass it off for his own at the house of Burke who has a mighty relish for a bad pun. But when the time comes for repeating it, he unluckily forgets the point, and falls into hapless confusion.

"That is the way to make 'em green." No one laughs. The guests look at each other in wonder. "I mean that is the road to turn 'em green," he blunders out. Still no laugh—and he starts up disconcerted and abruptly quits the table.

At the tavern he usually prefaces his jokes with a "Now I'll tell you a story of myself, which some people laugh at and some do not."

The poet and Beauclerc are seated one day at the theater next to Lord Shelburne, the minister, whom political scribbles have nicknamed Malagrida. "Do you know," says Goldsmith to his lordship, in the course of conversation, "that I never could conceive why they called you Malagrida, for Malagrida was a very good sort of a man."

This is too good a trip of the tongue for Beauclerc to let pass. He serves it up in his next letter to Lord Charlmont. He makes merry over it with his sarcastic compeer, Horace Walpole, who pronounces it "a picture of Goldsmith's whole life." Dr. Johnson alone growls forth a friendly defense. "Sir," says he, "it was a mere blunder in emphasis. He meant to say, I wonder they should use Malagrida as a term of reproach."

Rogers, the poet, meeting in later years a friend of Goldsmith's asks what he really was in conversation, "Sir," replies the old wiseacre, "he was a fool. The right word never came to him. If you gave him back a bad shilling, he'd say, 'Why, it's as good a shilling as ever was *born*. You know he ought to have said *coined*. *Coined*, sir, never entered his head. He was a fool, sir." (And yet Goldy is using a common Irishism. Swift, in his *Journal to Stella*, September 27, 1710, mentions: "I have the finest piece of Brazil tobacco for Dingley that ever was born.")

But Boswell calls him "un étourdi," Horace Walpole

"an idiot of parts, silly or piddling," and Tom Davies "an inexplicable existence in creation."

"Good heavens, Mr. Foote," exclaims a lively actress at the Haymarket, "what a humdrum kind of a man Doctor Goldsmith appears to be in our green room, compared with the figure he makes in his poetry."

"The reason for that, madam," replies the manager, "is the Muses are better companions than the Players. . . ."

At a literary dinner at Davies' the talk is entirely in the way of geniuses and of poetry. (Boswell has not seen warm victuals for four days and therefore plies a very bold knife and fork. It is inconceivable how heartily he eats and how comfortable he feels himself after the dinner.) Boswell asks Goldsmith, "And what do you think of Gray's odes? Are they not noble?"

Goldsmith. "Ah, the rumbling thunder! I remember a friend of mine was very fond of Gray. 'Yes,' said I, 'he is very fine, indeed, as thus:

> Mark the white and mark the red,
> Mark the blue and mark the green;
> Mark the colours ere they fade,
> Darting thro' the welkin sheen.

'O, yes,' said he, 'great, great!' 'True, Sir,' said I, 'but I have made the lines this moment.'"

Boswell. "Well, I admire Gray prodigiously. I have read his odes till I was almost mad."

Goldsmith. "They are terribly obscure. We must be historians and learned men before we can understand them."

Davies. "And why not? He is not writing to porters or carmen. He is writing to men of knowledge." (No doubt. But Gray's Pindarics are clogged with learning and need notes to explain them. While we're looking at the notes, our emotional response is chilled. The rhetoric is stagey. Goldy is right.)

The conversation continues.

Goldsmith. "Have you seen *Love in a Village?*"

Boswell. "I have. I think it a good pleasing thing."

Goldsmith. "I am afraid we will have no good plays now. The taste of the audience is spoiled by the pantomime of Shakespeare. The wonderful changes and shiftings."

Davies. "Nay, but you will allow that Shakespeare has great merit?"

Goldsmith. "No, I know Shakespeare very well." (Here Boswell says nothing but thinks Goldy a most impudent puppy. But now Goldy's vanity has hurried him into a rash and foolish statement.)

The following happens once in a large company which may serve as an instance to characterize the Doctor's manner of telling a story. Somebody says that one of Garrick's excellencies is his power in telling a story. This being universally agreed to excites Goldy's envy. "I do not see what difficulty there can be in telling a story well. I would undertake to tell a story as well as Mr. Garrick, and I will tell you one now, and I will do my best. There lived a cobbler—some people do laugh at this story and some do not; however, the story is this—there lived a cobbler in a stall. This stall was opposite our house, so I knew him very well. This cobbler a bailie came after, for I must tell you he was a very low fellow."

("But you was acquainted with him, you say. He used to be often at your house.")

"Ay, he used to come over to fetch our shoes when they wanted mending, but not as an acquaintance. I always kept the best company."

("Go on with your story, Doctor.")

"This cobbler was afraid of being arrested. Why, the very best company used to come in our house. Squire Thomson used to dine with us, who was one of the first men in the country. I remember his coach and six, which we used to see come galloping down the hill, and then my mother, who was a little woman, was quite hid at the head of the table behind a great sirloin of beef. You could but see the top of her head."

("Well, but go on, Doctor Goldsmith, with your story.")

"When the bailie came to and knocked at the door of the cobbler's stall in order to have it opened, the cobbler, being aware, answered in the voice of a child [here the Doctor changes his voice], 'Put your finger into the hole and lift up the latch,' which as soon as he had done, the cobbler with his knife cut the finger off, and still speaking in the child's voice, 'Put in the other finger, Sir, if you please. . . .'"

But if Goldsmith is sometimes foolish out of season, he never is, what is worse, wise out of season.

Perhaps too he recognizes that a friend may be indulging in a bit of humbug and tacitly consents to go along with the joke for the sake of the fun it will afford the company. Mary Horneck later declares emphatically "that on many occasions from the peculiar manner of his humor and assumed frown of countenance what is often uttered in jest is mistaken by those that do not know him for earnest."

But, undoubtedly, he is an anomaly to his friends. For they are ardent believers in decorum, expecting a distinguished man of letters to act like a distinguished man of letters and a clown to look and act like a clown. And here is Dr. Oliver Goldsmith, renowned and respected, acting like a fool.

Mrs. Thrale remarks: "Poor little Doctor how he does disgrace himself! and disgrace those parts but for the possession of which even the dog would be in haste to forsake his company."

(She dislikes him and complains about his curiosity. The first time he dines at her house he gravely asks Mr. Thrale how much a year he gets by his business. Thrale answers with singular propriety, "We don't talk of those things much in company, Doctor, but I hope to have the honor of knowing you so well that I shall wonder less at the question."

(One day, when he visits Johnson at her house while she is away, he sees a great cedar chest, and he is consumed with curiosity to know what is within. "What makes you so uneasy?" asks Johnson. "Why," says Goldsmith, "I long to pick the lock of that chest, so—do, Johnson, look if none of your keys will undo it." When Mrs. Thrale comes home and hears this folly, she opens the chest immediately and shows Goldsmith it is empty. "Marplot," she adds, "does nothing more ridiculous upon the stage."

(At another time he wanders into her boudoir and there he examines every box upon the toilet, every paper upon the card rack, everything in short "with an impudence truly Irish.")

Reynolds acknowledges that "to do justice to the world, a man seldom acquires the character of absurd without deserving it." And a recent biographer admits that although many of the stories of Goldsmith's alleged enviousness can be written off as deliberate attempts to amuse, the very persistence of the pattern suggests that he is plagued by the compulsive vanity to measure himself against other men. As David Garrick puts it: "Goldsmith would never allow a superior in any art from writing poetry down to dancing a hornpipe."

Even Burke cannot spare his simplicity and vanity nor refrain from practising upon them. He plays off a lively kinswoman as a raw Irish authoress arrived expressly to see "the great Goldsmith," to praise him and get his subscription to her poems. She smothers him with eulogiums, then reads some of her verses, appealing continually to the great Goldsmith to discover how he relishes them. Poor Goldy does all that a gallant gentleman can do in such a case—he praises the poems and he offers her his subscription. And it is not until she is gone that he abuses her poetry heartily.

Again, Burke and Colonel O'Moore, an Irish acquaintance, walking one day through Leicester Square on their way to dine with Reynolds observe Goldsmith, also on his way to the same dinner party, standing near a crowd of people who are staring and shouting at some foreign women in the windows of one of the hotels.

"Observe Goldsmith," says Burke to his friend, "and mark what passes between him and me by and by at Sir Joshua's."

They pass on, and are soon joined at Reynolds' by Goldsmith whom Burke receives very coolly. This vexes the poet, and he begs Burke to tell him how he has had the misfortune to offend him. Burke appears very reluctant to speak, but after a good deal of coaxing, remarks, "Really, sir, I am ashamed to keep company with one who can act as you have done in the square." With great earnestness, Goldsmith protests himself ignorant of what he means.

"Why," says Burke, "did you not exclaim, as you were looking up at those women, what stupid beasts the crowd must be for staring with such admiration at those painted Jezebels, while a man of your talents passed by unnoticed?"

"Surely, surely, my dear friend," exclaims Goldsmith, horror struck, "I did not say so?"

"Nay," returns Burke, "if you had not said so, how should I have known it?"

"That's true," answers Goldsmith, with great humility. "I am very sorry. It was very foolish. I do recollect that something of the kind passed through my mind, but I did not think I had uttered it."

But sometimes Goldsmith plays upon the simplicity of others, especially the Great Cham himself. They are supping cozily together at a tavern in Dean Street, Soho, kept by the singer, Jack Roberts, a protegé of Garrick's. Johnson delights in these gastronomical têtes-à-têtes and is expatiating in high good humor on rumps and kidneys, the veins of his forehead swelling with the ardor of mastication. "These," says he, "are pretty little things, but a man must eat a great many of them before he is filled."

"Ay, but how many of them," asks Goldsmith, "would reach to the moon?"

"To the moon! Ah! sir, that, I fear, exceeds your calculation."

"Not at all, sir, I think I can tell."

"Pray, then, sir, let us hear."

"Why, sir, one, *if it were long enough!*"

Johnson growls for a time at finding himself caught in such a schoolboy trap. "Well, sir," cries he at length, "I have deserved it. I should not have provoked so foolish an answer by so foolish a question."

CHAPTER 35

LISSOY

"MY LORD," replies Goldsmith to the Earl of Lisburne, who has questioned him on his neglect of the Muses to compile histories and write novels, "by courting the Muse I shall starve, but by my other labors I eat, drink, have good clothes, and can enjoy the luxuries of life."

Still, however, he finds time to court her among the green lanes and hedgerows in the rural environs of London, and on the 26th of May, 1770, she gives birth to his *The Deserted Village.*

The success is instantaneous and decisive. The first edition is swallowed up; in a few days a second is issued; in a few days more a third, and by the 16th of August, the fifth edition is hurried through the press.

He attains the pinnacle of his fame. The view from the pinnacle is fine, but the air is rarefied, and he breathes it with some discomfort and no little mental depression.

He can not rest until he makes a public acknowledgment of his regard for Reynolds, and so the poem is dedicated to him. "DEAR SIR—I can have no expectations, in an address of this kind, either to add to your reputation, or to establish my own. You can gain nothing from my

[244]

admiration, as I am ignorant of that art in which you are said to excel; and I may lose much by the severity of your judgment, as few have a juster taste in poetry than you. Setting interest, therefore, aside, to which I never paid much attention, I must be indulged at present in following my affections. The only dedication I ever made was to my brother, because I loved him better than most other men. He is since dead. Permit me to inscribe this Poem to you."

The increase of luxuries, the cumbrous pomp and power of wealth, the completion of the enclosure movement, and the removal of rural families from ancestral homes to crowded, industrial cities have all depopulated the country. But the poem is not just a lament for the sorry plight of the villagers; it is a prophecy of national doom and collapse. England is not heeding the lesson of history— luxuries are prejudicial to states and undo them. Like Rome, England is a land "adorn'd for pleasure," landgrabbing, vast estates, palatial country homes. The disorders of England are like the disorders of Rome—and Rome fell.

Of course Goldsmith prefers luxurious England of his own times to the primitive life of the Russians or the "noble savages" of Africa. This dual attitude towards luxury is firmly grounded in familiar Tory assumptions: an anti-Rousseauistic reverence for civilization, tradition, and what Burke means by prescription, class distinctions based on inheritance by blood of real property, and an antipathy to the rise of a new class wealthy with fluid capital. In contrast to the state of savagery, this luxurious state is to be preferred, yet this same state is in constant danger of decay and collapse. The new order has destroyed everything of importance in rural England—innocence, religion, education, social conviviality. Here the poem resembles Gray's *Elegy* in that it laments the passing of a society or of a way of life as poetically as the death of an individual. Once more Goldsmith looks back with fondness to his native village of Lissoy:

GOLDY

In all my wan'drings round this world of care,
In all my griefs—and God has giv'n my share—
I still had hopes my latest hours to crown,
Amid these humble bowers to lay me down;
To husband out life's taper at the close,
And keep the flame from wasting by repose;
I still had hopes, for pride attends us still,
Amid the swains to show my book learn'd skill,
Around the fire an ev'ning group to draw,
And tell of all I felt and all I saw;
And as a hare, whom hounds and horns pursue,
Pants to the place from whence at first she flew,
I still had hopes, my long vexations past,
Here to return—and die at home at last. . . .

And yet—a paradox beneath the placid surface of the author's verse—has not the poet discovered at last that you cannot go home again, because home no longer exists? In all Goldsmith's work, in all his thoughts is a nostalgic yearning for the family circle of his childhood with a sane awareness of its defects. The family has warmth, stability, comfort, innocence, mutual love. But like the college, it is essentially a retreat from the world. Its concerns are static—small and narrow: to hibernate between fireplace and easy chair. It eventually becomes every man's ideal of childhood—like the Deserted Village, a place of no return. But the wanderer is the adult in a dangerous but meaningful world.

"Sweet Auburn! loveliest village of the plain,
Where health and plenty cheer'd the lab'ring swain . . .
Thy sports are fled, and all thy charms withdrawn. . . ."

CHAPTER 36

WESTMINSTER ABBEY

"IF NONE but the truly great have a place in this awful repository," remarks Lien Chi Altangi, as he strolls with the Man in Black through Westminster Abbey, "a place like this will give the finest lessons of morality, and be a strong incentive to true ambition. I am told, that none have a place here but characters of the most distinguished merit."

The Man in Black seems impatient at his observations so Lien discontinues his remarks, and they walk on together to a particular part of the Abbey.

"There," says the gentleman, pointing with his finger, "that is the Poet's Corner. There you see the monuments of Shakespeare, and Milton, and Prior, and Drayton."

"Drayton," Lien replies, "I have never heard of him before—but I have been told of one Pope—is he there?"

"It is time enough," replies his guide, "these hundred years. He is not long dead—people have not done hating him yet."

"Strange," Lien cries, "can any be found to hate a man whose life was wholly spent in entertaining and instructing his fellow creatures?"

"Yes," says the Man in Black, "they hate him for that very reason. There are a set of men called answerers of

books, who take upon themselves to watch the republic
of letters and distribute reputation by the sheet. They
somewhat resemble the eunuchs in a seraglio, who are
incapable of giving pleasure themselves and hinder those
that would. These answerers have no other employment
but to cry out Dunce and Scribbler, to praise the dead
and revile the living, to grant a man of confessed abilities
some small share of merit, to applaud twenty blockheads
in order to gain the reputation of candor, and to revile the
moral character of the man whose writings they cannot
injure. Such wretches are kept in pay by some mercenary
bookseller, or more frequently the bookseller himself takes
this dirty work off their hands, as all that is required is to
be very abusive and very dull. Every poet of any genius
is sure to find such enemies. He feels, though he seems to
despise, their malice. They make him miserable here, and
in the pursuit of empty fame, at last he gains solid anxiety."

"Has this been the case with every poet I see here?"
Lien cries.

"Yes, with every mother's son of them," replies the Man
in Black, "except if he happened to be born a mandarine.
If he has much money, he may buy reputation from your
book answerers, as well as a monument from the guardians
of the temple."

Leaving this part of the Abbey, they walk on to take a
view of each particular monument in order. Lien is especially curious about one monument which appears more
beautiful than the rest.

"That," he says to his guide, "I take to be the tomb of
some very great man. By the peculiar excellence of the
workmanship and magnificence of the design, this must be
a trophy raised to the memory of some king who has saved
his country from ruin, or lawgiver, who has reduced his
fellow citizens from anarchy into just subjection."

"It is not requisite," replies his companion, smiling, "to
have such qualifications in order to have a very fine monument here. More humble abilities will suffice."

"What! I suppose then the gaining of two or three battles, or the taking half a score of towns, is thought a sufficient qualification?"

"Gaining battles or taking towns," replies the Man in Black, "may be of service, but a gentleman may have a very fine monument here without ever seeing a battle or a siege."

"This, then is the monument of some poet, I presume— of one whose wit has gained him immortality."

"No, sir," replies his guide, "the gentleman who lies here never made verses, and as for wit, he despised it in others, because he had none himself."

"Pray, tell me, then, in a word," says Lien peevishly, "what is the great man who lies here particularly remarkable for?"

"Remarkable, sir!" says his companion, "why, sir the gentleman that lies here is remarkable—very remarkable— for a tomb in Westminster Abbey. . . ."

CHAPTER 37

HICKEY,
THE SPECIAL ATTORNEY

"MY DEAR FRIEND," writes Goldsmith to Reynolds from France where he has gone with Mrs. Horneck and the young ladies, "we had a quick passage from Dover to Calais, which we performed in three hours and twenty minutes, all of us extremely seasick, which must necessarily have happened, as my machine to prevent seasickness was not completed. We were glad to leave Dover, because we hated to be imposed upon, so were in high spirits at coming to Calais, where we were told that a little money would go a great way.

"Upon landing, with two little trunks, which was all we carried with us, we were surprised to see fourteen or fifteen fellows all running down to the ship to lay their hands upon them. Four got under each trunk, the rest surrounded and held the hasps, and in this manner our little baggage was conducted with a kind of funeral solemnity, till it was safely lodged at the custom house. We were well enough pleased with the people's civility till they came to be paid. Every creature that had the happiness of but touching our trunks with their finger expected sixpence, and they had so pretty and civil a manner of demanding it that there was no refusing them.

"When we had done with the porters, we had next to speak with the custom house officers, who had their pretty civil ways too. We were directed to the Hotel D'Angleterre, where a *valet de place* came to offer his service, and spoke to me ten minutes before I once found out that he was speaking English. We had no occasion for his services, so we gave him a little money because he spoke English, and because he wanted it. I cannot help mentioning another circumstance. I bought a new ribbon for my wig at Canterbury, and the barber at Calais broke it in order to gain sixpence by buying me a new one."

This is not a very promising beginning, but the party passes on through Flanders and to Paris by way of Lisle. While stopping at a hotel in Lisle, they are drawn to the windows by a military parade in the square. The beauty of the Horneck girls immediately attracts the attention of the officers who break forth into enthusiastic speeches and compliments. Goldsmith is amused for a while, but at length, pretending impatience and anger, turns off from the window with the remark, "There are places where I am the object of admiration also." (This is not an instance of his vanity. He says it in a joke and with laughter.)

Travelling is a very different thing with Goldsmith, the poor student at twenty, and Goldsmith, the poet and professor at forty. Lying in a barn was no disaster then. There were no postillions to quarrel with, no landladies to be cheated by, no silk coat to tempt him into making himself look like a fool. Meat—when he could get it—was never too tough to be eaten, nor was he likely to have been poisoned by a dish of green peas. The world was his oyster then, which he opened with his flute.

He has risen into high life and acquired high-bred notions. He must be fastidious like his fellow travellers. He dares not be pleased with what pleased the vulgar tastes of his youth. And so one of his chief amusements is scolding at everything and every person he has left at home.

He is anxious to get back to the relish of manly conversation and the society of the brown table. A lurking thorn, too, is worrying him. He has outrun the constable—his expenses have gone far beyond his means. He is getting nervous about his arrears of work. He dares not think of another excursion yet, though Reynolds has proposed a joint excursion to Devonshire. He is already planning a new labor—he is even thinking of a new comedy.

Another circumstance helps to mar the pleasure he has promised himself. At Paris, the party is unexpectedly joined by a Mr. Hickey, a bristling attorney, who is well acquainted with Paris and its environs, and insists on playing cicerone on all occasions. Goldsmith and he do not relish each other, and they have several petty quarrels. The lawyer is too much a man of business for the poet and is disposed to manage everything.

He sends Hickey in a roar by protesting that all the French parrots he has heard spoke such capital French that he understood them perfectly, whereas an English parrot talking his own native Irish is quite unintelligible to him.

While he views the waterworks at Versailles with Hickey and the ladies, a question arises whether the distance from where they stand to one of the little islands is within the compass of a leap. Goldsmith sturdily maintains the affirmative—Hickey jeers. Whereupon the poet, remembering his prowess as a youth, attempts the leap, but falling short, tumbles into the water.

> Here Hickey reclines, a most blunt, pleasant creature,
> And slander itself must allow him good nature;
> He cherished his friend, and he relished a bumper,
> Yet one fault he had, and that one was a thumper.
> Perhaps you may ask if the man was a miser:

I answer, no, no, for he always was wiser.
Too courteous, perhaps, or obligingly flat?
His very worst foe can't accuse him of that.
Perhaps he confided in men as they go,
And so was too foolishly honest? Ah no!
Then what was his failing? Come tell it and burn ye.
He was—could he help it?—a special attorney.

CHAPTER 38

HAUNCH OF VENISON

ON HIS RETURN TO ENGLAND, Goldsmith receives news of his mother's death. He immediately dresses himself in a suit of clothes of gray cloth, trimmed with black, such as commonly is worn for half mourning. When he appears the first time after this at Sir Joshua's house, Frances Reynolds asks him whom he has lost and he answers, "A distant relation only."

A distant relation is no bad description of a mother from whom one has been separated and estranged for nearly twenty years. She loses the farm at Pallas and then her eyesight, and her bitterness grows sharp. Oliver longs for her approval and is acutely aware of her disapproval and his failure in her eyes. Perhaps that is why she is never reflected in his writings.

The devils are again driving him. Davies has published Parnell's poems with a life by Goldsmith as an introduction—a piece of job work, hastily got up for pocket money. Whatever its faults, it is successful, and the bookseller now commissions him to prepare an abridgment in one volume of his *History of Rome*—but first to write a work for which there is a more immediate demand. Davies is about to republish Lord Bolingbroke's *Dissertation on Parties*, selected for its hot party interest. To give it still greater currency, he engages Goldsmith to introduce it with a prefatory memoir.

But what is written proves very harmless in its way, with as little in it to concern Lord North as Mr. Wilkes, and of as small interest to the writer as to either.

"Doctor Goldsmith is gone with Lord Clare into the country," writes Davies to his friend the Reverend Granger, "and I am plagued to get the proofs from him of his life of Lord Bolingbroke." However, he does get them, and the book is published, without the *Dissertation*, in December.

Goldsmith continues with Lord Clare during the opening months of 1771—at Gosfield and at Bath. In the latter city an amusing incident occurs. The Duke and Duchess of Northumberland, occupying a house on one of the parades next door to Lord Clare's and similar to it, are surprised one day, when about to sit down to breakfast, to see Goldsmith enter the breakfast room from the street, and without noticing them, throw himself unconcernedly down on the sofa. The Duke and Duchess see his mistake and try to prevent any awkward embarrassment. They accordingly chat sociably with him about matters in Bath, until breakfast being served, they invite him to stay and partake of it. The truth at once flashes upon him, he starts up from the sofa, declines breakfast with profuse apologies, and retires in confusion.

At Gosfield there is beside the poet a crowd of humble cousins, card-ruined beaux, and captains on half pay all willing to make up Squire Gawky's retinue down to his country seat. Not one of these could not lead a more comfortable life at home in his little lodging of three shillings a week with his lukewarm dinner, served up between two pewter plates from a cook's shop. Yet, poor devils, they are willing to spend the winter in bondage merely to be thought to live among the great—though conscious they are taken down only to approve his lordship's taste upon every occasion, to tag all his observations with a "very true," to praise his stable, and descant upon his claret and cookery.

Gambling is the favorite amusement of Squire Gawky's party. The guests take wagers on anything—that Lord B—— will not be made Vice Admiral by such and such a date, that Mr. R—— will be found wearing a certain suit on a particular occasion, that the Duke of Q——, now seriously ill, will not survive on the first of next month. Then in the evening card playing at moderate stakes—bassett, ombre, loo, or whist.

Goldsmith finds his residence among the great not unattended with mortification. He is now accustomed to regard himself as a literary lion, and is annoyed at what he considers a slight on the part of Lord Camden. He complains of it on his return to town at a party of his friends. "I met him," he says, "at Lord Clare's house in the country, and he took no more notice of me than if I had been an ordinary man." The company laughs heartily.

"Nay, gentlemen," roars out Johnson, coming to the defense of the poet, "Dr. Goldsmith is in the right. A nobleman ought to have made up to such a man as Goldsmith, and I think it is much against Lord Camden that he neglected him."

After Goldsmith's return to London, the Squire sends from the spacious avenues of Gosfield Park an entire buck to his friend's humble quarters in the Temple.

THANKS, my lord, for your venison, for finer or fatter
Never ranged in a forest, or smoked in a platter;
The haunch was a picture for painters to study,
The fat was so white, and the lean was so ruddy;
Though my stomach was sharp, I could scarce help regretting
To spoil such a delicate picture by eating;
I had thoughts in my chambers to place it in view,
To be shown to my friends as a piece of virtu;
As in some Irish houses where things are so-so,
One gammon of bacon hangs up for a show,
But, for eating a rasher of what they take pride in,

Painted by E. M. Ward

Engraved by H. S. Sadd, N. Y.

DOCTOR JOHNSON RESCUING OLIVER GOLDSMITH FROM HIS
LANDLADY.

Painted by D. Gardner   Engraved by W. Dickinson

MRS. GWYNNE (THE JESSAMY BRIDE) and MRS. BUNBURY (LITTLE COMED
in the Characters of *The Merry Wives of Windsor*

They'd as soon think of eating the pan it is fried in.
But hold—let me pause—don't I hear you pronounce
This tale of the bacon a damnable bounce?
Well suppose it a bounce—sure a poet may try,
By a bounce now and then, to get courage to fly . . .
To go on with my tale; as I gazed on the haunch,
I thought of a friend that was trusty and staunch;
So I cut it and sent it to Reynolds undrest,
To paint it or eat it just as he liked best.
Of the neck and the breast I had next to dispose;
'Twas a neck and a breast that might rival Monroe's;
But in parting with these I was puzzled again,
With the how and the who and the where and the when.
There's Howard, and Coley, and H—rth, and Hiff,
I think they love venison—I know they love beef.
There's my countryman Higgins—oh! let him alone,
For making a blunder or picking a bone.
But hang it!—to poets who seldom can eat
Your very good mutton's a very good treat.
Such dainties to them their health it might hurt,
It's like sending them ruffles, when wanting a shirt. . . .

CHAPTER 39

MERRY-GO-ROUND

1.

VAUXHALL, RANELAGH, the Pantheon, and Mrs. Cornelys' are the rage of the town. Everybody flocks there—lords and liverymen, pinks and pickpockets, dukes and dustmen, drabs and duchesses, shopkeepers and squires—Ferdinand, Count Fathom, as well as my Lord Ogleby, Moll Flanders, Beau Tibbs, Lady Bellaston, Tabitha Bramble, and Tugwell the cobbler. The whole scene affords an admirable picture of high life below stairs and low life above.

There also struts Goldsmith in red heeled shoes to imitate the leading macaronis, an immense knot of artificial hair behind, a very small cocked hat, an enormous walking stick with long tassels, and extremely close cut jacket, waistcoat, and breeches. Like Charles Fox and Lord Carlisle, he masquerades as an exquisitely dressed running footman. Like them too, at the gaming table, he pulls off his embroidered clothes, dons a frieze great coat, and turns his coat inside out for luck. To save his laced ruffles, he puts on pieces of leather, such as are worn by footmen when they clean the knives. And to guard his eyes from the light and to prevent the tumbling of his hair, he wears

[258]

a high crowned straw hat with a broad brim and adorned with flowers and ribbons. Charles Fox borrows great sums from the Jewish moneylenders at exorbitant premiums. Charles calls his outward room, where the moneylenders wait till he rises, his Jerusalem chamber. . . .

Ranelagh is a vast amphi-theater erected in the center of a garden where everyone that loves eating, drinking, staring, or crowding is admitted for a half crown. Ranelagh has totally beat Vauxhall; everybody goes there; nobody goes anywhere else. My Lord Chesterfield is so fond of it that he says he orders all his letters to be directed thither. The floor is of beaten princes—that you can't set your foot down without treading on a Prince of Wales or a Duke of Cumberland. . . . The place is jammed with the gay, the rich, the happy, and the fair, glittering with cloth of gold and silver lace, embroidery, and precious stones.

The company is universal. There is His Grace of Grafton and the children out of the Foundling Hospital, my Lady Townshend and the kitten. The privileges of gazing upon lords and ladies, counts and countesses, attract the genteel, or those who wish to be considered so, in great numbers. These mortals never begrudge the money expended in coach hire, and always take good care, like Mr. and Mrs. Beau Tibbs, to sit in none but a genteel box, where they might see and be seen.

On entering the gentlemen customarily buy flowers for their own buttonholes, and flowers to present to their lady friends and admirers. They are then met by the strains of vocal and instrumental music. Choruses from Mr. Handel's most admired oratorios are interspersed with ballads by Mr. Dibdin, Mrs. Baddeley, and other famous performers of the day. Italian singers—so much the rage—are, of course, heard from time to time. But no one listens to the music—it is wasted on the desert air. The chief attraction is promenading:

GOLDY

The music was truly enchanting,
Right glad was I when I came near it,
But in fashion I found I was wanting,
'Twas the fashion to walk and not hear it.

In the evening half of the company follow one another's tail in an eternal circle, like so many blind asses
in an olive mill, where they can neither discourse, distinguish, nor be distinguished; while the other half are drinking hot water, under the denomination of tea, till nine or
ten o'clock at night, to keep them awake for the rest of the
evening.

Once the Prince makes his appearance and a com-
motion is raised. The ladies follow the Prince; the gentlemen pursue the ladies; the curious run to see what is the
matter; the mischievous run to increase the tumult; and
in two minues the boxes are deserted. The lame are over-
thrown; the well dressed demolished; and half the whole
company is contracted into one narrow channel and borne
along with the rapidity of a torrent to the infinite danger
of powdered locks, painted cheeks, and crazy constitutions.

The garden at Chelsea is the resort of fashion, but it
is to the garden at Lambeth—the new spring gardens of
Vauxhall—that London folk on pleasure bent betake themselves as a rule. There all classes, from the highest to the
lowest, can enjoy themselves freely and have a real good
time—without too much regard for the proprieties.

From Whitehall Stairs, the favorite starting place, you
take a wherry, so light and slender that you look like a
fairy sailing in a nutshell and row to Vauxhall. There is
the same crush of wherries, and the same confusion of
tongues at the landing place, and the same crowd of mud
larks and loafers come rushing into the water to offer their
unsolicited (but not gratuitous) services. Once free of
these, a few steps bring you to an unimposing entrance to

the garden—a gate or wicket in front of an ordinary looking house. Here either you exhibit your ticket or pay your shilling, hurry with a throb of anticipation down a darkened passage, and then—if you are young and unsophisticated—utter an involuntary exclamation of wonder, as with a sudden sound of muffled music, the many lighted enclosure bursts upon your view—tall elms and sycamores with colored lamps braced to the tree trunks or twinkling through the leaves, small alcoves with their inviting supper tables, brightly shining temples and pavilions, statues of Neptunes, mermaids, dolphins, placed in agreeable attitudes, the central quadrangle called the Grove, with its large pavilion, and the Grand Walk, the Cross Walk, and the Lovers' Walk, dark with shade of interlacing trees, a favorite haunt, not of peaceful lovers as of young rakes on the lookout for opportunities of horse play.

There are cocagnes, concerts, and lotteries, masquerades or ridottos, above all, private supper parties and—women. And what can one have for supper? Ham so thin that you can read a newspaper through it. It is currently reported that the expert carver at Vauxhall can cover an entire eleven acres with the slices from one ham. The waiters have to carry their plates in a certain position to prevent the wind from blowing away the wafer-like slices. Then there are chickens—no bigger than sparrows—and hung beef such as Sir Roger supped off when he visited the gardens. Drinks—burgundy, champagne, claret, red port (at 2s a bottle!), table beer at four pence for a quart mug, Burton ale (preferred by Sir Roger), and a specialty in the form of arrack punch. (Burke gets drunk and is ashamed of it; Goldy gets drunk and boasts of it, especially if it has been with a little whore or so who has allowed him to go in a coach with her.)

There are the women—the married or unmarried Lady of Quality who intrigues with as many as she pleases and still remains the Rt. Honourable; the draggle-tailed street walker who is a common woman and is liable to be sent to Bridewell—and the whore of high life who is a lady of pleasure and rolls in a gilt chariot.

There is a party of gentlemen and ladies of fashion who entertain the company at Vauxhall with the most charming harmony. The ladies play at crowing like cocks, and if any gentlemen of the party are within hearing, they answer them by braying like asses.

But the last night of the season is always the best night for the young bloods. On the last night there's always a riot, and the folks run about, and then there is such a squeaking and squalling, and all the lamps are broken, and the women run skimper scamper. . . .

2.

Sir Joshua is painting pretty, silly, self-indulging, self-destroying Sophia Baddeley. Mrs. Baddeley is the queen of the theater. She has a voluptuous face, large melting eyes, and full rosy lips. She is more celebrated for her beauty and gallantry than for her wit or professional skill. . . . She loves cats.

All the world is in expectation of the opening of the Pantheon, the new winter Ranelagh in Oxford Street. Mrs. Abington—exquisite figure, saucy air, and winning face— is sitting with Sir Joshua at the same time as Mrs. Baddeley. Both have their anxieties about the reception they are like to meet with at the new place of entertainment. At Almack's or at Mme. Cornelys' or at the Opera House masquerades, none are so welcome as the demireps, the mistresses, and the players. But the proprietors and managers of the Pantheon, it is whispered, have set up as censors and determine to exclude all women of slight character—and all the players. Lord Melbourne is at this moment the protector of pretty Mrs. Baddeley whom he loves "every minnitt" of his life, "Satterday, Sunday, and everyday"—and the young bloods vow that whoever is excluded from the Pantheon, Sophia Baddeley shall be let in.

At Almack's they meet and bind themselves to escort her and stand by her chair. And as they proceed in solemn procession to the masquerade, so many as fifty gentlemen hover about her. The constables allow the others to pass, but when Mrs. Baddeley follows, they cross their staves and civilly but resolutely say the orders are to admit no players. They put it in the politest way, for Mrs. Baddeley would have been excluded by her reputation, had her profession been unexceptionable. On this, the gallant escorts draw, compel the constables to give way at the sword's point, and raising their chivalrous blades, protect Mrs. Baddeley as she passes proudly to the Rotunda—blazing with lights, and surrounded with all the Gods and Goddesses of Olympus—in eighteenth century attire. Then the outraged gentlemen refuse to sheathe their swords or allow the music to proceed, till the managers come forward and humbly apologize—which they do.

A messenger is in waiting to inform Mrs. Abington of the result of Mrs. Baddeley's charge at the head of her guards—and she now makes her *entrée*. From that night any attempt to draw the line between degrees of vice is virtually relinquished.

Courtesans mingle with daughters of peers, Phrynes with the loveliest ladies of the court, and when, as it happens, attendance on some night is not great, the newspapers lament to see "such spirited exertions so poorly rewarded, as scarcely one person of distinction, or one *fille de joie* of note was present, to give a *ton* to the evening's entertainment."

And later an advertisement appears that "as it is not convenient for ladies always to carry the certificates of their marriages about them, the subscribers are resolved, in opposition to the managers, to protect the ladies to whom they give their tickets. . . ."

The Pantheon is the wonder of the age—the *locus classicus* of masquerades—a Balbec in all its glory. The pillars are of artificial giallo antico, the ceilings—even the passages—of the most beautiful stucco, the ballroom painted like Raphael's Loggia in the Vatican, and the dome, like the Pantheon in Rome, glazed. It costs £60,000.

Drums, festinos, hurricanes, and masquerades are held here. Fops, fools, gamesters, knaves, and lords combine each to his humor. Everything is allowed—champagne, dice, music—or your neighbor's spouse.

The dances most in vogue are the country dance and the minuet. Just before dancing begins, the ladies present throw down their fans upon the table. A gentleman then advances, takes up a fan, and invites the lady, to whom it belongs, to become his partner.

Like the taverns about Covent Garden, which are dedicated to Venus as well as Ceres and Liber, you may frequently see the jolly messmates of both sexes go in and come out in couples like the clean and unclean beasts in Noah's ark.

When not attending the gardens or the night clubs, Goldy and Sir Joshua are at Mrs. Cornelys' in Soho Square. This lady has commenced her career as a singer by the name of Pomperati. She has then become the "Heidegger of the Age" and now presides over the diversions of the *ton*. Her taste and invention in pleasures are singular. She takes Carlisle House, at Sutton Street, Soho Square, enlarges it, and establishes assemblies, and balls by subscription. At first she scandalizes people, but soon draws in both the righteous and ungodly. She goes on building and makes her house a fairy palace for balls, concerts, and masquerades. In a word, dogs, monkeys, ostriches, and all kinds of monsters are as frequently to be met with here as in the Covent Garden pantomimes. . .

A few years before, a celebrated lady endeavored to introduce a new species of masquerade by lopping off the exhuberance of dress, and she herself first set the example by stripping to the character of Iphigenia undressed for the sacrifice. But this project was not then sufficiently ripe for execution as a certain awkward thing called bashfulness was not yet banished from the female world.

What the above mentioned lady had the hardiness to attempt alone, is now to be set on foot by persons of fashion. And to the present enlightened times is reserved the honor of introducing a naked masquerade—however contradictory the term may seem. Ranelagh is the place pitched upon for their meeting, where it is proposed to have a masquerade *al fresco,* and the whole company to display all their charms *in puris naturalibus.* The Pantheon of the Heathen Gods, Ovid's *Metamorphoses,* and Titian's prints are to supply them with a sufficient variety of undressed characters. One set of ladies intends to personify water nymphs bathing in the canal, while a certain lady of quality who most resembles the Goddess of Beauty practices from a model of the noted statue of Venus de Milo. As for the gentlemen, they are to represent very suitably the forms of Satyrs, Pans, Fauns, and Centaurs. The beaux are to assume the semblance of beardless Apollos or admire themselves in the person of Narcissus—and our bucks are to act quite in character by running about stark naked with their mistresses and committing the maddest freaks. . . .

The beau of these days is—a thing, and a very absurd thing, to boot. There is nothing genuine about him. All that is expected of him is to drink deep, swear lustily, ride well, use an eyeglass, and to be able to shoe his own horse. It is likewise quite the thing to affect deafness and to lisp. A first rate buck is called a stag, but to earn this honorable epithet he must have made the grand tour, acquired the genteel oaths of every people he visited, and learned to damn eloquently in ten languages.

Of course, everything French is pronounced perfect—a mistress, a four-wheeled post chaise, and a French valet. The beau's dishes are all French. His conversation is so fantastic that every sentence he utters is almost as heterogeneous a mixture as a salmagundy. He never complains of the vapors, but tells you that he is much *ennuyé*. He does not affect to be genteel but *dégagé*. Nor is he taken with an elegant simplicity in a beautiful countenance, but breaks out in raptures on a *je ne sais quoi* and a certain naiveté. In a word, his head as well as his heels is entirely French and he is a thorough *petit maître*.

The art of combing the wig gracefully in public he studies with great assiduity and for that purpose carries a comb in an elegant case. Combing a wig is equivalent to twirling a moustache.

When he goes out to the dance, the ring, the play, he perfumes himself with oil of Venus, spirit of lavender, attar of roses, spirit of cinnamon or *eau de luce,* dabs his face with scented powder till it is as white as a miller's and plasters his hair with pomatum. Then he smears his upper lip with snuff.

> A coxcomb, a fop, a dainty milk sop
> Who essenc'd and dizen'd from bottom to top,
> Looks just like a doll for a milliner's shop.
> A thing full of prate and pride and conceit,
> All fashion, no weight,
> Who shrugs, and takes snuff, and carries a muff,
> A minnikin, finicking, French powder puff.

The macaronis, as the young ones about town are called, astonish the outside world by the gigantic scale of their play, the shortness of their coats, the looseness of their breeches, the height of their toupées, the smallness of their hats, and the size of their nosegays. They are in the habit of carrying two watches—one to indicate what time it is and the other to indicate what time it is not. They have a mincing air and whistle songs through their toothpicks.

Lastly comes the young blood—a baboon in men's clothes. Sherlock has instructed him in the use of the broadsword, and Broughton has taught him to box. He is a fine gentleman at assemblies, a sharper at the gaming table, and a bully at the casinos. He has not yet killed his man in the *honorable* way, but he has gallantly crippled several watchman, and most courageously run a drawer through the body. His scanty pay will not allow him to keep a mistress, but it is said he is privately married to a woman of the town. . . .

Goldsmith is walking along the Strand one day decked out in gay attire, with bagwig and sword, when two such coxcombs confront him, and one of them, pointing to the poet, calls out to his companion, "Look at that fly with a long pin stuck through it." Whereupon Goldy instantly calls aloud to the passersby. "Beware, ladies and gentlemen, of that brace of disguised pickpockets." And walking from the footpath into the coachway to give himself more room, and half drawing his sword, he beckons to the witty gentleman, armed in a like manner, to follow him. But the coxcomb declines the invitation, and sneaks away amid the hooting of the spectators.

Masquerading in an old English costume, Goldsmith attends the monthly ball at the Pantheon. Approximately two thousand persons are present. The fourteen rooms are ablaze with lights and decorations. The supper and wine are splendid. My lady Margaret Fordyce appears as Queen Elizabeth, Lady Villars as a Sultana sparkling with £30,000 worth of diamonds, Lady Gideon as a spinning girl, and Mrs. Bouverie and Mrs. Crewe as the two Merry Wives of Windsor. Facetious Mr. Southcote, in the character of a Smithfield butcher, keeps feeling his ribs from time to time and estimating his weight and value at the present high price of butcher's meat. Then there are Mrs. Fisher as Columbine, Captain Rice as a Billingsgate fishwoman, Mr. Talbot of Lincoln's Inn as a Stockwell clock, Mr. McDonald in full tartans and armed to the teeth, and the Horneck family, all as French dancers, in dresses of the same cut and fashion, and looking—notwithstanding the sex of one of them—like the three Graces. They are watched over by Goldsmith and Sir Joshua.

GOLDY

The wags single out the poet for their pleasure. Some, pretending not to know him, decry his writings and praise those of his despised contemporaries. Others laud his verses to the skies but purposely misquote and burlesque them. Others annoy him with parodies—while one young lady, who is dressed as a delicate macaroni thing, and whom he teases (as he supposes) with great success, silences his boisterous laugh by quoting his own line about the "loud laugh that speaks the vacant mind."

Still, despite these petty annoyances, Goldsmith is very happy—serving the Jessamy Bride and Little Comedy with supper, hurrying to get them wine, dancing with them, and importuning the female conjurers to tell their fortunes.

Sir Joshua retires early. And soon after Goldsmith sees the Hornecks to their carriages. But our bard is one of those determined visitors who breakfast on the remains of supper—astonishing the early dealers in Oxford Market as they troop to their chairs and coaches in the early May dawn, saluting the milk maids as they come in from the country, and watching the fiddlers and their zanies already stirring in the streets.

His name appearing in the newspapers among the distinguished persons present at one of these masquerades, his old enemy Kenrick serves him up a copy of anonymous verses:

TO DR. GOLDSMITH
On Seeing His Name In The List of Mummers At The Late Masquerade

How widely different, Goldsmith, are the ways
Of doctors now, and those of ancient days!
Theirs taught the truth in academic shades,
Ours in lewd hops and midnight masquerades.
So changed the times! say, philosophic sage,
Whose genius suits so well this tasteful age,
Is the Pantheon, late a sink obscene,
Become the fountain of chaste Hippocrene?

Or do thy moral numbers quaintly flow,
Inspired by th' Aganippe of Soho? . . .
Is this the good that makes the humble vain,
The good, philosophy should not disdain?
If so, let pride dissemble all it can,
A modern sage is still much less than man.

Goldsmith meets Kenrick at the Chapter Coffee House and calls him to sharp account for taking such liberty with his name. Kenrick shuffles and sneaks, protesting that he meant nothing derogatory to his character. Goldsmith, however, lets him know that another such outrage will be followed by personal chastisement.

Sir Joshua Reynolds, calling on the poet one morning, finds him walking about his room, kicking a bundle of clothes before him like a football.

"Why, sir," remarks Goldsmith, "this is an expensive masquerade dress which I have been fool enough to purchase, and as there is no other way of getting my money's worth, I am trying to take it out in exercise. . . ."

~~~~~~

CHAPTER 40

THE ROWLEY MANUSCRIPTS

ON ST. GEORGE'S DAY, April 23, 1771, the first annual dinner of the Royal Academy is held in the exhibition room. Sir Joshua, handsomely dressed, face beaming with pleasure, ear trumpet at hand, presides. And around him sit his fellow Academicians and five and twenty gentlemen of high position and distinguished taste who are his guests. On the walls are already hung the pictures which will be open to public inspection the following day.

Horace Walpole perhaps is also there. Long slender figure dressed in a lavender suit, waistcoat embroidered with silver, partridge silk stockings, gold buckles, and lace ruffles and frills. His eyes are dark, bright, lively—his forehead very pale and smooth. He enters the room in the style of affected delicacy—chapeau bras between his hands, as if he wishes to compress it, knees bent and feet on tiptoe as if afraid of a wet floor.

There is nothing natural about Horace Walpole—even his gait is formed upon a French dancing master's idea of the mincing of Agag, King of the Amalekites. . . .

He is near enough to Johnson and Goldsmith to hear their conversation. It is on the subject of some poems in manuscript, which sometime before, had been found in a chest in St. Mary Redcliffe, Bristol, and is said to be the work of one Rowley, a priest who lived in the fifteenth century. Dr. Goldsmith warmly affirms his belief in the authenticity of the poems and Johnson laughs at him. It is the moment for the supreme arbiter to interpose—"Forgeries," he cries, "all forgeries! I might, had I pleased, have had the honor of ushering this great discovery into the learned world, but I detected the fraud at once and declined to allow my name to be associated with such a thing."

Then Goldsmith informs him of the sequel to his trifling with the Rowley manuscripts—the death of the boy Chatterton. "The persons of honor and veracity who were present," says Walpole in after years, "will attest with what surprise and concern I thus first heard of his death. . . ."

(Later Goldsmith arranges to be introduced to George Catcott, the pewterer who sponsored Chatterton. Goldsmith desires to buy the manuscripts, but he lacks the necessary cash, and Catcott refuses to accept a promissory note. Eventually Goldsmith is persuaded that the poems are Chatterton's, but not before he has quarrelled with his friend Thomas Percy on the subject.)

But Walpole is avenged before the distinguished guests separate, and Goldsmith is put in his proper place. A short distance away from the poet is seated Moser, the Swiss, Keeper of the Academy. On seeing Dr. Johnson roll himself in his chair, as if about to speak, he shouts, "Hush, hush, the Toctor is going to zay zomething." Dr. Goldsmith is amazed that the way is being cleared for him. "No, no," shrieks Moser, "it is not you, but the great Toctor, I mean."

In the month of August there appears anonymously the *History of England*—in four volumes, compiled chiefly from Rapin, Carte, Smollett, and Hume, "each of whom," says Goldsmith in the preface, "has his admirers, in proportion as the reader is studious of political antiquities, fond of minute anecdote, a warm partisan, or a deliberate reasoner." It is a lively, readable piece of work, but it draws some sharp bobs from political scribblers. The Whig faction accuses him of being a Tory, and the Tory faction of being a Whig. . . . When a compiler draws upon four authors, he naturally incorporates into his work four sets of blunders.

Tom Davies becomes alarmed and takes the field full armed for his friend—and his property. Accordingly, a formal defense of the book appears in *The Public Advertiser*. "Have you seen," he writes to Granger, *An Impartial Account of Goldsmith's History of England?* If you want to know who was the writer of it, you will find him in Russell Street—but mum!"

Goldsmith seems concerned to discredit the Whigs as champions of liberty and on the other hand to establish both the loyalty of the Tories to the Revolution settlement and their superior worth to the people. We are no longer told that "the motives of a mob, though often wrong, are always honest."

Perhaps this attitude is due to Goldsmith's growing desire for a pension, for his spleen is directed against the kind of monarch under whom "men of real merit" are left to contempt and misery.

In the long run his moderate or slightly conservative position probably contributes to the success of the book. In fifty years it goes through twelve editions in its original four volume form and twice as many in the one volume abridgment that he makes later. Few of Goldsmith's works are more thoroughly read than the *History of England*.

To Bennet Langton, at his seat in Lincolnshire, where he has settled in domestic bliss, having the year previously married the Countess Dowager of Rothes, Goldsmith writes: "MY DEAR SIR—Since I had the pleasure of seeing you last, I have been almost wholly in the country, at a farmer's house, quite alone, trying to write a comedy. It is now finished, but when or how it will be acted, or whether it will be acted at all, are questions I cannot resolve. I am therefore so much employed upon that, that I

am under the necessity of putting off my intended visit to Lincolnshire for this season. Reynolds is just returned from Paris, and finds himself now in the case of a truant that must make up for his idle time by diligence. We have therefore agreed to postpone our journey till next summer, when we hope to have the honor of waiting upon Lady Rothes and you, and staying double the time of our late intended visit. We often meet and never without remembering you. I see Mr. Beauclerc very often both in town and country. He is now going directly forward to become a second Boyle, deep in chemistry and physics. Johnson has been down on a visit to a country parson, Dr. Taylor, and is returned to his old haunts at Mrs. Thrale's. Burke is a farmer, *en attendant* a better place, but visiting about too. Every soul is visiting about and merry but myself. And that is hard too, as I have been trying these three months to do something to make people laugh. There have I been strolling about the hedges, studying jests with a most tragical countenance. The *Natural History* is about half finished, and I will shortly finish the rest. God knows I am tired of this kind of finishing, which is but bungling work, and that not so much my fault as the fault of my scurvy circumstances. They begin to talk in town of the Opposition's gaining ground. The cry of liberty is still as loud as ever. I have published, or Davies has published for me, an Abridgement of the *History of England,* for which I have been a good deal abused in the newspapers, for betraying the liberties of the people. God knows I had no thought for or against liberty in my head, my whole aim being to make up a book of a decent size, that, as 'Squire Richard says, *would do no harm to nobody.* However, they set me down as an arrant Tory, and consequently an honest man. When you come to look at any part of it, you'll say that I am a sore Whig. God bless you, and with my most respectful compliments to her Ladyship, I remain, dear sir, your most affectionate humble servant,
OLIVER GOLDSMITH."

CHAPTER 41

THE FANTOCCINI

POOR KELLY's splendid career has come to an ignominious close. No sooner has his sudden success given promise of a rising man than the hacks of the ministry have laid hold of him. When Garrick announces his next comedy, *A Word to the Wise,* a word goes rapidly round the town to a wider audience, exasperated by his servile support of feeble and profligate rulers—and poor Kelly's fate is sealed. The play is hardly listened to. He has the melancholy satisfaction that it has fallen before liberty and Wilkes, not before laughter and wit, but the sentence is a decisive one.

No man, however, profits more by a sudden change of fortune in his favor. Prosperity causes a remarkable alteration in his conduct. From a low, petulant, absurd, and ill-bred censurer, he is transformed into a humane, affable, good-natured and well-bred man.

On the fall of Hugh Kelly, there arises a more formidable antagonist in the person of Richard Cumberland. He comes into the field with every social advantage. He is the son and grandson of a bishop; his mother is the celebrated Bentley's daughter; he has himself held a fellowship at Trinity and has acted as private secretary to Lord Halifax.

His first comedy, ushered in by a prologue, in which he

attacks all contemporary dramatists and compliments Garrick as "the immortal actor," is played at Covent Garden. Garrick being present and charmed by the unexpected compliment (for in earlier days he rejected a tragedy by Cumberland) makes himself known to the author, and a second comedy, *The West Indian,* in sentimental style, is secured for Drury Lane.

Cumberland thinks himself the creator of his own school and ignores the existence of poor Kelly. He vouchsafes ridiculous airs of patronage to men who stand above him. He professes a lofty indifference to criticism that tortures him—which makes Garrick call him a man without a skin. He abuses those dramatists most heartily whose notions he is readiest to borrow. And he has a stock of conceit which is proof against every effort to diminish it.

> Here Cumberland lies, having acted his parts,
> The Terence of England, the mender of hearts;
> A flattering painter, who made it his care
> To draw men as they ought to be, not as they are.
> His gallants are all faultless, his women divine,
> And comedy wonders at being so fine;
> Like a tragedy queen he has dizened her out,
> Or rather like tragedy giving a rout.
> His fools have their follies so lost in a crowd
> Of virtues and feelings, that folly grows proud;
> And coxcombs, alike in their failings alone,
> Adopting his portraits, are pleased with their own.
> Say, where has our poet this malady caught?
> Or wherefore his characters thus without fault?
> Say, was it that vainly directing his view
> To find out men's virtues, and finding them few,
> Quite sick of pursuing each troublesome elf,
> He grew lazy at last, and drew from himself?

Nevertheless Goldsmith is conscious of an opponent in the author of *The West Indian* and goes to the country to pursue his labor undisturbed. He takes lodgings for the

summer at a farmhouse near the six mile stone on the
Edgeware Road—and likes it so much that he returns to it
the following summer to finish his *Natural History*, carrying down his books in two returned postchaises. Bozzy
goes to see him, but he is not at home. Being curious to
see his apartment, however, he goes in and finds curious
scraps of descriptions of animals scrawled upon the walls
with a black lead pencil.

The farmhouse stands on a little hill, overlooking a
pretty country. The house is old fashioned and irregular,
but lodgeable and commodious. The greens and walks are
kept in the nicest order—and all is rural and romantic.

He takes the young folks of the family to see the strolling players at Hendon; he comes home one night without
shoes, having left them stuck fast in the mud; he has the
evil habit of reading in bed and of putting out the candle
by flinging his slipper at it.

He spends most of the time in his room, negligently
dressed, with his shirt collar open, busily writing. Sometimes in a fit of abstraction, he wanders into the kitchen
without noticing anyone, stands musing with his back to
the fire, and then hurries off again to scribble down on
paper a thought that has struck him.

He is fond of the humble place. The farmer's family
think him an odd character, and he is to them what
The Spectator appeared to the landlady and her children.
He is the Gentleman.

Although the farmhouse is Goldsmith's headquarters for
the summer, he absents himself for weeks at a time on
visits to Lord Clare and Mr. Langton at their country
seats. He visits town also to dine at the Club and enjoy the
amusements. On one occasion he accompanies Burke to
witness a performance of the Italian Fantoccini or Puppets
in Panton Street—the caprice of the town. When Burke
praises the dexterity with which one of them tosses a pike,
"Pshaw," says Goldsmith with some warmth, "I can do it
better myself."

The same evening they sup at Burke's lodgings, and in attempting to exhibit to the company how much better he can jump over a stick than the puppets, he breaks his shin. Foote, the Aristophanes of the stage, seeing the success of the Fantoccini, announces that he will produce a primitive puppet show at the Haymarket, to be entitled, "The Handsome Chambermaid or Piety in Pattens"—intended to burlesque the sentimental comedy which Garrick still maintains at Drury Lane. The whole town is agog with excitement.

"Will your puppets be as large as life, Mr. Foote?" demands a lady of rank.

"Oh, no, my lady," replies Foote, "not much larger than Garrick."

CHAPTER 42

BARTON FESTIVITIES

IN AUGUST OF 1771, Little Comedy marries Henry William Bunbury, Esquire, and shortly afterwards Goldsmith is invited to visit the couple at their seat, at Barton, in Suffolk.

How can he resist the temptation? His means are insufficient, but he procures an advance from Francis Newbery, Jr. (who has succeeded his father) on the promise of a new tale in the style of *The Vicar of Wakefield*. And so, his purse replenished, by hook or crook, he posts off to visit the bride at Barton.

He finds there a joyous household. Garrick is there, too, and assumes the part of master of the revels. He soon gives in to Doctor Goldsmith's "ridiculosity." "Come," Goldsmith says to him, "let us play the fool a little. . . ."

First, blind man's buff. "Hot cockles" succeeds next, "questions and commands" follows, and last of all they sit down to hunt the slipper. As every person may not be acquainted with this primeval pastime, it may be necessary to observe the following: that the company in this play plants itself in a ring upon the ground, all except one who stands in the middle, and whose business it is to catch a shoe which the others shove about under their hams from one to another, something like a weaver's shuttle. As it is impossible, in this case, for the lady who is up to face all the company at once, the great beauty of the play lies in hitting her a thump with the heel of the shoe on that side least capable of making a defense. It is in this manner that Little Comedy is hemmed in, and thumped about, all blowzed, in spirits, and bawling for "fair play" with a voice that might deafen a ballad singer— when confusion on confusion! who should enter the room but the Hornecks' two great acquaintances from town, Lady Blarney and Miss Carolina Wilhelmina Amelia Skeggs! Description would but beggar—therefore it is unnecessary to describe—this new mortification. To be seen by ladies of such high breeding in such vulgar attitudes! The party is stuck to the ground for some time, as if actually petrified with amazement.

The two ladies are uneasy to know what accident could have kept the girls from church the day before. The Jessamy Bride undertakes to be the prolocutor and delivers the whole in a summary way, only saying, "We were thrown from our horses." At which account the ladies are greatly concerned, but being told the family received no hurt, they are extremely glad; but being informed that they were almost killed by the fright, they are vastly sorry; but hearing that they had a very good night, they are extremely glad again. Nothing can exceed their friendship with the girls. Lady Blarney is particularly attached to Little Comedy; Miss Carolina Wilhelmina Amelia Skeggs (I love to give the whole name) takes a greater fancy to the Jessamy Bride.

There are other guests at Barton—Miss Squeeze and Beau Tibbs and Mr. Honeywood and Dr. Nonentity, a metaphysician. Most people think him a profound scholar, but as he seldom speaks, they cannot be positive in that particular. He generally spreads himself before the fire, sucks his pipe, talks little, drinks much, and is reckoned very good company. Then there is Tim Syllabub, a droll creature. He sometimes shines as a star of the first magnitude among the choice spirits of the age. He is reckoned equally excellent at a rebus, a riddle, a bawdy song, and a hymn for the Tabernacle. You will know him—in town, of course, for he has rigged himself out in a new suit and clean linen—by his shabby finery, his powdered wig, dirty shirt, and broken silk stockings.

Then there are Lady Fluff, Mr. Cheer (with laughing eyes and plump red cheeks) Squire Thornhill and Sophronia—the sagacious Sophronia—how shall I mention her? She was taught to love Greek and hate men from her very infancy. She rejected fine gentlemen because they were not pedants, and pedants because they were not fine gentlemen. Her exquisite sensibility taught her to discover every fault in every lover, and her inflexible justice prevented her pardoning them. Thus she rejected several offers, till the wrinkles of age overtook her, and now, without one good feature in her face, she talks incessantly of the beauties of the mind.

And lastly there is our wandering philosopher, Lien Chi Altangi, in a cut velvet coat of a cinnamon color, lined with pink satin, embroidered all over with gold—his waistcoat, which is cloth of silver, embroidered with gold likewise.

But heaven! Here comes Mr. Lofty, speaking to his servant—and Mrs. Horneck runs to meet him.

Lofty. "And if the Venetian ambassador, or that teasing creature the Marquis, should call, I'm not at home. Dam'me, I'll be pack horse to none of them. My dear madam, I have just snatched a moment—And if the expresses to his Grace be ready, let them be sent off; they're of importance. Madam, I ask a thousand pardons."

Mrs. Horneck. "Sir, this honor——"

Lofty. "And, Dubardieu! if the person calls about the commission, let him know that it is made out. As for Lord Cumbercourt's stale request, it can keep cold, you understand me. Madam, I ask ten thousand pardons.

Mrs. Horneck. "Sir, this honor——"

Lofty. "And, Dubardieu! If the man comes from the Cornish borough, you must do him, you must do him, I say. Madam, I ask ten thousand pardons—and if the Russian ambassador calls—but he will scarce call today, I believe. And now, madam, I have just got time to express my happiness in having the honor of being permitted to profess myself your most obedient, humble servant."

Mrs. Horneck. (gasping.) "Sir, the happiness and honor are all mine, and yet, I'm only robbing the public while I detain you."

Lofty. "Sink the public, madam, when the fair are to be attended. Ah, could all my hours be so charmingly devoted! Sincerely, don't you pity us poor creatures in affairs? Thus it is eternally—solicited for places here, teased for pensions there, and courted everywhere. I know you pity me. Yes, I see you do.

Mrs. Horneck. "Excuse me, sir. 'Toils of empires pleasures are,' as Waller says."

Lofty. "Waller, Waller, is he of the house?"

Mrs. Horneck. "The modern poet of that name, sir."

Lofty. "Oh, a modern! We men of business despise the moderns, and as for the ancients, we have no time to read them. Poetry is a pretty thing enough for our wives and daughters, but not for us. Why now, here I stand that know nothing of books. I say, madam, that I know nothing of books, and yet, I believe, upon a land carriage fishery, a stamp act, or a jag hire, I can talk my two hours without feeling the want of them. . . ."

Time for dinner. The guests gather in the hall. Fiddles sing; wax lights, fine dresses, fine plate, glitter and sparkle. The order of the table:

> At the upper end of the Table a dish of fish
> Afterwards removed for a Soop;
> Under that a Venison Pasty;
> And last, under the Venison Pasty, a Chine of Mutton
> On the further side, a little below the first dish
> A White Fricassee,

And under that, Bacon and Beans.
And on the near side, facing the White Fricassee, an Orange
Pudding
And on the same side, facing the Bacon and Beans
Tongue and Colliflowers.

Second Course.
At the upper end of the Table, Partridges,
Under that, Sweetmeat Tarts of all sorts,
And last under the Sweetmeat Tarts, Young
Rabbits.
On the further side, below the first dish,
Marrow Pasties;
And under that, Roasted Pigeons.
And on the near side, facing the Marrow Pasties,
Veal Sweetbreads.
And on the same side, facing the Roasted Pigeons,
A Dish of young peas.

Of course there is wine—and it is delicious, coming, as
Little Comedy explains, from her mother's cellar. The good
woman is equal to making wine out of anything that comes
to hand—orange, lemon, raisin, ginger, gooseberry, rasp-
berry, blackberry, currants, cowslips, sycamore, birch, wal-
nut, elder flower, balm, etc., etc.—and her storeroom is a
fortress provisioned for a siege.

Amid the laughter, bustle, and talk, the clinking of
glasses and the clatter of plates, Goldsmith holds forth on
the frivolity of fashion. "Today you are lifted on stilts—tomorrow you lower your heels and raise your heads. Your
clothes at one time are bloated out with whalebone—and
now you have laid your hoops aside and are become as
slim as mermaids. Ay, everything is in a state of continual
fluctuation. The train that's worn today—would you believe
it? We who are so fond of seeing our women with long
tails, at the same time dock our horses to the very rump.
It——"

Lofty. "Why, yes, madam, I believe Sir William had
some reason to confide in my judgment, one little reason,

perhaps. Why, madam—but let it go no further—it was I procured him his place——"

Goldsmith. "It—a lady's train——"

Lofty. "A mere bagatelle! a mere bagatelle!"

Goldsmith. "Is not bought but at some expense, and after it has swept the public walks for a very few evenings, is fit to be worn no longer. More silk must be bought in order to repair the breach, and some ladies of peculiar economy are thus found to patch up their tails eight or ten times in a season. Nay, I venture to affirm that a train may often bring a lady into the most critical circumstances, for should a rude fellow offer to come up to ravish a kiss, and the lady attempt to avoid it, in retiring she must necessarily tread upon her train, and thus fall fairly upon her back; by which means, everyone knows—her clothes may be spoiled. . . ."

The ladies laugh and clap their hands, the gentlemen chuckle. . . . Finally the cloth is drawn, the port goes round, and toasts are drunk with fervor. The King, the Prince of Wales, all the Royal family are honored in turn.

Then the guests retire to the ballroom. It so happens that there are not chairs enough for the whole company, and Mr. Thornhill immediately proposes that every gentleman shall sit upon a lady's lap. This Mrs. Horneck positively objects to, notwithstanding some looks of disapprobation from Goldsmith and Mrs. Bunbury. A servant is therefore dispatched for a couple of chair, which are soon provided. Conversation is brisk and lively, then slow and heavy by turns, Bunbury finally suggesting a few country dances. The music consists of two fiddles with a pipe and tabor. Goldy and the Jessamy Bride lead up the ball and the guests follow. The ladies of the town, Lady Blarney and Miss Carolina Wilhelmina Amelia Skeggs, strive hard to be easy, but without success. They swim, sprawl, languish, and frisk, but all will not do. After the dance has continued about an hour, as they are apprehensive of catching cold, they move to break up the ball. One of them expresses her sentiments upon this occasion in a very coarse manner, observing, "By Jingo, I am all of a muck of a sweat." Then the two ladies seat themselves in a corner of the room and talk of nothing but high life, and high-lived company, with other fashionable topics, such as pictures, taste, Shakespeare, and the musical glasses.

The rest of the company gathers closely round a cozy fire, cracks jokes, tells stories, and sings songs.

"Doctor Goldsmith, take your guitar, and thrum us a little song. 'The Lambs on the Green Hills'—I think you go through it very prettily."

"Does he so? Then let's have it."

"Up with it boldly, sir."

"Ay, a song! a song!"

"Silence, a song!"

> The lambs on the green hills stood gazing on me,
> And many strawberries grew round the salt sea,
> And many strawberries grew round the salt sea,
> And many a ship sailed the ocean.
>
> The bride and bride's party to church they did go,
> The bride she rode foremost, she bears the best show,
> But I followed after her with my heart full of woe,
> To see my love wed to another.
>
> The first place I saw her 'twas in the church stand,
> Gold rings on her finger and love by the hand,
> Says I, "My wee lassie, I will be the man,
> Although you are wed to another."
>
> The next place I seen her was on the way home,
> I ran on before her, not knowing where to roam,
> Says I, "My wee lassie, I'll be by your side,
> Although you are wed to another."
>
> The next place I seen her, 'twas laid in bride's bed,
> I jumped in beside her and did kiss the bride;
> "Stop stop," says the groomsman, "till I speak a word,

Will you venture your life on the point of my sword?
For courting so slowly you've lost this fair maid,
So begone, for you'll never enjoy her."

Oh, make my grave then both large, wide, and deep,
And sprinkle it over with flowers so sweet,
And lay me down in it to take my last sleep,
For that's the best way to forget her.

"Bravo! Bravo!"

"Very good upon my word."

"Come, here's Dr. Goldsmith's health, and may he one day be a bishop."

Lofty. (running up to Goldsmith). "Ah monsieur, si douce, si triste, si—er—ah! isn't it though, madame. Encore! encore!"

"Well, then, another song."

"Ay, another song!"

A glance from the Jessamy Bride.

> When lovely woman stoops to folly
>   And finds too late that men betray,
> What charm can soothe her melancholy,
>   What art can wash her guilt away?
>
> The only art her guilt to cover,
>   To hide her shame from every eye,
> To give repentance to her lover,
>   And wring his bosom—is, to die.

"Bravo! brav——"

"All I know of the matter is this, that it may be true, or may not be true, but this I can assure your Ladyship, that the whole rout was in amaze. His Lordship turned all manner of colors, my Lady fell into a *sound*, but Sir Tompkyn drawing his sword, swore he was hers to the last drop of his blood."

"Well," replies our Peeress Lady Blarney, "this I can

say, that the Duchess never told me a syllable of the matter, and I believe her Grace would keep nothing a secret from me. This you may depend upon as fact, that the next morning my Lord Duke cried out three times to his *valet de chambre,* Jernigan! Jernigan! Jernigan! bring me my garters."

During this discourse, Goldsmith turns his face to the fire, and at the conclusion of every sentence cries out, "Fudge," which amuses the company very much.

"Besides, my dear Skeggs," continues our Peeress, "there is nothing of this in the copy of verses that Dr. Burdock made upon the occasion."

"Fudge!"

"I am surprised at that," cries Miss Skeggs, "for he seldom leaves anything out, as he writes only for his own amusement. But can your Ladyship favor me with a sight of them?"

"Fudge!"

"My dear creature," replies our Peeress, "do you think I carry such things about me? Indeed, I was ever an admirer of all Dr. Burdock's little pieces; for, except what he does, and our dear Countess at Hanover Square, there's nothing come out but the most lowest stuff in nature—not a bit of high life among them."

"Fudge!"

"Your Ladyship should except," says the other, "your own things in the *Lady's Magazine.* I hope you'll say there's nothing low lived there? But I suppose we are to have no more from that quarter?"

"Fudge!"

"Why, my dear," says the lady, "you know my reader and companion has left me to be married to Captain Roach, and as my poor eyes won't suffer me to write myself, I have been for some time looking out for another. A proper person is no easy matter to find, and, to be sure, thirty pounds a year is a small stipend for a well-bred girl of character that can read, write, and behave in company.

As for the chits about town, there is no bearing them about one."

"Fudge!"

"That I know," cries Miss Skeggs, "by experience. For of the three companions I had this last half year, one of them refused to do plain work an hour in the day. Another thought twenty-five guineas a year too small a salary, and I was obliged to send away the third, because I suspected an intrigue with the chaplain. Virtue, my dear Lady Blarney, virtue is worth any price—but where is that to be found?"

"Fudge!"

CHAPTER 43

A LAMENT

"IN BED. Monday morning, February 10, 1772. W. Woodfall's Compliments to Doctor Goldsmith, his Proposal as to Price is agreed to. It was intended by W. W. to call on him this morning to inform him that it was wished by Mrs. Cornelys to have the entertainment consist of two parts. Both with a view of relieving the performers and preserving the auditors from dulness from too great a length of solemnity. . . . Doctor Goldsmith is himself, it is presumed, a Judge of Music. If any proper composition strikes him, his writing to it will be highly serviceable. The whole matter is at present but an idea. It is intended to perform something on the occasion of the Death of her late Royal Highness, the P. Dowager. . . ."

A young man of fortune, Joseph Cradock, living in Leicestershire, brings up with him to London his wife, a translation of one of Voltaire's tragedies, and introductions to celebrated people. He is very eager about plays and players, being a clever amateur musician and a private little Garrick. Goldsmith meets him at the house of Yates, the actor, and finding that he is a friend of Lord Clare, soon becomes intimate with him. He furnishes the embryo dramatist with a prologue and epilogue for his tragedy of

Zobeide, and Cradock, in return, arranges the music for the "Threnodia Augustalis," a lament on the death of the Princess Dowager of Wales, the political mistress of Lord Clare. The tragedy is played with some success at Covent Garden; the Lament is recited and sung at Mrs. Cornelys' rooms in Soho Square.

"Ah! Mr. Cradock!" cries Goldsmith on seeing the lettered ease of this amateur author and the time he can bestow on the elaboration of a manuscript, "think of me that must write a volume every month."

2.

A poor Irish youth, M'Veagh M'Donnell, stranded in London, throws himself—on a seat in the Temple Gardens, and willing to forget his miseries for a while, draws out from his pocket a book—a volume of Boileau. He has not been there long, when a gentleman, strolling about, passes near him, and observing, perhaps, something Irish about him, comes up and says, "Sir, you seem studious. I hope you find this a favorable place to pursue it."

"Not very studious, sir. I fear it is the want of society that brings me hither. I am solitary and unknown in the metropolis." And a passage from Cicero, occurring to him, he quotes it.

"You are a scholar, too, sir, I perceive."

"A piece of one, sir, but I ought still to have been in the college where I had the good fortune to pick up the little I know."

A long conversation follows. M'Donnell tells part of his history, and the gentleman, in return, desiring him to call soon, gives his address in the Temple. To M'Donnell's surprise he finds that the person is none other than the distinguished Doctor Goldsmith.

The young man keeps the appointment and is received very kindly. Dr. Goldsmith tells him that he is not rich, that he can give him little pecuniary aid, but that he will enable him to do something for himself. At least he can furnish him with some useful advice. "In London," Goldsmith continues, "nothing is to be got for nothing. You must work, and no man who chooses to be industrious need be under obligations to another, for here labor of every kind commands its rewards. If you think proper to assist me occasionally, I shall be obliged, and you will be placed under no obligation, until something more permanent can be secured for you."

Accordingly, M'Donnell is set about translating passages from Buffon for insertion in the *Animated Nature*.

On M'Donnell's advice, Goldsmith engages an amanuensis to take down from dictation his own compositions. But the experiment proves a failure. Goldsmith and the amanuensis sit looking at each other for some time, the one wondering what to say and the other wondering what to do. At length the author rises quietly, and going up to the young man, slips a guinea into his hand and dismisses him courteously.

CHAPTER 44

NESTOR

ANOTHER ACQUAINTANCE is General James Oglethorpe. Oglethorpe's ears, eyes, limbs, articulation and memory would suit a boy if a boy could recollect a century backward. His teeth are gone; he is a shadow, and a wrinkled one; but his spirits are in full bloom. He is quite a preux chevalier, heroic, romantic, etc. He flirts prodigiously. He has survived his times, but can outwalk men half his age. By 1785 he is one of the three persons still living who were mentioned by Mr. Pope. Lord Mansfield and Lord Marchmont are the other two. He has learned from Tomo-Chi-Chi how to live long, and he still lives on in a world of new things. Youngsters whisper with awe that in his youth he shot snipe in Conduit Street, near the corner of Bond Street. . . . He realizes our ideas of Nestor.

Burke talks a good deal of politics with Oglethorpe. He tells him later with great truth that he looks upon him as a more extraordinary person than any he has read of, for that he has founded the province of Georgia, has absolutely called it into being, and has lived to see it severed from the empire which created it and become an independent state.

The last mention we have of him is, when writing in

1785, but a very few days before his death, Miss Hannah More says, "I am just going to flirt a couple of hours with my beau General Oglethorpe. . . ."

His table is often the gathering place of men of wit and talent. Johnson is frequently there and delights in drawing from the General details of his various "experiences." He is anxious that he should give the world his life. "I know no man," says he, "whose life would be more interesting." Still the vivacity of the General's mind and the variety of his knowledge makes him skip from subject to subject too fast for the lexicographer. "Oglethorpe," growls he, "never completes what he says."

On April 10, 1772, Goldsmith dines in company with Johnson and Boswell at Oglethorpe's. After dinner when the cloth is drawn, Boswell fires up the brave old General with a question of the moral propriety of duelling.

"Undoubtedly," says the General with a lofty air, "a man has the right to defend his honor."

Goldsmith turns to Boswell. "I ask you first, sir, what would you do if you were affronted."

"I should think it necessary to fight."

"Why, then," replies Goldsmith, "that solves the question."

"No, sir," roars Johnson, "it does not solve the question. It does not follow that what a man would do is therefore right."

Boswell now says that he wishes to have it settled whether duelling is contrary to the laws of Christianity, and Johnson immediately enters on the subject. "Sir, as men become in a high degree refined, various causes of offence arise, which are considered to be of such importance that life must be staked to atone for them, though in reality, they are not so. A body that has received a very fine polish may be easily hurt. Before men arrive at this artificial refinement, if one tells his neighbor he lies, his neighbor tells him he lies; if one gives his neighbor a blow, his neighbor gives him a blow, but in a state of highly polished society, an affront is held to be a serious injury. It must therefore be resented, or rather a duel must be fought upon it, as men have agreed to banish from their society one who puts up with an affront without fighting a duel. Now, sir, it is never unlawful to fight in self defence. He, then, who fights a duel does not fight from passion against his antagonist, but out of self defence—to avert the stigma of the world and to prevent himself from being driven out of society. I could wish there was not that superfluity of refinement, but while such notions prevail, no doubt a man may lawfully fight a duel."

The General now tells an anecdote bearing on the subject. When he was a very young man, only fifteen, serving under Prince Eugene of Savoy, he was sitting in company at table with a Prince of Wurtemberg. The Prince took up a glass of wine and by fillip made some of it fly in Oglethorpe's face. Here was a nice dilemma. To have challenged him instantly might have fixed on himself the character of a drawcansir; to have taken no notice of it might have been considered as cowardice. So keeping his eye on the Prince, and smiling all the time, as if he took what his Highness had done in jest, he said, "My Prince, that's a good joke, but we do it much better in England"—and threw a whole glass of wine in the Prince's face.

"Il a bien fait, mon Prince," cried an old general present. "Vous l'avez commencé." (He has done right, my Prince. You commenced it.) And thus all ended in good humor.

Dr. Johnson says, "Pray, General, give us an account of the siege of Belgrade." Upon which the General, pouring a little wine upon the table, and drawing his lines and parallels, describes everything with a wet finger. "Here were we—here were the Turks," etc.—to which Johnson listens with eager attention, poring over the plans and diagrams with his usual purblind closeness.

A question is now started how far people who disagree in a capital point can live in friendship together. Johnson says they may. Goldsmith says they cannot, as they have not the *idem velle atque idem nolle*, the same likings and aversions.

"Why, sir," returns Johnson, "you must shun the subject as to which you disagree. For instance, I can live very well with Burke. I love his knowledge, his genius, his diffusion and affluence of conversation, but I would not talk to him of the Rockingham party."

"But, sir," retorts Goldsmith, "when people live together who have something as to which they disagree and which they want to shun, they will be in the situation mentioned in the story of Bluebeard, 'You may look into all the chambers but one.' But we should have the greatest inclination to look into that chamber, to talk of that subject."

"Sir," thunders Johnson, "I am not saying that *you* could live in friendship with a man from whom you differ as to some point. I am only saying that *I* could do it."

The conversation turns upon ghosts. General Oglethorpe tells the story of a Colonel Prendergast, an officer in the Duke of Marlborough's army, who predicted among his comrades that he would die on a certain day. The battle of Malplaquet took place that day—the Colonel was in the thick of it, but came out unhurt. The firing had ceased, and his brother officers, while they were yet in the field, jestingly asked him where was his prophecy now. "The day is not over," Prendergast answered gravely. "I shall die notwithstanding what you see." Soon afterwards, there came a shot from a French battery, to which the order for a cessation of firing had not reached, and he was killed upon the spot. Colonel Cecil, who took possession of his effects, found in his pocket the following solemn entry.

[Here the date] "Dreamt—or was told by an apparition. Sir John Friend meets me." [Here the very day on which he was killed was mentioned.] Prendergast had been connected with Sir John Friend who was executed for high treason.

This story is well received. Goldsmith remarks that his brother, the clergyman, had assured him of his having seen an apparition. And Johnson repeats what his old friend Mr. Cave, the printer at St. John's Gate, "an honest man and a sensible man," has told him—that he also saw a ghost.

"And pray, sir," asks Boswell, "what did he say was the appearance?"

"Why, sir," answers Johnson, "something of a shadowy being."

CHAPTER 45

THE MISCHANCES OF LOO

"MADAM—I read your letter with all that allowance which critical candor could require, but after all find so much to object to, and so much to raise my indignation, that I cannot help giving it a serious answer. I am not so ignorant, my dear Mrs. Bunbury, as not to see there are many sarcasms contained in it, and solecisms too. (Solecism is a word that comes from the town of Soleis in Attica, among the Greeks, built by Solon, and applied as we use the word Kidderminster for curtains from a town also of that name—but this is learning you have no taste for!) I say, madam, there are many sarcasms in it, and solecisms also. But not to seem an ill-natured critic, I'll take leave to quote your own words, and give you my remarks upon them as they occur. You begin as follows—

'I hope, my good doctor, you soon will be here,
And your spring velvet coat very smart will appear,
To open our ball the first day of the year.'

"Pray, madam, where did you ever find the epithet 'good' applied to the title of doctor? Had you called me 'learned doctor,' or 'grave doctor,' or 'noble doctor,' it might be allowable, because they belong to the profession. But, not to cavil at trifles, you talk of 'my spring velvet coat' and advise me to wear it the first day in the year, that is, in the middle of winter!—a spring velvet coat in the middle of winter!! That would be a solecism indeed! and yet to increase the inconsistence, in another part of your letter you call me a beau. Now, on one side or other, you must be wrong. If I am a beau, I can never think of wearing a spring velvet in winter, and if I am not a beau, why then, that explains itself. But let me go on to your two next strange lines—

'And bring with you a wig that is modish and gay,
To dance with the girls that are makers of hay.'

"The absurdity of making hay at Christmas you yourself seem sensible of. You say your sister will laugh, and so indeed she well may! The Latins have an expression for a contemptuous kind of laughter, '*naso contemnere adunco*,' that is, to laugh with a crooked nose. She may laugh at you in the manner of the ancients if she thinks fit. But now I come to the most extraordinary of all extraordinary propositions, which is, to take your and your sister's advice in playing at loo. The presumption of the offer raises my indignation beyond the bounds of prose. It inspires me at once with verse and resentment. I take advice! and from whom? You shall hear—

First let me suppose, what may shortly be true,
The company set and the word to be Loo;
All smirking and pleasant, and big with adventure,
And ogling the stake which is fixed in the center.
Round and round go the cards, while I inwardly damn
At never once finding a visit from Pam,
I lay down my stake, apparently cool,
While the harpies about me all pocket the pool.
I fret in my gizzard, yet, cautious and sly,
I wish all my friends may be bolder than I.
Yet still they sit snug, not a creature will aim

By losing their money to venture at fame.
'Tis in vain that at niggardly caution I scold,
'Tis in vain that I flatter the brave and the bold;
All play their own way, and they think me an ass. . . .
'What does Mrs. Bunbury?' . . . 'I, Sir? I pass.'
'Pray what does Miss Horneck? take courage, come do' . . .
'Who, I? let me see, sir, why I must pass too.'
Mr. Bunbury frets, and I fret like the devil,
To see them so cowardly, lucky, and civil.
Yet still I sit snug, and continue to sigh on,
Till, made by my losses as bold as a lion,
I venture at all, while my avarice regards
The whole pool as my own . . . 'Come, give me five cards.'
'Well done!' cry the ladies, 'Ah, doctor, that's good!
The pool's very rich, . . . Ah! the doctor is loo'd!'
Thus foiled in my courage, on all sides perplext,
I ask for advice from the lady that's next.
'Pray, ma'am be so good as to give me your advice;
Don't you think the best way is to venture for't twice!'
'I advise,' cries the lady, 'to try it, I own . . .
Ah! the doctor is loo'd! Come, doctor, put down.'
Thus, playing and playing, I still grow more eager,
And so bold, and so bold, I'm at last a bold beggar.
Now, ladies, I ask, if law matters you're skilled in,
Whether crimes such as yours should not come before
            Fielding:
For giving advice that is not worth a straw,
May well be called picking of pockets in law.
And picking of pockets, with which I now charge ye,
Is, by quinto Elizabeth, Death without Clergy.
What justice, when both to the Old Bailey brought!
By the Gods, I'll enjoy it, tho' 'tis but in thought!
Both are placed at the bat, with all proper decorum,
With bunches of fennel and nosegays before 'em;
Both cover their faces with mobs and all that,
But the judge bids them angrily, take off their hat.
When uncovered, a buzz of inquiry runs round,
'Pray, what are the crimes?' . . . 'They've been pilfering
            found!'
'But pray, who have they pilfered?' . . . 'A doctor, I hear.'

'What, yon solemn faced, odd looking man that stands near?'
'The same.' . . . 'What a pity! How does it surprise one,
Two handsomer culprits I never set eyes on!'
Then their friends all come round me with cringing and
       leering,
To melt me to pity, and soften my swearing.
First Sir Charles advances with phrases well strung,
'Consider, dear Doctor, the girls are but young.'
'The younger the worse,' I return him again,
'It shows that their habits are all dyed in grain.'
'But when they're so handsome, one's bosom it grieves.'
'What signifies *handsome,* when people are *thieves?*'
'But where is your justice? their cases are hard.'
'What signifies *justice?* I want the *reward.*'

   "'There's the parish of Edmonton offers forty pounds;
there's the parish of St. Leonard Shoreditch offers forty
pounds; there's the parish of Tyburn, from the Hog-in-the-
pound to St. Giles' watch house, offers forty pounds—I shall
have all that if I convict them!'

    'But consider their case, . . . It may yet be your own!
    And see how they kneel! Is your heart made of stone?'
    This moves! . . . so at last I agree to relent,
    For ten pounds in hand, and ten pounds to be spent.

   "I challenge you all to answer this. I tell you, you cannot. It cuts deep. But now for the rest of the letter, and
next—but I want room—so I believe I shall battle the rest
out at Barton some day next week. I don't value you all!
O.G."

CHAPTER 46

BLUES

THIS HAPPENS TO BE a Dilletanti Sunday, and Sir Joshua rarely misses one of the Society's pleasant dinners at the Star and Garter, where he is sure to find old friends and congenial companions. Here he can discuss good wine and pictures with Lord Mulgrave and Mr. Bouverie, bow to Lord Palmerston's or the Duke of Devonshire's praises of his last imported antique, hear Mr. Fitzpatrick's or George Selwyn's freshest *bon mot,* and raise his eyebrows at the news that Lord Holland is thinking of paying off Chas. Fox's debts, which his club friends put at something above a £100,000. Perhaps he takes part in a discussion of the dresses for the Henri Quatre and Charles the Second Quadrilles at the next Almack's, hears speculations as to the authorship of the Heroic Epistle just now the rage at the Court end of the town, and shifts his trumpet as Lord Spencer expatiates on the last Andrea Sacchi which he has bought for a Guido. He has besides to beat up for votes for his new friend, Mr. Luke Gardiner, who is a candidate for the Dilettanti and comes forward for the ballot tonight. . . . There is a great deal of wit and virtu talked, a great deal of laughing, a great deal of wine drunk, in all of which Sir Joshua takes his part genially— but temperately.

He is in time to attend Mrs. Ord's *conversazione* at

[300]

eight. Mrs. Ord is the clever wife of a wealthy Northumbrian gentleman, and though only a surgeon's daughter, has made her way to the front rank of the blues. Here Sir Joshua is certain to meet the literary lions of the day, Johnson roaring supreme among them, a bishop or two, a sprinkling of lawyers. There will drop in his friend Doctor Goldsmith, already launched away in a career of social dissipation—dining and supping out, at clubs, at routs, at theaters; a guest with Johnson at the Thrale's, an object of Mrs. Thrale's lively sallies, a lion at Mrs. Vesey's and Mrs. Montagu's where some of the high-bred bluestockings pronounce him "a wild genius" and others, peradventure, "a wild Irishman." There will drop in besides during the evening, some of the fashionable wits and noblemen of the Dilettanti Club who mix with the literary society of the time—Topham Beauclerc, Lord Palmerston, Lord Lucan, Lord Mulgrave, Lord Ossory—and even George Selwyn may saunter in like a man walking in his sleep and drop out one of his mots, the pungency of which is doubled by the languid gravity of the speaker. More formidable than the gentlemen is the closely packed circle of ladies in high *têtes*—crowned with queer caps or lappets or other fabrics of lace and ribbon—long stomachers, ample ruffles, and broad stiff skirts of substantial flowered silk or rich brocade. There will be Mrs. Montagu with her thin, keen, intelligent face, her grand air, her bright eyes, and her blaze of diamonds, talking formally and pompously to the Duchess of Portland and Lady Spencer, flanked perhaps by Mrs. Chapone, with a face like a Gorgon but a model of the proprieties and decorums—and an oracle as having sat at the feet of Richardson; or Mrs. Carter, the lady who knows Greek and has translated Epictetus and corresponds with the masters of colleges and bishops, or Mrs. Lennox, another literary lady, but less favored than Mrs. Carter, for her translations of Greek are through French.

Mrs. Montagu likes flattery and loves to drape and pose herself as the Chief Muse of a new British Parnassus.

When she entertains, she fascinates her guests with Chinese
rooms, Athenian rooms, feather rooms, rooms decorated by
Angelica Kauffmann, and other gorgeous apartments in her
house on Hill Street and in her palace in Portman Square.
She has her rivals, to be sure, but she carries away the bell,
thanks to her name, her diamonds, her dinners—and her
determination.

The younger and more cheerful part of the society,
however, edge away from this deep blue section of Mrs.
Ord's circle and gather where the flighty, deaf, and short-
sighted Mrs. Vesey rattles out her incomparable Irish bulls
and unconscious blunders with imperturbable good humor.

At home Mrs. Vesey entertains her friends in the blue
room or green room, and often in her little dressing room,
which Mrs. Carter calls, "the unostentatious receptacle of
liberal society." She collects her party from the Baltic to
the Po, for there is a Russian nobleman, an Italian virtuoso,
and General Paoli. . . . Mrs. Montagu may be brilliant in
diamonds, solid in judgment, critical in talk, stiff in character, chaste and instructive, but Mrs. Vesey is a withered
old lady with the heart of a child. She moves about her
crowded assemblies, like a fairy crone, her parchment skin
seamed and shrivelled with age, her ear trumpet dangling
from her neck, while she distributes her promiscuous company, pats her guests on the arm, breaks up their cliques,
and squares the social circle. Horace Walpole bursts into
momentary enthusiasm—"What English heart ever ex-
celled hers?" She touches everyone into good spirits with
the wave of her fairy wand. She is the good Mrs. Vesey—
uttering gentle, amiable, elegant sentiments in a tone of
voice originally intended for a cherub. When excitedly
denouncing second marriages, she can quite overlook the
fact that she herself has been married twice. "Bless me, my
dear! I had quite forgotten it."

But at Mrs. Ord's there is metal more attractive still.
In spite of the bankruptcy hanging over her husband's
head, Mrs. Thrale bandies epigrams and quotations with

wits and bookish men and rivals the most attractive of
women by the charms of her slight, brisk, active figure,
her bright black eyes, her white teeth and animated countenance. She is more modern than her sisters—she romps
with learning and plays blind man's buff with the sages.
She is gay, wayward, natural, bright—an exorciser of melancholy.

Both beaux and wits gather round where Mrs. Cholmondeley by her badinage and her beauty reminds one
of her lovely and witty sister, Peg Woffington.

Sir Joshua comes upon a party talking scandal—a coali-
tion of prudery, debauchery, sentiment, history, Greek,
Latin, French, Italian, and metaphysics—all except the second, understood by halves, by quarters, or not at all.

But Sir Joshua escapes from this group only to fall on—
a party of critics.

"I'm convinced Dr. Guzzle, 'tis a poor paltry book,"
cries a little black man. "I'm told too that Ratsbane,
Screechowl, and Hawkeye abuse it."

"But my dear Doctor, have you had time to peruse it?"

"Oh, yes, I have skimmed it. 'Tis terrible trash—an olio
of nonsense."

"Sir, depend on't, good Mr. Shuttlecock's pamphlet, just
now published, soon will make an end on't."

"Gude, sir," cries a Scot, springing up and presenting
his snuff box, "you're quite o' my mind. . . ."

All the pride of London—every wit and witness—is here
at Mrs. Ord's. Cards, singing, and dancing have been banished from her evening entertainments, and undisturbed
conversation has been substituted as the staple. Like Mrs.
Vesey she abhors formality and makes her guests draw
chairs about a large table in the middle of the room. She
is able to mix her ingredients, and for this Doctor Burney
pronounces her an excellent cook. . . .

The ladies sit late and St. Martin's may be striking the
hour of two as Sir Joshua's carriage turns the west corner
of Leicester Fields on the way home. . . .

GOLDY

Dr. Johnson is indignant. "There is nothing served about there, neither tea, nor coffee, nor lemonade, nor anything whatever, and depend upon it, sir, a man does not love to go to a place from whence he comes out exactly as he goes in. . . ."

CHAPTER 47

LAMENTATIONS OF JEREMIAH

THE EXCITEMENT OF SOCIETY, the excitement of composition, the anxiety about his debts bring on a fever which forces Goldsmith to bed. As a remedy he quacks himself with James's powders.

Difficulties are increasing. His *Animated Nature,* though not finished, has been entirely paid for, and the money spent. The sum advanced by Garrick on Newbery's note still hangs over him as a debt. The tale on which Newbery lent two or three hundred pounds previous to the Barton excursion has proved a failure. The bookseller is urgent for a settlement of his account. The perplexed author has nothing to offer him in liquidation but the copyright of the comedy which he has in his portfolio. "Though to tell you the truth, Frank," says he, "there are great doubts of its success."

The manuscript is submitted to Colman, and a long and baffling negotiation takes place, Colman retaining the play in his hands many months without coming to a decision. Thus matters stand in January, 1773, when Goldsmith, fretting that the theatrical season is passing away, writes with renewed earnestness to him:

"To George Colman, Esq.

"DEAR SIR—I entreat you'll relieve me from that state

[305]

of suspense in which I have been kept for a long time. Whatever objections you have made or shall make to my play, I will endeavor to remove and not argue about them. To bring in any new judges, either of its merits or faults, I can never submit to. Upon a former occasion, when my other play was before Mr. Garrick, he offered to bring me before Mr. Whitehead's tribunal, but I refused the proposal with indignation. I hope I shall not experience as harsh treatment from you as from him. I have, as you know, a large sum of money to make up shortly; by accepting my play, I can readily satisfy my creditor that way. At any rate, I must look about to some certainty to be prepared. For God's sake take the play, and let us make the best of it, and let me have the same measure, at least, which you have given as bad plays as mine. I am your friend and servant,

OLIVER GOLDSMITH."

In reply the manuscript is returned with disparaging remarks and suggested alterations scored on the blank leaves, but with the intimation that the promise of the theater shall be kept and the play acted notwithstanding. Smarting from vexation at Colman's criticisms, Goldsmith submits them to his friends who pronounce them trivial, unfair, and contemptible, and hint that Colman, being a dramatic writer himself, may be actuated by jealousy. The play is then sent, with Colman's comments written on it, to Garrick, but he has scarce done so, when Johnson interferes, represents the evil that may result from an apparent rejection of it by Covent Garden, and promises to go immediately to Colman and have a talk with him on the subject. Goldsmith, therefore, pens the following note to Garrick:

"DEAR Sir—! I ask you many pardons for the trouble I gave you yesterday. Upon more mature deliberation, and the advice of a sensible friend, I began to think it indelicate in me to throw upon you the odium of confirming Mr. Colman's sentence. I therefore request you will send my play back by my servant; for having been assured of having it acted at the other house, though I confess yours in every respect more to my wish, yet it would be folly in me to forego an advantage which lies in my power of appealing from Mr. Colman's opinion to the judgment of the town. I entreat, if not too late, you will keep this affair a secret for some time.

"I am, dear sir, your humble servant,

OLIVER GOLDSMITH."

Johnson's talk with the manager of Covent Garden is successful. "Colman," he says, "was prevailed on at last, by much solicitation, nay a kind of force" to bring forward the comedy.

Still the manager is indiscreet enough to express the opinion that it will fail miserably. The plot, he says, is bad, the interest is not sustained—it dwindles and dwindles and at last goes out like the snuff of a candle.

The effect of his croaking is soon apparent in the theater. Actors and actresses take their tone from the manager and throw up their parts. Two of the most popular actors, Woodward and Gentleman Smith, to whom are assigned the parts of Tony Lumpkin and Young Marlow, refuse to act them. Friends advise the postponement of the comedy. "No," says Goldsmith, giving to his necessity the braver look of independence, "I'd rather my play were damned by bad players than merely saved by good acting." Finally substitutions are made.

A famous company attends the rehearsals. Poor Shuter quite loses his presence of mind at the appearance of so many ladies. Johnson attends them; Reynolds, his sister and the whole Horneck family; Cradock, Murphy, Colman, and the members of the Club.

The manager continues his croaking. He has set his face against success. He will not suffer a new scene to be painted; he refuses to furnish even a new dress and is careful to spread his forebodings as widely as he can.

Colman is not a false or ill-natured man. He has des-

paired of the comedy from the first and thinks it a kind
of mercy to help it out of, rather than into, the world. And
so he accompanies it with an *obligato* that resembles the
Lamentations of Jeremiah.

With a manager so disposed, at every step there is, of
course, a stumble. Murphy volunteers an epilogue, but the
lady (Mrs. Bulkley) who is not to speak it makes objection
to the lady (Miss Catley) who is. The author writes an
epilogue to bring in both, and the lady first objected to,
objects in turn. A third epilogue is then written by poor
Goldsmith, to which Colman thinks proper to object as
too bad to be spoken. Cradock meanwhile sends a fourth
from the country, which is rejected for a similar reason
(but politely printed with the comedy as having "arrived
too late"). And Goldsmith finally tries his hand at a fifth
which, though it is permitted to be spoken, is thought "a
mawkish thing."

"We are all in labor for a name for Goldy's play," says
Johnson. What now stands as the second title, *The Mis-
takes of a Night* is originally the only one, but it is thought
undignified for a comedy. "The Old House a New Inn" is
suggested but dismissed as awkward. Reynolds announces
what he thinks so capital a title that he threatens if it is
not adopted to go and help damn the play, and he triumphantly names it, "The Belle's Stratagem," an elegant title
but not considered applicable. This name, however, is still
under discussion, when Goldsmith, in whose ear lingers,
perhaps, a line of Dryden's, hits upon *She Stoops to
Conquer*.

"Stoops, indeed?" is Horace Walpole's comment. "So
she does! that is, the Muse. She is draggled up to the knees,
and has trudged, I believe, from Southwark Fair."

The evil bodings of Colman still continue. They are
even communicated in the box office to the servant of the
Duke of Gloucester, who has been sent to engage a box.
An angry remonstrance with Goldsmith follows.

In the meantime, Foote's *Primitive Puppet Show* entitled the *Handsome Housemaid or Piety in Pattens* is brought out at the Haymarket. All the world, fashionable and unfashionable, crowds to the theater. Haymarket is crammed with carriages. The doors are burst open by the mob from without. The burlesque is a *succès de stupeur*, and sentimental comedy receives its quietus. Even Garrick, who has befriended it, now gives it a kick, as he sees it going downhill, and sends Goldsmith a humorous prologue for his play.

CHAPTER 48

TING-TING-A-LING

MONDAY, MARCH 15, 1773. At last the eventful day arrives, and Goldsmith's friends are summoned to a dinner at the St. James's Coffee House. Johnson takes the chair at the head of a long table and is the life and soul of the party. There are present the Burkes, Sir Joshua Reynolds, Fitzherbert, Caleb Whitefoord, and a phalanx of North British applauders, under the banner of Major Mills—all good men and true. Among them is the very worthy Adam Drummond, who is gifted with the loudest and most contagious laugh that ever echoed from human lungs. The neighing of the horse of Hystaspes' son is a whisper to it, and the thunder of the theater cannot drown it—but Adam Drummond knows no more than the cannon on a battery when to give his fire.

Goldsmith is extremely nervous. He shakes hands twice with Richard Burke and asks him if he has heard that the King of Sardinia is dead. He hopes that the death of the King of Sardinia will not have a depressing effect upon the playgoers. Edmund Burke assures him gravely that he need not be apprehensive on that score as the frequenters of the pit are not likely to be melancholy over the decease of a potentate whose name they probably never heard. Goldsmith shakes his head doubtfully, and says he will try and hope for the best, but still. . . .

[310]

Finally everything is arranged—the signals agreed upon, the posts allotted, the cues given—and the friends file out of the coffee house and march to the theater. Goldsmith goes the opposite way. . . .

"Bill o' the play, sir?" buzz the urchins at you like flies. Prentice lads are laughing and pushing and the seam-stresses are shrinking and blushing. Impudent orange girls are going and coming. There is a babel of chatter. A beau sniffs at a bouquet of flowers, looks around with a smirk, and ogles the ladies.

"Look—look—there's that devil Wilkes—you can tell him by the squint." He wears a scarlet suit edged with gold.

Hugh Kelly looks all the blacker in black. The prim looking person in the corner is Ossian Macpherson. And near him, in a lavender suit, waistcoat embroidered with a little silver, is Lord Ossory. That regal person in the box is the Duke of Gloucester in a coat of pale purple turned up with lemon color, embroidered all over with pearls as big as peas. Ah! rolling and blinking here too with the rest of his party comes sturdy old Johnson dressed in his best clothes. He is talking to hale, fresh, farmer-like Thrale, and occasionally glaring at Macpherson who slinks farther in the corner.

"The cast? Poor, very poor, indeed! Why can't they get Woodward or Gentleman Smith?"

"Lee Lewes—who's Lewes?—Harlequin?—Dubellamy?—Quick?—Nobodies—never heard of them."

"Stay, I saw Quick once in Beau Mordecai. Yes, Quick is not bad. Mrs. Green, too, is comical. But Shuter . . ."

"Ah! Shuter's the man all right for my money."

"Then there's little Bulkley . . ."

But from the orchestra come the first squeaks of a fiddle—then the bass awakes and gives a growl—the horn dashes in with wide-eyed surprise—and the music begins with a crash and flourish. Away to the zenith it goes swelling while the audience keeps time by banging on the seats or tapping on the boxes.

Ting-ting-a-ling, ting-ting-a-ling, from the stage. The fans cease to whirr, the house for a minute grows still, as if nought but wax figures are in it. Then an actor steps out, and all eyes glisten.

"Who is it?"

"Hush!"

"The Prologue! Why, he's sobbing."

"Hush! Listen!"

Enter Hr. Woodward, dressed in black and holding a handkerchief to his eyes.

> Excuse me, sirs, I pray—I can't yet speak—
> I'm crying now—and have been all the week.
> "'Tis not alone this mourning suit," good masters,
> "I've that within"—for which there are no plasters!
> Pray, would you know the reason why I'm crying?
> The Comic Muse, long sick, is now a-dying!
> And if she goes, my tears will never stop,
> For as a player, I can't squeeze out one drop.
> I am undone, that's all—shall lose my bread—
> I'd rather, but that's nothing—lose my head . . .
> One hope remains—hearing the maid was ill
> A *doctor* comes this night to show his skill.
> To cheer her heart and give her muscles motion,
> He in *five draughts* prepared, presents a portion.
> A kind of magic charm—for be assured,
> If you will swallow it, the maid is cured.
> But desperate the Doctor, and her case is,
> If you reject the dose and make wry faces!
> This truth he boasts, will boast it while he lives,
> No poisonous drugs are mixed in what he gives.
> Should he succeed, you'll give him his degree;
> If not, within he will receive no fee!
> The College *you*, must his pretensions back,
> Pronounce him *regular*, or dub him *quack*.

The comedy opens. A chamber in an old fashioned house. Enter Mr. and Mrs. Hardcastle.

Mrs. Hard. "I vow, Mr. Hardcastle, you're very particular. Is there a creature in the whole country but ourselves, that does not take a trip to town now and then, to rub off the rust a little? There the two Miss Hoggs, and our neighbor Mrs. Grigsby, go to take a month's polishing every winter.

Hard. "Ay, and bring back vanity and affectation to last them the whole year. I wonder why London cannot keep its own fools at home! In my time, the follies of the town crept slowly among us, but now they travel faster than a stage coach. Its fopperies come down not only as inside passengers, but in the very basket.

Mrs. Hard. "Ay, your times were fine times indeed; you have been telling us of them for many a long year. Here we live in an old rumbling mansion, that looks for all the world like an inn, but that we never see company. Our best visitors are old Mrs. Oddfish, the curate's wife, and little Cripplegate, the lame dancing master—and all our entertainment your old stories of Prince Eugene and the Duke of Marlborough. I hate such old fashioned trumpery."

Hard. "And I love it. I love everything that's old—old friends, old times, old manners, old books, old wine, and I believe, Dorothy (taking her hand), you'll own I have been pretty fond of an old wife." . . . and on and on . . .

All eyes are fixed on Dr. Johnson who sits in a side box, and when he laughs every one feels himself at liberty to roar. But Adam Drummond, planted in an upper box above the stage, and in full view of the pit, follows his signals with so comic a rattle that he engrosses more attention than the actors. At length the pit takes offence and begins to hiss. The phalanx of British applauders, however, drowns them out.

Johnson sends Steevens out to hunt for Goldsmith. Steevens goes on foot from coffee house to coffee house, from Jack's in Dean Street to the Old Bell in Westminster, but fails to discover his friend in one of them. An hour and a quarter he spends in this way. Finally he hastens to the Mall in St. James's Park, crowded with dandies combing their wigs, and decoy ducks, fashionably dressed, occasionally giving vent to a very audible, "What charming weather for Ranelagh." In their midst is Goldsmith wandering up and down like a troubled spirit. Steevens urges him to return as his presence is needed.

They enter the stage door at the opening of the fifth act and hear a solitary hiss at the improbability of Tony Lumpkin's trick on his mother in persuading her she is forty miles off on Crackskull Common when she is in her own garden.

"What's that? What's that?" cries Goldsmith to the manager, in great agitation.

"Pshaw Doctor," replies Colman sarcastically, "don't be frightened at a squib, when we've been sitting these two hours on a barrel of gunpowder."

"Did it make you laugh?" the author asks Northcote, Sir Joshua's assistant, who applauded lustily in the gallery.

"Exceedingly," is the answer.

"Then that is all I require," and Goldsmith gives him half a dozen tickets for his first benefit night.

The comedy runs to the end of the season. The tenth night is by royal command, and the twelfth is the season's closing night, March 31. But it runs many merry nights a second season and makes thousands of honest people merry every season since. The author gets from four hundred to five hundred pounds.

Colman is taunted and squibbed out of town—and takes refuge in Bath:

To George Colman, Esq.

On the Success of Dr. Goldsmith's New Comedy

Come Coley, drop those mourning weeds,
    Nor thus with jokes be flamm'd,
Tho' Goldsmith's present play succeeds,
    His next may still be damn'd.

As this has 'scaped without a fall,
    To sink his next prepare,

New actors hire from Wapping Wall,
     And dresses from Rag Fair.

For scenes let tatter'd blankets fly,
     The prologue Kelly write,
Then swear again the piece must die
     Before the author's night.

Should these tricks fail, the lucky elf,
     To bring to lasting shame,
E'en write the best you can yourself,
     And print it in *his name*.

The comedy is immediately put to press and dedicated to Johnson. "DEAR SIR—By inscribing this light performance to you, I do not mean so much to compliment you as myself. It may do me some honor to inform the public that I have lived many years in intimacy with you. It may serve the interests of mankind also to inform them that the greatest wit may be found in a character, without impairing the most unaffected piety."

From James Boswell of Auchinleck (he deliberately misdates the letter; he is on his way to London but wants for his archives a letter from the author of *She Stoops to Conquer*): "While you are in the full glow of theatrical splendor, while all the great and the gay in the British metropolis are literally hanging upon your smiles, let me see that you can *stoop to write* to me. . . . Pray, write directly. Write as if in repartee. . . ."

"My Dear Sir," replies Goldy, "I thank you for your kind remembrance of me, for your most agreeable letter, and for your congratulations." (Boswell has been in town two days and the letter goes off to Scotland to wait five weeks for his return).

"I believe I always told you that success upon the stage was great cry and little wool. It has kept me in hot water these three months, and in about five weeks hence I suppose I shall get my three benefits. I promise you, My Dear Sir, that the stage earning is the dirtiest money that ever a poor poet put in his pocket, and if my mind does not very much alter, I have done with the stage. . . ."

Boswell stops in at Brick Court in the Temple as he passes along one morning. Goldsmith is not up, and he is shown into the dining room and library. When Goldsmith learns who his caller is, he roars out from his bed, "Boswell!" Boswell runs to him, and they have a "cordial embrace." Then while Boswell sits on the side of the bed, the two men chat about the success of *She Stoops to Conquer* and a scandalous newspaper article intimating that Johnson is the father of the eldest Thrale boy. "Now," says Goldsmith, "is not this horrid?" Boswell agrees that it is "ludicrous nonsense"—it might be believed by strangers. "The assertions of a newspaper are taken up insensibly. I long believed Burke to be a Jesuit."

Boswell goes into the dining room, Goldsmith rises and comes to breakfast, and Boswell sits by him. On a table he finds a letter from Francis Gentleman full of gratitude to Goldsmith and enclosing a promissory note for fifteen pounds. Boswell reflects that Goldsmith is "the most generous hearted of men" and "and now that he has a huge supply of gold by his comedy all the needy draw upon him."

But a passage in Goldsmith's letter may explain the real incentive of Boswell's visit. The poet openly writes:

"I am still left the only *Poet Militant* here and in truth I am very likely to be *militant* till I die, nor have I even the prospect of an hospital to retire to.

"I have been three days ago most horribly abused in a newspaper, so, like a fool as I was, I went and thrash'd the Editor. I could not help it. He is going to take the law of me. However, the press is now so scandalously abusive that I believe he will scarcely get damages. I don't care how it is; come up to town and we shall laugh it off whether it goes for or against me."

CHAPTER 49

THE EVANS AFFRAY

(For *The London Packet*)

TO DR. GOLDSMITH

VOUS VOUS NOYEZ PAR VANITÉ.

"Sir—The happy knack which you have learned of puffing your own compositions, provokes me to come forth. You have not been the editor of newspapers and magazines not to discover the trick of literary *humbug,* but the gauze is so thin that the very foolish part of the world sees through it, and discover the doctor's monkey face and cloven foot. Your poetic vanity is as unpardonable as your personal. Would man believe it, and will woman bear it, to be told that for hours the great Goldsmith will stand surveying his grotesque oran-outang's figure in a pier glass? Was but the lovely H——k as much enamored, you would not sigh, my gentle swain, in vain. But your vanity is preposterous. How will this same bard of Bedlam ring the changes in the praise of Goldy! But what has he to be either proud or vain of? *The Traveller* is a flimsy poem, built upon false principles—principles diametrically opposite to liberty. What is *The Good Natured Man* but a poor water gruel dramatic dose? What is *The Deserted Village* but a pretty poem of easy numbers, without fancy, dignity, genius or fire? And, pray, what may be the last *speaking pantomime,* so praised by the doctor himself, but an incoherent piece of stuff, the figure of a woman with a fish's tail, without plot, incident or intrigue? We are made to laugh at stale, dull jokes, wherein we mistake pleasantry for wit, and grimace for humor, wherein every scene is unnatural and inconsistent with the rules, the laws of nature and the drama; viz., two gentlemen come to a man of fortune's house, eat, drink, etc., and take it for an inn. The one is intended as a lover for the daughter; he talks with her for some hours; and when he sees her again in a different dress, he treats her as a bar girl, and swears she squinted. He abuses the master of the house, and threatens to kick him out of his own doors. The squire, whom we are told is to be a fool, proves to be the most sensible being of the piece, and he makes out a whole act by bidding his mother lie close behind a bush, persuading her that his father, her own husband, is a highwayman, and that he has come to cut their throats; and to give his cousin an opportunity to go off, he drives his mother over hedges, ditches, and through ponds. There is not, sweet, sucking Johnson, a natural stroke in the whole play but the young fellow's giving the stolen jewels to the mother, supposing her to be the landlady. That Mr. Colman did no justice to this piece, I honestly allow; that he told all his friends it would be damned, I positively aver; and from such ungenerous insinuations, without a dramatic merit, it rose to public notice, and it is now the ton to go and see it, though I never saw a person that either liked it or approved it, any more than the absurd plot of Home's tragedy of Alonzo. Mr. Goldsmith, correct your arrogance, reduce your vanity, and endeavor to believe, as a man, you are of the plainest sort: and as an author, but a mortal piece of mediocrity.

> Brise le miroir infidèle
> Qui vous cache la vérité.
>   TOM TICKLE"

Goldsmith would have treated the dog's vomit as he treated other previous explosions—with contemptuous indifference—had not Master Snarley—yow dragged in the name of the Jessamy Bride. But now he is in a high state of excitement and indignation, and accompanied by a friend, Captain Higgins of the Marines, he repairs to Paternoster Row, to the shop of Evans, the publisher, who, he supposes, is the editor of the paper. This Thomas Evans is a hard-headed, eccentric man. He has so violent a quarrel with his son that he literally allows him, a year and a half before his own death, to perish in the streets; he separates from his wife because she sides with her son in the quarrel; and he threatens to disinherit his heirs if they refuse to bury him without a coffin or shroud and limit his expenses to 40s.

Evans is summoned by his assistant Harris from an adjoining room. Goldsmith announces his name. "I have called," adds he, "in consequence of a scurrilous attack made upon me, and an unwarrantable liberty taken with the name of a young lady. As for myself, I care little, but her name must not be sported with."

Evans declares his utter ignorance of the matter, says he will speak to the editor, and as he stoops as though to look for the libel, Goldsmith strikes him smartly with his cane across the back, crying out as he does so, "You know well enough, you rascal, what I mean." Evans, a stout, high-blooded Welshman, returns the blow with interest. In a sudden scramble, the lamp hanging overhead is broken, the combatants covered with oil, and the affray brought to a somewhat ludicrous pause. Then from the adjoining room there steps no less a person than Kenrick, the author of the libel, who separates the parties, and sends Goldsmith home in a coach greatly battered and disfigured.

When he gets to his chambers, it happens that Beau and Garrick call to carry him off to the Club, and Beau, who has all the sportive talents of Charles II and loves a little mischief, persuades the Doctor to go all bruised as he is to show the world how little he is affected by the late encounter. The astonishment of the company can be imagined when in the midst of some ingenious literary discussion, the door is banged open, and the bloody figure of the unfortunate bard enters, followed by his two conductors enjoying the surprise of their associates. The doctor has every attention paid him which his painful situation requires, but even the most serious are amused at the oddity of the spectacle. From civility and tenderness, however, the members repress their smiles till the bard notices the constrained silence, and suffering great pain in body and mind, desires leave to retire "as he finds he only makes the company melancholy." This unfortunate suggestion overcomes all delicacy. To be grave any longer exceeds their power. The poor doctor is no sooner withdrawn than a roar bursts forth which it is impossible to restrain. . . .

Evans starts a suit against Goldsmith for assault, but is finally prevailed upon to compromise, the poet contributing fifty pounds to a Welsh charity.

Newspapers make themselves merry over the combat. Some censure Goldsmith for invading the sanctity of a man's house, others accuse him of being guilty of the very offence that he now resents in others. This draws from him the following reply.

"To The Public.

"Lest it should be supposed that I have been willing to correct in others an abuse of which I have been guilty myself, I beg leave to declare, that, in all my life, I never wrote or dictated a single paragraph, letter, or essay in a newspaper, except a few moral essays under the character of a Chinese, about ten years ago, in the *Ledger,* and a letter, to which I signed my name in the *St. James' Chronicle.* If the liberty of the press, therefore, has been abused, I have had no hand in it.

"I have always considered the press as the protector of our freedom, as a watchful guardian, capable of uniting the weak against the encroachments of power. What concerns the public most properly admits of a public discussion. But of late the press has turned from defending public interest to making inroads upon private life, from combating the strong to overwhelming the feeble. No condition is now too obscure for its abuse, and the protector has become the tyrant of the people. In this manner the freedom of the press is beginning to sow the seeds of its own dissolution. The great must oppose it from principle, and the weak from fear, till at last every rank of mankind shall be found to give up its benefits, content with security from insults.

"How to put a stop to this licentiousness, by which all are indiscriminately abused, and by which vice consequently escapes in the general censure, I am unable to tell. All I could wish is that, as the law gives us no protection against the injury, so it should give calumniators no shelter after having provoked correction. The insults which we receive before the public, by being more open, are the more distressing; by treating them with silent contempt we do not pay a sufficient deference to the opinion of the world. By recurring to legal redress we too often expose the weakness of the law, which only serves to increase our mortification by failing to relieve us. In short, every man should singly consider himself as the guardian of the liberty of the press, and, as far as his influence can extend, should endeavor to prevent its licentiousness becoming at last the grave of its freedom.

OLIVER GOLDSMITH."

Boswell reads this article in a newspaper which he finds at Dr. Johnson's. The Doctor is not at home at the time, and Bozzy and Mrs. Williams, in a critical conference over the letter, suppose from the style that it was written by the lexicographer himself. The latter on his return soon undeceives them. "Sir," says he to Boswell, "Dr. Goldsmith would no more have asked me to write such a thing as that for him than he would have asked me to feed him with a spoon or to do anything else that denoted his imbecility.

I as much believe that he wrote it as if I had seen him do it. Sir, had he shown it to any one friend, he would not have been allowed to publish it. He has, indeed, done it very well, but it is a foolish thing well done. I suppose he has been so much elated with the success of his new comedy, that he has thought every thing that concerned him must be of importance to the public."

"I fancy, sir," rejoins Boswell, "this is the first time that he has been engaged in such an adventure."

"Why, sir," laughs Johnson, "I believe it is the first time he has *beat;* he may have *been beaten* before. This, sir, is a new plume to him."

CHAPTER 50

DINNERS AND CONVERSATION

IT IS HOLY WEEK, a time during which Johnson is particularly solemn in his manner and strict in his devotions. Boswell assumes, of course, an extra devoutness on the present occasion and attempts to deal out some second-hand homilies for the edification of Goldsmith.

"Sir," says the poet in reply, "as I take my shoes from the shoemaker, and my coat from the tailor, so I take my religion from the priest."

A few days later, the ninth of April, Boswell repairs to his Fleet Street place of worship to keep Good Friday with Dr. Johnson, in orthodox style. He breakfasts with him on tea and cross buns, goes to church with him in the morning and evening, fasts in the interval, and reads with him in the Greek New Testament. Then he complains of the sore rebuff he has met with in the course of his religious exhortations to the poet and laments that the latter should indulge in "this loose way of talking."

"Sir," replies Johnson, "Goldsmith knows nothing—he has made up his mind about nothing."

Johnson, however, blows hot as well as cold, according to the humor he is in. Boswell observes some time later, in a tone of surprise, that Goldsmith has acquired more fame than all the officers of the last war who were not generals. "Why, sir," answers Johnson, "you will find ten thousand fit to do what they did before you find one to do what Goldsmith has done. You must consider that a thing is valued according to its rarity. A pebble that paves the street is in itself more useful than the diamond upon a lady's finger."

On the thirteenth of April the three dine alone with General Oglethorpe and his family and discuss the question of the degeneracy of the human race. Goldsmith asserts the fact and attributes it to luxury.

Johnson. "Sir, in the first place, I doubt the fact. I believe there are as many tall men in England now, as ever there were. But, secondly, supposing the stature of our people to be diminished, that is not owing to luxury, for, sir, consider to how very small a proportion of our people luxury can reach. Our soldiery, surely, are not luxurious, who live on sixpence a day, and the same remark will apply to almost all the other classes. Luxury, so far as it reaches the poor, will do good to the race of people. It will strengthen and multiply them. Sir, no nation was ever hurt by luxury, for, as I said before, it can reach but to a very few. I admit that the great increase of commerce and manufactures hurts the military spirit of a people, because it produces a competition for something else than martial honors—a competition for riches. It also hurts the bodies of the people, for you will observe there is no man who works at any particular trade, but you may know him from his appearance to do so. One part or other of his body being more used than the rest, he is in some degree deformed, but, Sir, that is not luxury. A tailor sits cross-legged, but that is not luxury."

Goldsmith. "Come, you're just going to the same place by another road."

Johnson. "Nay, sir, I say that is not *luxury*. Let us take a walk from Charing Cross to Whitechapel, through, I suppose, the greatest series of shops in the world. What is

[324]

there in any of these shops (if you except the gin shops)
that can do any human being any harm?"

Goldsmith. "Well, sir, I'll accept your challenge. The
next shop to Northumberland House is a pickle shop."

(Goldsmith in naming a pickle shop means that the
pickle as an appetizer is used to stimulate an "artificial"
appetite by those who have lost their "natural" appetite
through surfeiting.)

Johnson. "Well, sir, do we not know that a maid can in
one afternoon make pickles sufficient to serve a whole
family for a year? Nay, that five pickle shops can serve all
the kingdom? Besides, sir, there is no harm done to anybody by the making of pickles, or the eating of pickles."

After this fooling, they drink tea with the ladies, and
Goldsmith sings Tony Lumpkin's song from *She Stoops to
Conquer* to a very pretty Irish tune, the *Humours of Bal-
lamagairy.* He had designed the song for Miss Hardcastle,
but as Mrs. Bulkley, who played the part, could not sing,
it was left out.

> Ah me! when shall I marry me?
>   Lovers are plenty, but fail to relieve me.
> He, fond youth, that could carry me,
>   Offers to love, but means to deceive me.
>
> But I will rally, and combat the ruiner;
>   Not a look not a smile shall my passion discover.
> She that gives all to the false one pursuing her
>   Makes but a penitent, loses a lover.

Two days later the three friends meet again at the table
of General Paoli, the hero of Corsica, whose glory is out of
all proportion to the smallness of his country. Among the
guests is Signor Martinelli of Florence, author of a *History
of England* in Italian, printed in London.

The question is debated whether Martinelli should continue his *History of England* to the present day.

Goldsmith. "To be sure, he should."

Johnson. "No, sir, he would give great offence. He would have to tell of almost all the living great what they do not wish told."

Goldsmith. "It may, perhaps, be necessary for a native to be more cautious, but a foreigner who comes among us without prejudice, may be considered as holding the place of a Judge and may speak his mind freely."

Johnson, "Sir, a foreigner, when he sends a work from the press, ought to be on his guard against catching the error and mistaken enthusiasm of the people among whom he happens to be."

Goldsmith. "Sir, he wants only to sell his history and to tell truth: one an honest, the other a laudable motive."

Johnson. "Sir, they are both laudable motives. It is laudable in a man to wish to live by his labors, but he should write so as he may *live* by them, not so as he may be knocked on the head. I would advise him to be at Calais before he publishes his history of the present age. A foreigner who attaches himself to a political party in this country is in the worst state that can be imagined. He is looked upon as a mere intermeddler. A native may do it from interest."

Boswell. "Or principle."

Goldsmith. "There are people who tell a hundred political lies every day and are not hurt by it. Surely, then, one may tell truth with safety."

Johnson. "Why, sir, in the first place, he who tells a hundred lies has disarmed the force of his lies. But besides, a man had rather have a hundred lies told of him than one truth which he does not wish should be told."

Goldsmith. "For my part, I'd tell truth and shame the devil."

Johnson. "Yes, sir, but the devil will be angry. I wish to shame the devil as much as you do, but I should choose to be out of the reach of his claws."

Goldsmith. "His claws can do you no harm when you have the shield of truth."

They talk of the King's coming to see Goldsmith's new play. "I wish he would," says Goldsmith, adding, however, with an affected indifference, "Not that it would do me the least good."

Johnson. "Well then, sir, let us say it would do *him* good, (laughing). No, sir, this affectation will not pass—it is mighty idle. In such a state as ours, who would not wish to please the Chief Magistrate?"

Goldsmith. "I do wish to please him. I remember a line in Dryden,

'And every poet is the monarch's friend.'

It ought to be reversed."

Johnson. "Nay, there are finer lines in Dryden on this subject:

'For colleges on bounteous Kings depend,
And never rebel was to arts a friend"

General Paoli. "Successful rebels might be."

Martinelli. "Happy rebellions."

Goldsmith. "We have no such phase."

General Paoli. "But have you not the *thing?*"

Goldsmith. "Yes, all our *happy* revolutions. They have hurt our constitution, and will hurt it, till we mend it by another HAPPY REVOLUTION"—a sturdy sally of Jacobitism wondered at by Boswell and relished by Johnson.

General Paoli mentions a passage in Goldsmith's play which he construes into a compliment to a lady of distinction whose marriage with the Duke of Gloucester has excited the strong disapprobation of the King.

Boswell, to draw Goldsmith out, thinks the compliment unintentional. The poet smiles and hesitates. But the General comes to his relief. "Monsieur Goldsmith," says he, "est comme la mer, qui jette des perles et beaucoup d'autres belles choses, sans s'en apercevoir." (Mr. Goldsmith is like the sea, which casts forth pearls and many other beautiful things without perceiving it.)

"Très bien dit et très élégamment" (very well said and very elegantly), exclaims Goldsmith delighted.

Boswell speaks highly of Mr. Harris of Salisbury as being a very learned man and a good Grecian.

Johnson. "I am not sure of that. His friends give him out as such, but I know not who of his friends are able to judge of it."

Goldsmith. "He is what is much better—he is a worthy humane man."

Johnson. "Nay, sir, that is not to the purpose of our argument. That will as much prove that he can play upon the fiddle as well as Giardini as that he is an eminent Grecian."

Goldsmith finding he has got in a scrape dexterously turns the conversation. "The greatest musical performers," says he, "have but small emoluments. Giardini, I am told, does not get above seven hundred a year."

"That is indeed but little for a man to get," observes Johnson, "who does best that which so many endeavor to do. There is nothing, I think, in which the power of art is shown so much as in playing on the fiddle. In all other things we can do something at first. Any man will forge a bar of iron, if you give him a hammer, not so well as a smith but tolerably. A man will saw a piece of wood, and make a box, thought a clumsy one, but give him a fiddle and fiddle stick, and he can do nothing."

They have an argument six days later at Mr. Thrale's, on the subject of suicide. "Do you think, sir," says Boswell, "that all who commit suicide are mad?"

"Sir," replies Johnson, "they are not often universally disordered in their intellects, but one passion presses so upon them that they yield to it and commit suicide, as a passionate man will stab another. I have often thought," he adds, "that after a man has taken the resolution to kill himself, it is not courage in him to do anything, however desperate, because he has nothing to fear."

"I don't see that," observes Goldsmith."

Johnson. "Nay, but my dear sir, why should you not see what every one else does?"

"It is," replies Goldsmith, "for fear of something that he has resolved to kill himself, and will not that timid disposition restrain him?"

"It does not signify," pursues Johnson, "that the fear of something made him resolve—it is upon the state of his mind, after the resolution is taken, that I argue. Suppose a man, either from fear, or pride, or conscience, or whatever motive, has resolved to kill himself. When once the resolution is taken he has nothing to fear. He may then go and take the King of Prussia by the nose at the head of his army. He cannot fear the rack who is determined to kill himself. When Eustace Budgel was walking down to the Thames, determined to drown himself, he might, if he pleased, without any apprehension of danger, have turned aside, and first set fire to St. James's palace."

On April 29, the same party, with Reynolds, Langton, and Thrale, dines at General Oglethorpe's. The conversation passes from Garrick to the custom of eating dogs at Otaheite, and then turns to literary subjects. Goldsmith speaks slightingly of the character of Mallet.

"Why sir," remarks Johnson, "Mallet had talents enough to keep his literary reputation alive as long as he himself lived, and that, let me tell you, is a good deal."

"But," persists Goldsmith, "I cannot agree that it was so. His literary reputation was dead long before his natural death. I consider an author's literary reputation to be alive only while his name will ensure a good price for his copy from the booksellers. I will get you (leaning over the table and pointing to Johnson) a hundred guineas for anything whatever that you shall write, if you put your name to it. . . ." Johnson does not reply but begins to praise *She Stoops to Conquer.*

CHAPTER 51

BALLOTING

"Sir," says brisk little Davy Garrick to Sir Joshua Reynolds, who is speaking to him of the Club, "I like it much. I think I shall be of you."

When Sir Joshua mentions this to Johnson, he is much displeased with the actor's conceit. "He'll be of us," he growls, "how does he know we will *permit* him? The first Duke in England has no right to hold such language."

When Sir John Hawkins speaks favorably of Garrick's pretensions, "Sir," replies Johnson, "he will disturb us by his buffoonery."

In the same spirit, he declares to Mr. Thrale that if Garrick applies for admission, he will blackball him. "Who, sir?" exclaims Thrale, with surprise, "Mr. Garrick—your friend—your companion—blackball him!"

"Why, sir," replies Johnson, "I love my little David dearly—better than all or any of his flatterers do, but surely one ought to sit in a society of ours,

'Unelbowed by a gamester, pimp, or player.'"

The exclusion from the Club is a sore mortification to Garrick, though he bears it without complaining. Yet he continually asks questions about it—what is going on there—whether he is ever the subject of conversation.

By degrees the rigor of the Club is relaxed. Some of the

members grow negligent. Beauclerc loses his right of membership by failing to attend. On his marriage, however, with the blonde goddess, Lady Diana Spencer, daughter of the second Duke of Marlborough and recently divorced from Viscount Bolingbroke (a very trying gentleman and a restless bully), he has claimed and regained his seat in the Club. The family lives in princely style both at their summer quarters at Muswell Hill and on great Russell Street, where the library set in a great garden reaches half way to Highgate. . . . Lady D is exceedingly fair to see. She is handsome and agreeable and ingenious beyond the ordinary rate. She proves herself one of those odd and rare women who take to their husband's old friends (!) . . .

Goldsmith proposes to increase the number of members in the Club. "It will give," he says, "an agreeable variety to our meetings, for there can be nothing new amongst us. We have travelled over each other's minds."

"Sir," remarks Johnson, piqued at the suggestion, "you have not travelled over my mind, I promise you."

Sir Joshua, less confident in the exhaustless fecundity of his mind, acknowledges the force of Goldsmith's suggestion, and several new members are therefore added. The first, to his great joy, is David Garrick, and there is a celebration in honor of the election, when the hospitable brewer of Southwark has a table laid in one of his new brewing coppers, and beefsteaks dressed at the furnace are set before Johnson, Reynolds, Goldsmith, Garrick, Burke, and the Italian Baretti. Another new member is Beauclerc's friend, Lord Charlemont, a famous book collector, and a still more important one is Mr. (afterwards Sir William) Jones, a young lawyer of the Temple and a distinguished scholar. Burke proposes Mr. Agmondesham Vesey, husband of the bluestocking, introducing his name with the remark that he is a man of gentle manners.

"Sir," interrupts Johnson, "you need say no more. When you have said a man of gentle manners, you have said enough."

Nevertheless when Vesey, with schoolboy gentleness of talk, introduces one day the subject of Catiline's conspiracy, Johnson withdraws his attention and thinks about Tom Thumb.

A fifth candidate is now in agitation—proposed by Johnson on the 23rd of April (when Goldsmith is in the chair) and strenuously seconded by Beauclerc. This is no other than James Boswell.

The club members are surprised, but Johnson is resolute and has but one answer to all who object. "If they had refused, sir," he says afterwards to Boswell, "they knew they'd never have got in another. I'd have kept them all out."

On Friday, April 30, 1773, when the ballot is to take place, Beauclerc gives a dinner at his house in the Adelphi. They do not stay long, however, but go off in a body to the Club, leaving Boswell at Beauclerc's till the fate of his election is announced to him. He sits in a state of anxiety which even the charming conversation of Lady Di cannot entirely dissipate. But in a short time he receives the welcome tidings of his election, hastens to Gerrard Street, and is "introduced to such a society as can seldom be found." He now for the first time sees Burke, and at the supper table sit Johnson, Garrick, and Goldsmith, Mr. Jones and Dr. Nugent, Reynolds, Lord Charlemont, Langton, Chamier, Vesey, and Beauclerc.

As he enters, Johnson rises, places himself behind a chair, and leaning on it as on a desk or pulpit, gives Bozzy a mock solemn charge, pointing out the conduct expected of him as a good member of the Club—what he is to do, and especially what he is to avoid, including in the latter, no doubt, all those petty, prying, questioning, gossiping, babbling habits, which have so often grieved the spirit of the lexicographer.

CHAPTER 52

DOCTORS MAJOR AND MINOR

"FRIDAY, MAY 7, 1773. I dined with him this day at the house of my friends, Messieurs Edward and Charles Dilly, booksellers (and dissenters) in the Poultry: there were present, their elder brother Mr. Dilly of Bedfordshire, Dr. Goldsmith, Mr. Langton, Mr. Claxton, Reverend Dr. Mayo, a dissenting minister, the Reverend Mr. Toplady, and my friend the Reverend Mr. Temple." (A notation of Boswell.)

The conversation turns upon the natural history of birds. *Johnson.* "I think we have a good evidence for the migration of woodcocks as can be desired. We find they disappear at a certain time of the year, and appear again at a certain time of the year, and some of them when weary in their flight, have been known to alight on the rigging of ships far out at sea."

One of the company observes that some of them have been found in summer in Essex. *Johnson.* "Sir, that strengthens our argument. Some being found shows that if all remained, many would be found. A few sick or lame ones may be found."

Goldsmith. "There is a partial migration of the swallows—the stronger ones migrate, the others do not."

Johnson revives the question of instinct and reason. "Birds," says he, "build by instinct; they never improve; they build their first nest as well as any one they ever build."

Goldsmith. "Yet we see if you take away a bird's nest with the eggs in it, she will make a slighter nest and lay again."

Johnson. "Sir, that is because at first she has full time and makes her nest deliberately. In the case you mention she is pressed to lay, and must therefore makes her nest quickly, and consequently it will be slight."

Goldsmith. "The nidification of birds is what is least known in natural history, though one of the most curious things in it."

This easy flow of gossip does not satisfy Boswell. He sees a great opportunity, with a dissenting person present, of making Johnson "rear," and so straightway he introduces the subject of toleration.

Johnson disagrees, of course, with Mayo, and when the dissenting minister puts to him, as a consequence of his argument, that the persecution of the first Christians must be held to have been perfectly right, Johnson frankly declares himself ignorant of any better way of ascertaining the truth than by persecution on the one hand and endurance on the other.

"But," asks Goldsmith at this point, "how is a man to act, sir? Though firmly convinced of the truth of his doctrine, may he not think it wrong to expose himself to persecution? Has he a right to do so? Is it not, as it were, committing voluntary suicide?"

"Sir, as to voluntary suicide, as you call it," retorts Johnson, "there are twenty thousand men in an army who will go without scruple to be shot at and mount a breach for five pence a day."

"But," persists Goldsmith, "have they a moral right to do this?"

Johnson evades the question. "Sir, if a man is in doubt

whether it would be better for him to expose himself to martyrdom or not, he should not do it. He must be convinced that he has a delegation from heaven."

"Nay," repeats Goldsmith, unconscious that he is pressing disagreeably on Johnson. "I would consider whether there is the greater chance of good or evil upon the whole. If I see a man who had fallen into a well, I would wish to help him out, but if there is a greater probability that he shall pull me in than that I shall pull him out, I would not attempt it. So were I to go to Turkey, I might wish to convert the Grand Signor to the Christian faith, but when I considered that I should probably be put to death without effectuating my purpose in any degree, I should keep myself quiet."

To this Johnson replies by enlarging on perfect and imperfect obligations, and by repeating that a man, to be a martyr, must be persuaded of a particular delegation from Heaven.

"But how," still persists Goldsmith, "is this to be known? Our first reformers, who were burnt for not believing bread and wine to be Christ——"

"Sir," interrupts Johnson loudly, "they were not burnt for not believing bread and wine to be Christ, but for insulting those who did believe it."

What with his dislike of reforming Protestants and his impatience of contradiction, Johnson has now become thoroughly roused, and so recklessly seizes the field that none can dispossess him.

Goldsmith sits in nervous agitation from a wish to get in and shine. Finding himself still excluded, however, he takes his hat to go away, but remains for a time with it in his hand, like a gamester who at the end of a long night lingers for a while to see if he can have a favorable opening to finish with success. Once he begins to speak and finds himself overpowered by the loud voice of Johnson, who is at the opposite end of the table and does not perceive his attempt. Whereupon he throws down his hat in a passion, and looking angrily at Johnson, exclaims in a bitter tone, "Take it."

Just then Toplady, beginning to speak, and Johnson uttering some sound as if about to interrupt him, "Sir,' exclaims Goldsmith, venting his own envy and spleen, "the gentleman has heard you patiently for an hour; pray allow us now to hear him."

"Sir," replies Johnson, sternly, "I was not interrupting the gentleman. I was only giving him a signal of attention. Sir, you are impertinent."

Goldsmith makes no reply, but after some time goes away, having another engagement.

That evening, as Boswell is on his way to the Club with Johnson and Langton, he remarks, "It is a pity that Goldsmith on every occasion, endeavors to shine, for by it he so often exposes himself." Langton contrasts him with Addison who, content with the fame of his writings, acknowledged himself unfit for conversation, and on being taxed by a lady with silence in company, replied, "Madam, I have but ninepence in ready money, but I can draw for a thousand pounds." Boswell observes that Goldsmith has a great deal of gold in his cabinet but, not content with that, is always taking out his purse.

"Yes, sir," chuckles Johnson, "and that so often an empty purse."

When they arrive at the Club, they find Goldsmith in company with Burke, Garrick, and other members, but sitting apart, and silently brooding over Johnson's reprimand to him after dinner. Johnson notices this, and whispers, "I'll make Goldsmith forgive me." Then with a loud voice, "Dr. Goldsmith" he calls out, "something passed today where you and I dined—I ask your pardon."

Goldsmith answers quickly, "It must be much from you, sir, that I take ill."

And so, the difference over, they are on as easy terms as ever, and Goldsmith rattles away as usual.

They are dining one evening with the Reverend George

Graham, a Master of Eton, who, notwithstanding the so-
briety of his cloth, has got intoxicated to about the pitch
of looking at one man and talking to another. "Doctor,"
cries he in an ecstasy of devotion, but goggling by mistake
upon Goldsmith, "I should be glad to see you at Eton."

"I shall be glad to wait upon you, sir," replies
Goldsmith.

"No, no!" cries the other eagerly, "'tis not you I mean,
Doctor *Minor*, 'tis Doctor *Major* there."

For the rest of the evening Goldsmith is as irascible as
a hornet. "That Graham," he remarks afterwards, "is
enough to make one commit suicide. . . ."

"Why, what wouldst thou have, dear Doctor?" says
Johnson laughing at a squib in the *St. James Chronicle*
which has coupled himself and his friend as the pedant
and his flatterer in *Love's Labour's Lost*, and at which
poor Goldsmith is fretting and fuming, "Who the plague
is hurt with all this nonsense, or how is a man the worse,
I wonder, in his health, purse, or character, for being
called Holofernes?"

"How you may relish being called Holofernes," replies
Goldsmith, "I do not know, but I do not like at least to
play Goodman Dull!"

CHAPTER 53

THE CHAMPION OF
CHRISTIANITY

GOLDSMITH IS IN DEBT. Some new scheme must be devised to provide for the past and future. He has undertaken to write a *History of Greece* in two volumes for William Griffin, but the sum advanced has been swallowed up by his obligations. It now occurs to him to edit a *Popular Dictionary of Arts and Sciences,* in a number of volumes. For this he receives promises of support from powerful hands. Johnson is to contribute an article on ethics; Burke a resumé of his *Essay on the Sublime and Beautiful,* an essay on the Berkleyan system of philosophy, and others on political subjects; Sir Joshua Reynolds an essay on painting; and Garrick, while he undertakes on his own part to furnish an essay on acting, engages Dr. Burney to contribute an article on music. Goldsmith is to edit the whole.

He draws up a prospectus of the plan and submits it to the booksellers—but it is rejected. Davies who represents the craft on this occasion lets us into the secret of their refusal. "The booksellers, notwithstanding they have a very good opinion of his abilities, yet are startled at the bulk, importance, and expense of so great an undertaking, the fate of which is to depend upon the industry of a man

[338]

with whose indolence of temper and method of procras-
tination they have long been acquainted."

Goldsmith, by his heedlessness, certainly has given
them reasons for some such distrust. Works unfinished but
paid for have been suspended to make way for some job
that is to provide for present necessities. These in turn
have been as hastily executed, and the whole, however
pressing, shoved aside on some sudden call to amusement.

On one occasion, when he is hard at work on his
Natural History, Cradock and Dr. Percy are hurriedly summoned to finish some pages which lie upon his table, he
being detained by another engagement at Windsor. The
friends meet by appointment at his rooms in the Temple,
where they find everything in disorder—costly books, and
uncorrected proof sheets scattered about on the floor and
tables.

The subject in hand relates to birds. "Do you know
anything about birds?" asks Dr. Percy smiling. "Not an
atom," replies Cradock; "do you?" "Not I! I scarcely know
a goose from a swan. However, let us try what we can do."
They set to work and complete their friendly task—and
only when Goldsmith returns are they informed that he
has been out on a party with some literary ladies.

At another time, as he is pushing on doggedly through
the second volume of his *Grecian History,* Edward Gibbon,
the historian, calls. "You are the man of all others I wish
to see," cries the poet. "What was the name of that Indian
King who gave Alexander the Great so much trouble?"

"Montezuma," replies Gibbon sportively. Goldsmith is
putting the name down on paper, when Gibbon pretends
to recollect himself and gives the true name, Porus.

The failure of Goldsmith's projected *Dictionary* unusually depresses him. His once trim chambers fall into a
grievous disorder. He flies into a passion with the servants,
though he instantly repents. From such friends as visit
him, he makes little concealment of his affairs. His own
distress sharpens his sensibility to the distress of others.

He is playing whist one evening at the house of Sir William Chambers in Berners Street when all at once he throws down his cards, hurries out of the room and into the street. He returns in an instant, resumes his seat, and the game goes on. Sir William, after a little hesitation, ventures to ask the cause of his sudden withdrawal.

"Was—the room too warm for you, sir?"

"Not at all," replies Goldsmith, "but in truth I could not bear to hear that unfortunate woman in the street, half singing, half sobbing, for such tones could only arise from the extremity of distress. Her voice grated painfully on my ear and jarred my frame, so that I could not rest until I had sent her away."

It occurs to some friends to agitate the question of a pension for him. The application is met by a firm refusal. His talent is not a marketable one. Has he not refused to become a ministerial hack when offered a *carte blanche* by Parson Scott? Besides George III has his hands too full with his political singing birds—with Grenville, Townshend, Pitt, Burke, North, and the rest, and with his House of Commons and John Wilkes—to find time to listen to Oliver Goldsmith.

In the meantime the Scottish professor Beattie comes up to London with the somewhat trumpery *Essay on Truth* under his arm, and throws the orthodox world into a paroxysm of contagious ecstasy. He is cried up as the great champion of Christianity—as a battery of assault against Voltaire and Hume. Though the noise cannot make Beattie a tolerable philosopher, it makes him for the time a very perfect social idol. He is embraced as "the long delayed avenger of insulted Christianity." He is so caressed and invited and treated and liked and flattered by the great that even Dr. Johnson can see nothing of him. Then the King sends for him, praises his essay, and gives him £200 a year.

"Everyone," says Mrs. Thrale, "loves Dr. Beattie but

Goldsmith, who says he cannot bear the sight of so much applause as we all bestow upon him."

"Here's such a stir," he exclaims to Johnson one day, "about a fellow that has written one book and I have written many."

"Ah, Doctor!" retorts Johnson to his discontented, disregarded, unpensioned friend, "there go two and forty sixpences, you know, to one guinea." Whereat lively Mrs. Thrale claps her hands with delight and poor Goldsmith sulks in a corner. (Being an author he has no business to be thin skinned, and should rather have been shelled like a rhinoceros.)

Reynolds accompanies Beattie to Oxford, partakes with him in an honorary doctorship of civil law, and on their return, paints his fellow doctor in Oxonian robes with the *Essay of Truth* under his arm and at his side the angel of Truth overpowering and chasing away the demons of infidelity, sophistry, and falsehood—the last represented by the plump broadbacked Hume, the second by the lean and piercing face of Voltaire, and the first bearing a remote resemblance to Gibbon.

"It is unworthy of you," he says to Sir Joshua, "to debase so high a genius as Voltaire before so mean a writer as Beattie. Beattie and his book will be forgotten in ten years, while Voltaire's fame will last forever. Take care it does not perpetuate this picture to the shame of such a man as you."

CHAPTER 54

"GOLDSMITH'S PARLAVER"

"WE HAVE A NEW COMEDY HERE," writes
Beauclerc to Lord Charlemont of Kelly's *School for Wives*,
tried under an assumed name, "which is good for nothing.
Bad as it is, however, it succeeds very well, and almost
killed Goldsmith with envy."

What is killing Goldsmith is not envy. His health is
impaired and his spirits depressed. He is deep in debt. He
is peevish and irritable. He is too proud to seek sympathy
or relief from his friends, and so he buries his troubles in
his bosom. Sir Joshua notices his state of mind and takes
him to Vauxhall and Ranelagh and other places of amusement. They saunter along the lighted avenues, watch the
cabinet ministers and their daughters, the royal dukes and
their wives, the agreeable young ladies (with gentlemen of
eighty-two), and all the red-heeled macaronis.

At Beauclerc's house he plays the game of Dumb
Crambo with Garrick. The poet sits on Garrick's knee, and
a tablecloth is pinned under his chin and brought behind
Garrick to hide both their faces. Garrick with his hands on
each side of the cloth waves them in burlesque fashion,
tapping his heart and putting his hand to Goldy's head
and nose at the wrong time, while the poet, in his Irish
brogue, declaims some of the heroic soliloquies of Ad-

[342]

dison's *Cato*. They keep an immense party laughing till they shriek.

Cradock comes up to town towards autumn, when all the fashionable world is in the country, to give his wife the benefit of a skillful dentist—and takes lodgings in Norfolk Street to be near his friend. He finds Goldsmith much altered and very low. The poet wishes him to look over and revise some of his works, but Cradock suggests a subscription edition of his two celebrated poems, the *Traveller* and the *Deserted Village*. Goldsmith readily gives him his private copies, saying sadly, "Pray, do what you please with them." But he rather submits than encourages, and the plan falls through.

"Oh, sir," say the two sisters Gun, milliners, who live at the corner of Temple Lane and are among Goldsmith's creditors, "sooner persuade him to let us work for him gratis than suffer him to apply to any other. We are sure that he will pay us if he can."

Towards the end of the year he receives another Christmas invitation to Barton. But his purse is empty and the booksellers have already advanced full payments to him. As a last resource, he applies to Garrick. The old loan of forty pounds has never been paid, and Newbery's note pledged as a security has never been taken up. An additional loan of sixty pounds is now asked for, thus increasing the loan to one hundred. To insure the payment, he now offers the transfer of the *Good Natured Man* to Drury Lane with such alterations as Garrick may suggest. Garrick in reply evades the offer of the altered comedy, hints significantly of a new one which Goldsmith has talked of writing for him, and offers to furnish the money required on Goldsmith's own acceptances.

"MY DEAR FRIEND—I thank you. I wish I could do something to serve you. I shall have a comedy for you in a season, or two at furthest, that I believe will be worth your acceptance, for I fancy I will make it a fine thing. You shall have the refusal—I will draw upon you one month after date for sixty pounds, and your acceptance will be ready money, part of which I want to go down to Barton with. May God preserve my honest little man, for he has my heart. Ever, OLIVER GOLDSMITH."

Garrick hastily folds up the letter and endorses across it, "Goldsmith's parlaver."

But the poet turns his back on his Temple quarters and forgets his troubles in the family circle and a Christmas fireside at Barton.

CHAPTER 55

RETALIATION

BARTON FESTIVITIES ARE OVER, and Gold-
smith is back at his abode in the Temple working at his
tasks. His *Animated Nature* so long delayed, is announced
for publication. He is completing his *Grecian History* and
is making another abridgment of his *History of England*
for schools. He is revising his *Inquiry into Polite Learning*
for a pittance of five guineas, and is arranging his *Survey
of Experimental Philosophy* begun eight years before. He
is translating the comic romance of Scarron. . . .

He again makes an effort to rally his spirits by getting
into society, but the gayeties of society are scarce medicine
for the mind. At length, wearied by the distractions of town
life, he resolves to retire into the country and to spend but
two months of the year in London. He accordingly arranges to sell his right in the Temple and in the month of
March goes to his country lodgings at Hyde.

He belongs to an association of literary men, some of
them members of the Club, who dine together occasionally
at the St. James's Coffee House. Once a whim seizes the
company to write epitaphs on "The late Dr. Goldsmith."
Pens and ink are called for, and several epitaphs are
thrown off in a playful vein. Much laughter follows. Garrick offhand writes the following:

GOLDY

Here lies Nolly Goldsmith, for shortness call'd Noll,
Who wrote like an angel but talk'd like poor Poll.

When Goldsmith next attends the coffee house, the epitaphs are read to him and he is called upon for a retaliation. He remains silent a few moments, then promises to comply, but begs for a little time.

At Edgeware he composes a series of sketches in which the characters of his distinguished intimates—the Burkes, Garrick, Whitefoord, Hickey, Cumberland, and Douglas—are admirably hit off with a mixture of generous praise and good-humored railery. He is the skilful *maître d'armes* with a button on his foil who makes point after point without wounding. But there is chalk on the button and it leaves its mark wherever it touches his antagonist. Before he is done with them they are pretty well pitted. There are only chalk marks, to be sure, but they indicate the skill which he has at command. His friends conceive a great respect for him.

During the process of composition several of the retaliatory epitaphs become known to those retaliated upon. They—Garrick in particular—therefore recompose their epitaphs on him.

Here, Hermes, says Jove, who with nectar was mellow,
Go fetch me some clay—I will make an odd fellow:
Right and wrong shall be jumbled, much gold and some dross,
Without cause be he pleased, without cause be he cross;
Be sure, as I work, to throw in contradictions,
A great love of truth, yet a mind turn'd to fictions,
Now mix these ingredients, which warm'd in the baking,
Turn'd to learning and gaming, religion and raking.
With the love of a wench, let his writings be chaste;
Tip his tongue with strange matters, his lips with fine taste
That the rake and the poet o'er all may prevail,
Set fire to the head and set fire to the tail;
For the joy of each sex on the world I'll bestow it,
This scholar, rake, Christian, dupe, gamester, and poet.

The Life and Times of Oliver Goldsmith

Though a mixture so odd, he shall merit great fame,
And among brother mortals be Goldsmith his name,
When on earth this strange meteor no more shall appear,
You, Hermes, shall fetch him, to make us sport here. . . .

CHAPTER 56

EXEUNT

Here Reynolds is laid, and to tell you my mind,
He has not left a wiser or better behind.
His pencil was striking, resistless, and grand;
His manners were gentle, complying, and bland;
Still born to improve us in every part,
His pencil our faces, his manners our heart.
To coxcombs averse, yet most civilly steering:
When they judged without skill, he was still hard of hearing.
When they talk'd of their Raphaels, Corregios, and stuff,
He shifted his trumpet, and only took snuff.
By flattery unspoiled——

And here Goldsmith's hand fails and he lays down his
pen. A sudden attack of his old illness warns him to seek
advice in London. He arrives in the city in the middle of
March, obtains temporary relief, and is again amongst his
friends and in his old haunts. But he is still left struggling
with symptoms of a low nervous fever.

On Friday, the 25th of March, he is specially anxious
to attend the Club (Charles Fox, Sir Charles Bunbury,
George Steevens, and Dr. Fordyce have just been elected),
but in the afternoon he feels so ill that he is forced to take
to his bed, and at eleven o'clock at night a surgeon apothecary named Hawes, who lives in the Strand, and whom

Goldsmith is in the habit of consulting, is sent for. He finds the poet with flushed face, bright wide open eyes, tossing restlessly in his four post bed—complaining of a violent headache, his tongue moist, his pulse ninety, and his mind made up that he shall be cured by James's fever powders.

Hawes implores him not to think of it, urging its probable danger of exhausting his strength. The patient is still obstinate. Dr. Fordyce soon arrives and adds his warning, but it is unavailing. And a boy is sent out for a packet of the powders.

The patient gets worse, suffering severe fits of vomiting and diarrhea. Another physician, Dr. Turton, is called into consultation. A week passes. Goldsmith's appetite is gone, his strength fails him, he cannot sleep. He is so weak that a want of sleep may in itself be fatal. Then it occurs to Dr. Turton to put a pregnant question to the patient.

"Your pulse, sir, is in greater disorder than it should be, from the degree of fever which you have. Is your mind at ease?"

"No, it is not," replies Goldsmith.

These are the last words he utters. The end comes suddenly and unexpectedly. He falls into a deep sleep, but awakes in strong convulsions which continue without intermission. He sinks rapidly and by a quarter before five o'clock, on the morning of Monday, the fourth of April, 1774, in his forty-fifth year, Oliver Goldsmith is dead.

When Burke is told he bursts into tears. Reynolds is in his studio when the messenger comes to him, but he at once lays down his brush, leaves the room, and does not reenter it for the rest of the day.

"Was ever poet so trusted before?" exclaims Dr. Johnson when he hears his friend's debts amount to two thousand pounds. The idea pleases him. To be able to owe two thousand pounds is the next best thing to having it.

The staircase of Brick Court is crowded with mourners—outcasts of the city whom Goldsmith has befriended, and members of the Club. His coffin is reopened at the request of Miss Mary Horneck and her sister, and a lock is cut from his hair.

A public funeral is at first proposed and Lords Shelburne and Louth, Reynolds, Burke, Beauclerc, and Garrick are designated as pall bearers. But it is afterwards felt that a private ceremony better becomes the circumstances in which he died.

And so five days after his death, at five o'clock, on the evening of Saturday, the ninth of April, the remains of Oliver Goldsmith are privately interred in the burying ground of the Temple Church.

Reynold's nephew, Palmer, attends as chief mourner, and is accompanied by Mr. John Day and his relative Robert Day, and by Mr. Hawes and his friend Mr. Etherington.

These are unexpectedly joined on the morning of the funeral by Hugh Kelly, who in the presence of great sorrow only remembers happier and more friendly days and is seen still standing weeping at the grave as the others move away. . . .

"Chambers, you find, is gone far, and poor Goldsmith is gone much farther," writes Johnson to Bennet Langton in Lincolnshire three months later. "He died of a fever, exasperated, as I believe, by the fear of distress. He raised money and squandered it by every artifice of acquisition and folly of expense. But let not his frailties be remembered; he was a very great man. . . ."

Reynolds suggests a monument to the poet's memory in Westminster Abbey. It is executed by Nollekens and consists of a medallion portrait and tablet, and is placed over the south door, between the monuments of Gay and the Duke of Argyll. Johnson furnishes a Latin inscription which is read at the table of Sir Joshua Reynolds. So many objections are raised that it is resolved to submit them to Johnson in the form of a round robin, such as mutinous sailors adopt at sea when a grievance is started, and no one wishes to stand first or last in remonstrance with the captain.

After stating the great pleasure with which the intended epitaph has been read and the admiration it created for its masterly style "considered abstractedly," the round robin goes on to say that its circumscribers are yet of opinion that the character of Goldsmith as a writer, particularly as a poet, is not perhaps delineated with all the exactness which Dr. Johnson is capable of giving it, and that, therefore, with deference to his superior judgment they humbly request he will at least take the trouble of revising it and of making such alterations and additions as he shall think proper upon a further perusal. "But if we might venture to express our wishes they would lead us to request that he would write the epitaph in English rather than in Latin, as we think that the memory of so eminent an English writer ought to be perpetuated in the language to which his works are likely to be so lasting an ornament."

Sir Joshua agrees to carry the round robin to Dr. Johnson who receives it with much good humor. "I am willing," he says, "to modify the sense of the epitaph in any manner the gentlemen please—but I never will consent to disgrace the walls of Westminster Abbey with an English inscription."

Seeing the names of Dr. Warton and Edmund Burke among the signers, "I wonder," he says, "that Joe Warton, a scholar by profession, should be such a fool—and I should have thought that Mund Burke would have had more sense."

The Latin is accordingly placed on the marble where it now remains. Translated it reads:

OF OLIVER GOLDSMITH

A Poet, Naturalist, and Historian,
Who left scarcely any style of writing untouched,
And touched nothing that he did not adorn;
Of all the passions,

GOLDY

Whether smiles were to be moved, or tears,
A powerful yet gentle master,
In genius sublime, vivid, versatile,
In style, elevated, clear, elegant—
The love of companions,
The fidelity of friends,
And the veneration of readers,
Have by this monument honored the memory. . . .

CHAPTER 5 7

EPILOGUE

HAZLITT MEETS MARY HORNECK at North-
cote's painting room, more than fifty years after, as Mrs.
Gwynne, the widow of a General Gwynne of the army. She
is at the time upwards of seventy years of age. Still, he says,
she is beautiful, beautiful even in years. After she has gone,
Hazlitt remarks how handsome she still is.

"I do not know," says Northcote, "why she is so kind
as to come to see me, except that I am the last link in the
chain that connects her with all those she most esteemed
when young—Johnson, Reynolds, Goldsmith—and remind
her of the most delightful period of her life."

"Not only so," observes Hazlitt, "but you remember
what she was at twenty, and you thus bring back to her
the triumphs of her youth—that pride of beauty, which
must be the more fondly cherished as it has no external
vouchers, and lives chiefly in the bosom of its once lovely
possessor. In her, however, the Graces have triumphed
over time. She was one of Ninon de l'Enclos' people, of
the last of the immortals. I could almost fancy the shade
of Goldsmith in the room, looking round with complacency. . . ."

BIBLIOGRAPHY

Of course I owe a vast debt to "Goldy."
I have quoted, paraphrased, and included in the body of
the text the most winning part of his writing. Scholars
will know where, and others may not. But does it matter?
I also wish to acknowledge the kind permission of
McGraw-Hill Book Company, Inc. to quote excerpts from
Boswell's London Journal, 1762–63, edited by Frederick A.
Pottle (New York, 1950) and *Sir Joshua Reynolds' Portraits,* edited by Frederick W. Hilles (New York, 1952).
The ballads sung are, no doubt, based on earlier versions.

Allen, Robert J., *The Clubs of Augustan London* (Cambridge,
    Mass., 1933).
Barnouw, A. J., "Goldsmith's Indebtedness to Justus van Effen,"
    Modern Language Review, VIII (1913), 314-23.
Battestin, Martin C., "Fielding's Changing Politics and *Joseph
    Andrews,*" *Philological Quarterly* XXXIX (Jan. 1960), 39-55.
Beattie, James, *London Diary, 1773,* ed. by Ralph S. Walker
    (Aberdeen, 1946).
Bell, Howard J., "Goldsmith and the Pickle Shop," *Modern
    Language Notes,* LVII (1942), 121-22.
Bell, Howard J., Jr., "*The Deserted Village* and Goldsmith's
    Social Doctrines," *PLMA* LIX (1944), 747-72.
Bell, Walter G., "Fleet Street in Seven Centuries" (London,
    1912).
Bernbaum, Ernest, *The Drama of Sensibility* (Boston and London, 1915).

Besant, Sir Walter, *London in the Eighteenth Century* (London, 1902).

Biron, H. C., "Smelfungus," *National Review*, LXXV (March-August, 1920), 344-53.

Black, William, *Goldsmith* (New York, 1879).

Boswell, James, *Private Papers of James Boswell from Malahide Castle*, prepared for the press by Geoffrey Scott and Frederick A. Pottle, 18 Vols. (Mount Vernon, New York, 1928-1934).

Boswell, James, *Journal of a Tour to the Hebrides*, prepared for the press by Frederick A. Pottle and Chas. H. Bennett (New York, 1936).

Boswell, James, *The Life of Samuel Johnson*, ed. by G. B. Hill, rev. by L. F. Powell, 6 vols. (Oxford, 1934-1950).

Boswell, James, *Boswell's London Journal, 1762-1763* (New York, 1950).

Brandes, Georg, *Wolfgang von Goethe*, trans. by Allen W. Porterfield, Vol. I (New York, 1924).

"Broadsheet Ballads, Being a Collection of Irish Popular Songs," with an introduction by Padraic Colum (Dublin, 1913).

Brown, Jos. E., "Goldsmith's Indebtedness to Voltaire and Justus van Effen," *Modern Philology*, XXIII (1926), 273-84.

Brown, Jos. E., "Goldsmith and Johnson on Biography," *Modern Language Notes*, XLII (1927), 168-71.

Bruce, Henry, *Life of General Oglethorpe* (New York, 1890).

Campbell, Thomas, *A Philosophical Survey of the South of Ireland* (Dublin, 1778).

Clifford, James L., *Hester Lynch Piozzi (Mrs. Thrale)* (Oxford, 1941).

Collison-Morley, Lacy, *Giuseppe Baretti* (London, 1909).

Colman, George, and Thornton, Bonnell, *The Connoisseur* (Oxford, 1767).

Colman, George, Jr., *Random Records*, 2 vols. (London, 1830).

Cone, Carl B., *Burke and the Nature of Politics* (University of Kentucky Press, 1957).

Cooper, H. C., *James Oglethorpe* (New York, 1904).

Cradock, Joseph, *Literary and Miscellaneous Memoirs*, Vol. I (London, 1828).

Crane, R. S., and Friedman, Arthur, "Goldsmith and the *En-*

cyclopédie," *Times Literary Supplement* (May 11, 1933), p. 331.

Dahl, Curtis, "Patterns of Disguise in *The Vicar of Wakefield*," *ELH*, XXV (June, 1958), No. 2, 90-104.

Daniel, Robert N., *An Investigation of Certain Elements of the Goldsmith Tradition* (University of Chicago, Chicago, 1911).

Davidson, Levette J., "Forerunners of Goldsmith's *The Citizen of the World*," *Modern Language Notes*, XXXVI (1921), 215-20.

De Quincey, Thomas, *Dr. Samuel Parr and Other Writings* (Boston, 1873).

Dictionary of National Biography, ed. by Leslie Stephen and Sidney Lee (London and New York, 1885-1900).

Dixon, W. Macneile, *Trinity College, Dublin* (London, 1902).

Dobson, Austin, *Oliver Goldsmith, a Memoir* (New York, 1889).

Dobson, Austin, *Eighteenth Century Vignettes* (New York, 1893).

Dobson, Austin, *Miscellanies* (New York, 1898).

Dobson, Austin, *David Garrick and His Contemporaries*, ed. by Brander Matthews and Laurence Hutton (Boston, 1900).

Eberlein, H. D., and Richardson, A. E., *The English Inn—Past and Present* (Philadelphia, 1926).

Elwin, Rev. Whitwell, *Some Eighteenth Century Men of Letters*, ed. by Warwick Elwin, Vol. II (London, 1902).

Encyclopedia Britannica, 14th edition (New York and London, 1929).

Essays on Goldsmith by Scott, Macaulay, and Thackeray, with an introduction by G. E. Hadow and notes by C. B. Wheeler (Clarendon Press, 1918).

European Magazine and London Review, XXIV (1793), 170-71.

Fielding, Henry, *The Works of Henry Fielding, Esq.*, ed. by James P. Browne, Vol. X (London, 1871).

Fielding, Henry, Sir Alexander Drawcansir's *Covent Garden Journal*, 2 vols, ed. by G. E. Jensen (New Haven, 1915).

Forster, John, *The Life and Times of Oliver Goldsmith*, 2 vols. (London, 1871).

Forster, John, *Footnotes to the Life and Times of Oliver Goldsmith*, 2 vols. (London, 1871).

Frank, Maude, *Mistake at the Manor* (New York, 1915).

Freeman, William, *Oliver Goldsmith* (London, 1951).

Friedman, Arthur, "Goldsmith and the *Weekly Magazine*," *Modern Philology*, XXXII (Feb. 1935), No. 3, 281-99.

Friedman, Arthur, "Goldsmith and the Marquis D'Argens," *Modern Language Notes*, LIII (1938), 173-76.

Friedman, Arthur, "Goldsmith and Steele's *Englishman*," *Modern Language Notes*, LV (1940), 294-96.

Friedman, Arthur, "Goldsmith's Contributions to the *Critical Review*," *Modern Philology*, XLIV (Aug. 1946), No. 1, 23-52.

Fussell, Jr., Paul, "William Kenrick, Eighteenth Century Scourge and Critic," *Journal of the Rutgers University Library*, XX (June, 1957) No. 2, 42-59.

Gassman, Byron, "French Sources of Goldsmith's *The Good Natur'd Man*," *Philological Quarterly*, XXXIX (1960), 56-65.

Gaussen, Alice C. C. *Percy, Prelate and Poet* (London, 1908).

Golden, Morris, "The Family Wanderer Theme in Goldsmith," *ELH*, XXV (Sept. 1958), No. 3, 181-93.

Goldsmith, Oliver, *Works*, ed. by J. W. M. Gibbs, 4 vols. (London, 1884).

Goldsmith, Oliver, *She Stoops to Conquer*, ed. by Austin Dobson (New York, 1899).

Goldsmith, Oliver, *Miscellaneous Works* with biographical introduction by David Masson (London, 1919).

Goldsmith, Oliver, *New Essays by Oliver Goldsmith*, ed. by Ronald S. Crane (Chicago, 1927).

Goldsmith, Oliver, *The Collected Letters of Oliver Goldsmith*, ed. by Katherine Balderston (Cambridge, 1928).

Goldsmith, Oliver, *Complete Poetical Works*, ed. by Austin Dobson (Oxford, 1911).

Grant, Alexander, *The Story of the University of Edinburgh*, 2 vols. (London, 1884).

Guiney, Louise I., *A Little English Gallery* (New York, 1894).

Gwynn, Stephen, *Memorials of an Eighteenth Century Painter* (James Northcote) (London, 1898).

Gwynn, Stephen, *Oliver Goldsmith* (New York, 1935).

Hammer, Carl, Jr., "Goethe's Estimate of Oliver Goldsmith," *Journal of English and Germanic Philology*, XLIV (1945), 131-38.

Harper, Charles G., *Stage Coach and Mail in Days of Yore*, Vol. I (London, 1903).

Haydon, Frances, "Oliver Goldsmith as Biographer," *South Atlantic Quarterly*, XXXIX (1940), 50-57.

Hubbard, Elbert, *Little Journeys to the Homes of Good Men and Great* (New York, 1895).

Hume, David, *Private Correspondence* (London, 1820).

Hutton, James, *A Hundred Years Age* (London, 1857).

Irving, Washington, *Oliver Goldsmith* (New York, 1903).

Jenks, Tudor, *In the Days of Goldsmith* (New York, 1907).

Kenny, Robert W., "Ralph's *Case of Authors*," *PMLA*, LII (1937), 104-13.

Kent, Elizabeth E., *Goldsmith and His Booksellers* (Ithaca New York, 1933).

Knapp, Mary E., Comment in *Johnsonian News Letter*, XIX (June, 1959), No. 2, 11-12.

Leslie, Charles R., and Taylor, Tom, *Life and Times of Sir Joshua Reynolds*, 4 vols. (London, 1865).

Loftie, Rev. W. J., "Oliver Goldsmith at Hyde House Farm," in *Poet's Country*, by Andrew Lang (Phila., 1907).

Lovejoy, Arthur O., "Goldsmith and the Chain of Being," *Journal of the History of Ideas*, VII (Jan., 1946), No. 1, 91-98.

Lucas, Frank L., *The Search for Good Sense* (London, 1958).

Lynd, Robert, *Dr. Johnson and Company* (New York, 1928).

Lynskey, Winifred, "The Scientific Sources of Goldsmith's *Animated Nature*," *Studies in Philology*, XL (1943), 33-57.

Lynskey, Winifred, "Goldsmith and the Warfare in Nature," *Philological Quarterly*, XXIII (Oct., 1944), 333-42.

Lynskey, Winifred, "Goldsmith and the Chain of Being," *Journal of the History of Ideas*, VI (June, 1945), 363-74.

Mac Dermot, H. E., "Goldsmith as a Talker," *Queen's Quarterly*, LI (Summer, 1944), 184-93.

Maxwell, Constantia, *Dublin under the Georges* (London, 1936).

Maxwell, Constantia, *A History of Trinity College, Dublin, 1591-1892* (Dublin, 1946).

Miner, Earl, "The Making of 'The Deserted Village,'" *The Huntington Library Quarterly*, XXII (February, 1959), 125-42.

Molloy, Fitzgerald, *Sir Joshua and His Circle* (London, 1906).

Moore, Frank Frankfort, *The Jessamy Bride* (New York, 1906).

Moore, Frank Frankfort, *The Life of Oliver Goldsmith* (London, 1910).

Murray, Grace A., *Personalities of the Eighteenth Century* (London, 1927).

Nettleton, George Henry, *English Drama of the Restoration and Eighteenth Century* (New York, 1928).

Nicoll, Allardyce, *A History of Eighteenth Century Drama, 1750-1800* (Cambridge, 1927).

Paschal, Father, "Goldsmith as a Social Philosopher," *The Irish Ecclesiastical Record*, Fifth Series, XXXV (1930), 113-24.

Percy, Thomas, *The Life of Oliver Goldsmith* (London, 1774).

Pitman, James H., *Goldsmith's Animated Nature* (Oxford, 1924).

Pottle, Frederick A., "James's Powders," *Notes and Queries*, CXLIX (1925), 11-12.

Price, Laurence M., "The Works of Oliver Goldsmith on the German Stage, 1716-1795" *Modern Language Quarterly*, V (1944), No. 4, 481-86.

Prior, James, *The Life of Oliver Goldsmith*, 2 vols. (London, 1837).

Prior, James, *Life of the Right Honourable Edmund Burke* (London, 1867).

Reynolds, Sir Joshua, *Portraits* (New York, 1952).

Reynolds, W. Vaughan, "Goldsmith's Critical Outlook," *Review of English Studies*, XIV (1938), 155-72.

Russell, W. Clark, *Representative Actors, A Collection of Criticisms, Anecdotes, Personal Descriptions, etc.* (London, 18–?).

Salpeter, Harry, *Dr. Johnson and Mr. Boswell* (New York, 1929).

Samuels, Arthur P. I., *The Early Life, Correspondence, and Writings of the Rt. Hon. Edmund Burke, LL.D.* (Cambridge, 1923).

Scott, Temple, *Oliver Goldsmith, Bibliographically and Biographically Considered* (New York, 1928).

Seeber, Edward D., "Goldsmith's American Tigers," *Modern Language Quarterly*, VI (December, 1945), No. 4, 417-20.

GOLDY

Seeber, Edward D., and Remak, Henry H. H., "The First French Translation of 'The Deserted Village,'" *Modern Language Review*, XLI (1946), 62-67.

Seitz, R. W., "Goldsmith and the *Literary Magazine*," *Review of English Studies*, V (1929), 410-30.

Seitz, R. W., "Goldsmith and the *Annual Register*," *Modern Philology*, XXXI (1933), 183-94.

Seitz, R. W., "The Irish Background of Goldsmith's Social and Political Thought," *PMLA*, LII (1937), 405-11.

Seitz, R. W., "Some of Goldsmith's Second Thoughts on English History," *Modern Philology*, XXXV (1938), 279-88.

Sherbo, Arthur, "A Manufactured Anecdote in Goldsmith's *Life of Richard Nash*," *Modern Language Notes*, LXX (1955), 20-22.

Shou-Yi, Chên, "Oliver Goldsmith and His Chinese Letters," *T'ien hsia Monthly*, VIII (1939), 34-52.

Smeaton, Oliphant, *Tobias Smollett* (New York, 1897).

Smith, Hamilton J., *Oliver Goldsmith's The Citizen of the World*, Yale Studies in English, LXXI (1926), (New Haven, Conn., 1926).

Smollett, Tobias, *Roderick Random* (London, 1890).

Stauffer, Donald, *The Art of Biography in Eighteenth Century England* (Princeton, 1941).

Street Ballads, A Collection of 238 Songs Mainly Printed in Dublin, 18–? (possibly 1869-1870). From this collection I have chosen "Banks of Boyne" listed as "a new song," but most likely based on an earlier popular version.

Stubbs, John William, *The History of the University of Dublin* (Dublin and London, 1889).

Swaen, A. E. H., "Fielding and Goldsmith in Leiden," *Modern Language Review*, I (1906), 327-28.

Sydney, William Connor, *England and the English in the Eighteenth Century*, 2 vols. (Edinburgh, 1891).

Tallentyre, S. G., *The Friends of Voltaire* (London, 1906).

Thaler, Alvin, *Shakespeare to Sheridan* (Cambridge, 1922).

Thrale, Mrs. Hester Lynch, *Thraliana*, 2 vols., ed. by Katherine C. Balderston (Oxford, 1951).

Timbs, John, *Clubs and Club Life in London* (London, 1872).

Tinker, Chauncey B., *The Salon and English Letters* (New York, 1915).

Tinker, Chauncey B., *The Letters of James Boswell*, 2 vols. (Oxford, 1924).

Tinker, Chauncey B., *Young Boswell* (Boston, 1922).

Turberville, A. S., *English Men and Manners in the Eighteenth Century* (Oxford, 1926).

Walker, Hugh, "Wise Men Who Have Passed for Fools," *Yale Review*, April, 1916.

Waller, John F., *Boswell and Johnson* (London, 1881).

Walpole, Horace, *The Yale Edition of Horace Walpole's Correspondence*, ed. by W. S. Lewis and others, Vols. I, II, XI, XV, XVI, XXVIII (New Haven, Conn., 1937-1955).

Walsh, John E., *Sketches of Ireland Sixty Years Ago* (Dublin, 1847).

Wardle, Ralph M., *Oliver Goldsmith* (University of Kansas Press, Lawrence, Kansas, 1957).

Whiteside, James, *Essays and Lectures: Historical and Literary* (Dublin, 1868).

Wichelns, Herbert A, "Burke's Essay on the Sublime and Its Reviewers," *Journal of English and Germanic Philology*, XXI (1922), 645-61.

Williams, Iolo A., *Seven Eighteenth Century Bibliographies*, (London, 1924).

Winstanley, John, *Poems* (Dublin, 1742).

INDEX

[362]

Pilkington, Jack, 109, 127-128, 215
Powell, Mr., 204
Prendergast, Col., 294
Public Ledger, 117-119, 143, 320
Purdon, Edward, 102, 109, 215

Ranelagh, 258-260, 265, 342
Reynolds, Frances, 148, 164-165
Reynolds, Sir Joshua, 120, 139, 147-148, 150, 151; founds the Club, 152; 162, 164, 173, 190-191, 196, 207, 218, 219, 220; at his dinner table, 234-237; 241, 244-245, 250, 252, 262, 264, 267, 269, 270, 273, 300, 303, 307, 310, 329, 330-332, 338, 341, 342; verses on Reynolds, 348; 349, 350-352, 353
Richardson, Samuel, 74-76, 153
Robertson, Dr. William, 212, 225-226
Robin Hood Society, 124-130
Rock, Dr. Richard, 173
Rogers, Samuel, 237
Rosciad, 120, 138-139, 177
Roscommon, 19, 26, 38, 45, 89
Rouelle, 63
Rousseau, 195

Scott, Parson, 200-201
Selwyn, George, 139, 157, 300, 301
Sentimental Comedy, 195-196, 309
Shebbeare, John, 119
Shelburne, Lord, 237, 350
Shuter, Ned, 202, 204-206, 307, 311
Sidebotham, Mrs., 174
Skeggs, Carolina Wilhemina Amelia, 279-287
Sleigh, Dr., 74
Smart, Christopher, 82
Smiglecius, 31, 32
Smollett, Dr. Tobias, 79, 80, 114-115, 116-117, 138, 153, 271
Steele, Sir Richard, 195

Steevens, George, 140, 157, 313, 348
Sterne, Laurence, 120, 147, 153, 178, 212
St. James Chronicle, 320, 337
St. Paul's, 231-233
Swift, Jonathan, 237

Thrale, Henry, 328, 329, 330, 331
Thrale, Mrs. Hester Lynch, 240-241, 273, 301-304, 340-341
Toplady, Rev. Mr., 333-336
Trinity College, Dublin, 26-32, 34-36
Turk's Head Tavern, 152
Turton, Dr., 349

Vauxhall, 258-262, 342
Vesey, Agmondesham, 331-332
Vesey, Mrs., 169, 301-304, 331
Voltaire, 66-67, 116, 119, 340, 341

Walford, Miss, 202
Walpole, Horace, 81, 105, 107, 118, 120, 147, 148, 157, 211-212, 237-238, 270-271, 302, 308
Walpole, Sir Robert, 80, 153
Warburton, Bishop William, 139
Welch, Gallows, 34-35
West, Richard, 32
Westminster Abbey, 217, 247-249
White's, 15, 28
Wilcox, bookseller, 80
Wilder, Theaker, 30, 31-32, 35-36
Wilkes, John, 146, 194, 200, 212, 255, 274, 311, 340
Wilkie, bookseller, 109-110
William, schoolmaster's servant, 77-78
William III, 28
Williams, Miss, 165, 321
Wine Office Court, 161
Winstanley, John, 30-31
Woodfall, W., 288
Woodward, Mr., 311, 312

Young, Edward, 75, 154